Praise for *Game Plan*

"While Washington sleeps, America's enemies are amassing at the gates of our economy. When their attacks are unleashed, everything will change in the blink of an eye. How will you protect yourself and your family? Kevin Freeman offers an unflinching look at the very scary, all-too-real threats we face, along with coolheaded advice on how to invest with confidence in an increasingly dangerous world. This book is worth its weight in gold. Read it now, and thank Kevin Freeman later."
—Brad Thor, #1 *New York Times* bestselling author of *Hidden Order*

"Kevin Freeman understands the threat of financial terrorism as well as anyone. You'd have to be negligent to ignore his timely advice about protecting your family from the economic attacks that are clearly on the horizon."
—Frank Keating, president and CEO, American Bankers Association, and former governor of Oklahoma

"As Kevin Freeman points out, America faces a global economic war that threatens your family, your job, and your life savings. Yet despite his five-year effort to warn Washington, willful blindness seems to be preventing our leadership from protecting you. *Game Plan* reveals the hidden truth about the economic threats and provides the actionable steps you should take to protect your family."
—Lt. Gen. William G. "Jerry" Boykin (U.S. Army, Ret.), former commander of Special Forces Command and the Green Berets and former deputy under secretary of defense for intelligence

"*Game Plan* is an important look at one of the most significant threats to U.S. security: cyberattacks and other efforts designed to cripple the economy. Must reading for those interested in protecting national security."
—Bill Gertz, senior editor, Washington Free Beacon, and national security columnist, *Washington Times*

"Kevin Freeman is a national treasure. His ability to synthesize economic and national security is unsurpassed—and of incalculable importance in the conflict of our time: the War for the Free World."
—Frank Gaffney, president and founder, Center for Security Policy

"The threat of financial terrorism is very real, and nobody knows that threat more thoroughly than Kevin Freeman. In this book, he'll tell you how to deal with the possibility of financial collapse, and give you hope for the future, too."

—Ben Shapiro, *New York Times* bestselling author of *Bullies: How the Left's Culture of Fear and Intimidation Silences America*

"Kevin Freeman's writing reminds me of the Pauline passage: 'for the light makes everything visible…. Awake, O sleeper, rise up from the dead….' Kevin calls all of us to 'wake up' and recognize that our country's financial life hangs in the balance. A must-read for all who want to see their way through the darkness of our times."

—Everett Piper, president, Oklahoma Wesleyan University

"Kevin Freeman is a long-time family friend. He wrote a business plan for my father, Sir John Templeton, in 1990, and helped build the Templeton Private Client Group from its inception. *Game Plan* shares his insight on economic threats facing the United States economy and how you can prepare your family and your business. Kevin is considered one of the world's leading experts on the issues of economic warfare and financial terrorism. His analysis is brilliant, and I hope you will find it as valuable as I have."

—Dr. John M. Templeton Jr., president and chairman, John Templeton Foundation

"As a Texas legislator, I relied heavily on Kevin Freeman's knowledge about financial terrorism. By teaming up with him, we were able to draft legislation that would protect the Lone Star State in case of economic collapse or terrorism at the federal level. He has become the nation's foremost expert on this topic. Kevin Freeman has followed up his exceptionally important book *Secret Weapon* with *Game Plan*. You will want to read it, study it, and make sure that you and those around you do indeed have a game plan for a potential financial crisis."

—Matt Krause, Texas House of Representatives, District 93

"Kevin's work is a new National Security Primer. If our elected leaders, national security, intelligence, and military officials ignore this well-researched analysis, 9/11 could look like child's play. I hope, moreover, that our technology and industry leaders (who by virtue of daily global challenges understand this remarkable vector) will start lively chatter in their communities about the nature of this potentially immense and perhaps imminent calamity. Serious scholars should ask, 'Why have we missed this series of interlocking threats?' Academia owes the nation a rigorous review of this work. It simply cannot be ignored. Markets matter. Our nation matters. This book matters."

—Hon. Thomas W. O'Connell, former assistant secretary of defense, special operations, 2003–7

"The U.S. government's acknowledged debt is about $17 trillion. Analysts such as Boston University economics professor Laurence Kotlikoff place our government's true liabilities closer to $211 trillion. A major transformation is coming, and the sharks of the world are circling. We know this because hostile regimes and non-state actors have said so in their communications. The spirit of American independence and modern technology still hold out the potential to provide a return to free markets and greater liberty, private entrepreneurship, and personal responsibility. Read *Game Plan* and choose your destiny. Kevin Freeman may be the Western world's foremost authority willing to speak publicly about economic warfare."

—Chris Graham, editor of the *Counter Terrorist*, former commander of a U.S. military anti-terrorism unit, former intelligence officer, www.chrisgrahamauthor.com

"Kevin Freeman is one of the smartest men I know. You ignore him at your peril."

—Rod Martin, founder and executive chairman, Advanced Search Laboratories, and former special counsel, PayPal

"Impressive, alarming, hopeful, practical, and a must-read! In these uncertain times, Kevin has offered us all a gift, if you are wise enough to read this book!"

—Ginni Thomas, the Daily Caller

"Economic warfare is among the least recognized but most threatening risks we face. Kevin Freeman has sounded the alarm. It is incumbent on America to pay heed and respond. Reading *Game Plan* will help you protect yourself and your family."

—Steve Malzberg, Newsmax TV

"Once again, Kevin Freeman provides sound information and advice on how to survive the inevitable financial crisis that we will all eventually face. I strongly recommend you read *Game Plan* so you are prepared for what is ahead."

—Jonathan Bernis, president and CEO, Jewish Voice Ministries International

"Kevin Freeman's passion for protecting the economic security of our country and its way of life is clearly reflected by his most recent writing. His key finding that the U.S. faces a credible, significant, and extant financial threat should be considered a call to action for our most senior government, business, and military leaders. If our leaders don't heed his warning, they will repeat their failure to act decisively on similar warnings about al Qaeda's intentions and capabilities in the 1990s. This threat, however, is even more ominous, more immediate, and deadlier."

—S. C. Zidek, assistant professor, Mercyhurst University, Institute for Intelligence Studies

"Kevin Freeman brilliantly unveils the imminent threat that economic jihad poses to the West's financial system. Everyone wanting to preserve the rights, freedoms, opportunities, and prosperity handed down through Western civilization needs to read *Game Plan*."

—William J. Federer, author of *What Every American Needs to Know about the Qur'an: A History of Islam & the United States*

"The American economy has protected Western civilization for the past century. Our foreign policy, our military preparedness, and our very lives depend on it. It is today clearly under attack from capable enemies, as Kevin Freeman explains in detail. Most importantly, he tells us what we can do to win the battle."

—Lt. Gen. Ed Soyster (U.S. Army, Ret.), former director of the Defense Intelligence Agency

"*Game Plan* is a compelling, essential primer for those who are prudent enough to want to understand how to prepare our country and themselves for the "Third Phase" of the assault on our financial systems by America's enemies. Kevin Freeman teaches what policy makers and you can do to protect our country and our families from the new weapons of mass destruction already in the hands of those who have every intention to harm us."

—Becky Norton Dunlop, vice president, the Heritage Foundation, and former deputy assistant to President Ronald Reagan

"Read this book! Discover what the Islamists, Iran, China's People's Liberation Army, the Russian government, and just plain criminals have in store for Americans—and learn how you can prepare your game plan to deal with the consequences of the game plans of the bad guys."

—George S. Dunlop, former principal deputy assistant secretary of the army

"America's national security remains at risk as unwarranted euphoria returns to the U.S. stock exchanges and official threat analysis rejects the very existence of a global economic war against the American people. Kevin Freeman's work is a quantum leap forward—he identifies the threats and unearths the most likely perpetrators, alerting investors to structure defensive portfolio strategies in response to such financially fatal realities. If you have capital at risk, this is a must-read!"

—Maj. Patrick Maloy (USMC, Ret.)

"*Game Plan* points to looming, well-documented threats from not only al Qaeda, which remains focused on exploiting America's economic vulnerabilities, but from other foes like Russia, China, Iran, North Korea, and Venezuela. So far, the U.S. government has largely turned a blind eye to warnings from financial experts like Kevin Freeman, refusing to confront these threats. With the life savings and investments of so many Americans at risk, it is critical that every concerned citizen understand what is at stake."

—Margaret Hemenway, former official at the
Department of Defense, at NASA, and on Capitol Hill

"The most perilous danger of terrorism is the unseen one. The myopic focus on preventing mass-murder attacks makes us vulnerable to broader, stealthier threats against our institutions. None of those is more consequential than the threat to our economy, and no one lays bare that threat with keener insight than Kevin Freeman."

—Andrew C. McCarthy, former federal prosecutor and bestselling author

"Kevin Freeman's brilliant analysis is frightening. The clear message is Wake up! Financial terrorism has the potential to change a prosperous way of life, 'de-Americanize' the world, and change the face of history. Albert Einstein said, 'A foolish faith in authority is the worst enemy of truth.' The 'authorities' of the free, democratic world appear blind to the truth and asleep at the switch. Like the scientific leadership that shunned the revolutionary principles of quantum mechanics and relativity in Einstein's era, our leadership is turning a blind eye to cyberterrorism and economic warfare. I urge attention to the clarion call in this book to avoid serious damage to a political and social structure that transformed the world for the better."

—Peter G. Traber, M.D., CEO, Galectin Therapeutics,
and professor of medicine

"Kevin Freeman describes an economic Armageddon just around the corner, largely of our own making, that our enemies are actively preparing to exploit. If you were worried about the Fed, the weak dollar, and the prospect of hyperinflation before, *Game Plan* will show you how to transform those fears into a responsible plan of action. For starters, we must—and can—become energy independent by transforming safe, abundant, American natural gas into methanol to power our automobiles."

—Kenneth R. Timmerman, author and former GOP congressional candidate

"After more than a decade in law enforcement I can attest that no single person has provided a clearer and more definitive explanation of the threats facing this nation and the challenges hindering today's law enforcement agencies than Kevin Freeman. Through his tireless research Freeman has educated countless law enforcement officials on the once unrecognized threat of financial terrorism. His innovative research has also been invaluable during ongoing criminal investigations, involving international, federal, and local law enforcement agencies."

—Eamon Blanchard, law enforcement investigator

"Economic warfare is real, and Kevin Freeman shows us how it works."

—Jeff Nyquist, author of *Origins of the Fourth World War*

"Kevin Freeman's *Game Plan* appropriately includes in his exhaustive analysis of economic problems facing America the existential threat from a manmade or natural electromagnetic pulse (EMP) event, which could shut down the electric power grid indefinitely. The relatively small cost of insurance to protect the electric power grid against that threat is an economic no-brainer."

—Ambassador Henry F. Cooper, chairman, High Frontier,
and former director of the Strategic Defense Initiative

"Talk about a wake-up call! Kevin Freeman's *Game Plan* sets forth a well-documented and highly plausible threat that could send twenty-first-century America back to the eighteenth century literally in a flash. It's enough to keep the average American from ever sleeping again! On the positive side, however, he also describes some relatively easy and inexpensive protective measures that can minimize the damage to our financial, electrical, and social infrastructures. It's a game plan that we ignore at our very substantial peril."

—Colin A. Hanna, president, Let Freedom Ring

"I've known Kevin Freeman since the time he first raised his concerns about the risks of financial warfare. He has consistently gotten it right and has been consistently ahead of the pack in doing so. For those with financial assets to protect, this book is a must-read."

—Stephen Coughlin, senior fellow, Center for Security Policy, and former consultant to the Joint Chiefs of Staff

"Benjamin Franklin warned centuries ago, 'Think what you do when you run in debt, you give to another power over your liberty.' War is about exploiting vulnerabilities. Kevin Freeman alerted us to our economic vulnerabilities in *Secret Weapon*. In *Game Plan*, he warns that our liberty is imperiled by a concerted exploitation of these vulnerabilities. The State of Utah is working to heed his warning."

—Ken Ivory, Utah state representative and author of *Where's the Line? How States Protect the Constitution*

"Kevin Freeman's latest book comes at a critical time in human history. Bill Clinton's famous campaign motto was 'It's the economy, stupid!' The Jihadists' approach to destroying America is to destroy the American economy. Kevin's masterly *Secret Weapon* revealed the enemy's insidious plans to bring down Wall Street and the United States and therefore the world economy. Now he prepares us for what is coming, including Chinese disinvestment in the dollar and Russia's continuing competition with the United States for preeminence. Hosea 4:6 says, 'My people are destroyed for lack of knowledge.' Kevin Freeman's *Game Plan* gives us the knowledge to save us from being destroyed."

—Dennis Avi Lipkin (a.k.a. Victor Mordecai), author

"What does the risk of economic warfare mean to our economy and your own personal finances? *Game Plan* by Kevin Freeman is a must-read for understanding the imminent financial risks we face and what you can do about them."

—Eric M. Jackson, award-winning author of
The PayPal Wars and CEO of CapLinked

"I traveled extensively with Kevin Freeman, to the DIA, FBI, and halls of Congress. It would have been un-American not to help a patriot like Kevin in his attempt to warn our leaders and his fellow citizens. Economic warfare is a serious threat, but no one in Washington wants to address it. Perhaps they are too busy lining their own pockets while our nation collapses. Rumor has it that a large think tank has been awarded a 'study to nowhere' on the issue. Typical Washington. A senior DoD official told me that addressing this problem doesn't fit the political narrative. Obviously those 'public servants' defining the narrative are not really concerned about national security or this nation's citizens. Events prove this. Read the book before they ban it. It is destined to become a collector's item."

—David Hemenway, citizen soldier, Washington navigator

"It's a new century, and *Game Plan* by Kevin Freeman reveals the emergence of a new kind of war that the United States is ill prepared to take on. Freeman describes in painstaking detail how the very foundations of our society are in peril, yet the American political class remains in denial. If you have time to read only one book in 2014, read this one. Your way of life depends on it."

—Gil Amelio, retired technologist, inventor, author, and transformative
CEO of National Semiconductor and Apple Computer

"Kevin Freeman has hit another home run with his new book, *Game Plan*. He is one of the preeminent thinkers of our generation. His extensive research integrates the long-term historical perspective with the current perspective. He understands the economic as well as the military threat to our national security. The danger is not only from international terror with guns and bullets, but also in the financial and economic realm. Read it and become enlightened!"

—Hon. Allen B. Clark, former assistant secretary of Veterans Affairs

GAME PLAN

GAME PLAN

How to Protect Yourself from the
Coming Cyber-Economic Attack

KEVIN D. FREEMAN

REGNERY
Publishing, Inc.
An Eagle Publishing Company • Washington, DC

Cataloging-in-Publication data on file with the Library of Congress
ISBN 978-1-62157-200-8

Published in the United States by
Regnery Publishing, Inc.
One Massachusetts Avenue NW
Washington, DC 20001

www.Regnery.com

Manufactured in the United States of America

10 9 8 7 6 5 4 3 2 1

Books are available in quantity for promotional or premium use. Write to Director of Special Sales, Regnery Publishing, Inc., One Massachusetts Avenue NW, Washington, DC 20001, for information on discounts and terms, or call (202) 216-0600.

Distributed to the trade by
Perseus Distribution
250 West 57th Street
New York, NY 10107

Dedicated to He who proclaims true Liberty (Isaiah 61:1),
a cause worthy of our lives, our fortunes, and our sacred honor.

Contents

Introduction

More than five years ago, I alerted the Pentagon that a war was under way. It was a new kind of war—unlike any we were prepared to face. And it almost ended our way of life, although few understood that reality at the time or since.

Our enemies have telegraphed the how and why of this new kind of war for almost a decade. The Chinese People's Liberation Army even produced a book, *Unrestricted Warfare*, about new techniques to defeat a superpower, mocking our inability to recognize, let alone address, the threat. One of the best ways to break America, the Chinese know, is to hit our economy by waging financial warfare.

The 9/11 attacks—direct and physical—took a page from the Chinese PLA playbook. *Unrestricted Warfare* specifically mentions attacking

America by blowing up the World Trade Center,[1] and Osama bin Laden acknowledged that his primary aim was to weaken our financial system.[2]

The second attack was subtler but more devastating. The first sign of the looming battle was the rapid and unprecedented run-up in oil prices. At the start of 2007, oil was trading for about fifty dollars per barrel on international markets. By June 2008 the price had soared to almost $150 per barrel despite a slowing global economy. Hundreds of billions of dollars flowed from the West to the Middle East, weakening us financially at the worst possible time—just as a housing bubble was about to burst. What drove up prices? Some blame China's economic growth, although Chinese demand accounted for only a small part of the price increases. In fact, massive purchases of "paper oil" in the financial markets, much of it by Middle Eastern sovereign wealth funds, pushed prices to unsustainable levels. These orders, hidden behind financial instruments, caused a huge transfer of wealth that nearly crippled our economy. It couldn't have been scripted better.

Unrestricted Warfare prescribes other stealthy financial attacks, including a man-made stock market crash. That is where my Pentagon warnings began—in the frightening days of September 2008. The ensuing financial panic and stock market decline—the worst since the Great Depression—bore all the hallmarks of an economic attack. Unnamed entities using financial instruments targeted systemically critical American financial companies, setting off a cascade of failures. Nearly every week new companies were taken to the brink of disaster. When Lehman Brothers went down, the whole system nearly followed.

It was George Soros, the man credited with "breaking the Bank of England" and accused of destroying whole economies, who attributed the failure of Lehman Brothers and other mainstay American firms to a "bear raid"—a deliberate attack intended to destroy a company's stock price and viability.[3] It was Soros who explained that the bear raids were conducted using complex financial instruments such as credit default swaps and short selling.[4] And it was Soros who recognized that the failure of Lehman almost brought down the entire financial system in one devastating blow.[5] Most important, George Soros was the man whom *Unrestricted Warfare* describes as a model for twenty-first-century financial warfare.[6] Soros knew what was happening as it went down. And even though we have no reason to believe that he was behind the bear raids, we do know he was aware and profitably reacted.[7]

I explained all of this in a formal report to the Pentagon in 2009[8] and in my last book, *Secret Weapon: How Economic Terrorism Brought Down the U.S. Stock Market and Why It Can Happen Again*. My conclusions have since been validated by other government reports,[9] and a former Treasury official has acknowledged the reality of economic warfare and the targeting of America.[10] The Department of Defense has even run a war-game simulation that demonstrated conclusively that properly executed economic attacks could devastate the dollar and destroy our economy.[11]

So what have we done to prepare? Alarmingly enough, almost nothing. Instead, we have rolled up additional trillions of dollars in new debt, and the Federal Reserve has been pumping out money like crazy. The stage has been set for what I originally described as a Phase Three attack on the U.S. dollar. A substantial devaluation of our currency would leave us, like Greece, at the mercy of creditors and the global financial system. This is where *Game Plan* begins. The first section provides a "Who's Who" of American enemies intent on our destruction and fully aware of our vulnerability. I then explain how the next attack may take place and how it would affect you.

The second section is about how to respond as the economic war unfolds. Unfortunately, there's no way of telling precisely how the next attack will take place. While we can be certain that there will be attacks, it is impossible to predict how the economy and markets will react. Will the next weapon be an electromagnetic pulse that wipes out the electric grid? Will it be a cyberattack that destroys all financial records and data? Or an old-fashioned takedown of the currency, like the one George Soros inflicted on the British pound and perhaps on the Malaysian ringgit?[12] While any of these, or some combination, is possible, exactly how and when the attack occurs will make a profound difference in the impact. One type of attack might produce a deflationary depression, while another might cause a hyperinflationary spiral. The national reaction to the attack will influence how damaging it is.

This book is called *Game Plan* because there is no pat answer for every threat. When a coach prepares his team for the season, he must plan for a variety of opponents and produce a unique strategy for each. My goal is to review the threats and consider a variety of investment and personal options to address them. Should you put all your money in gold? Is it time to abandon stocks? What about the safety of bonds, guaranteed investments, or hedge funds? I will explore each major asset category and consider whether and when it might have a role in protecting your life savings. As George Soros was prepared to profit in spite of the 2008 collapse, you must strategically plan to move as the investment markets respond.

The last section of *Game Plan* will help you pull together a personalized strategy and give you hope for the future. I will even explore some solutions to problems at the national level. In addition, I'll share some practical approaches that can provide you with personal confidence as you face the serious challenges of the day. More important, I will discuss some key spiritual truths to sustain us even in the darkest of times.

America was attacked in 2001 and again in 2008. We are still suffering from those attacks. *Secret Weapon* explained in detail how the attack of 2008 happened, who was involved, and what would come next. There are many signs that a third attack is imminent. *Game Plan* is your companion to *Secret Weapon*, taking the research to the next level, personalizing it for individuals, and providing a strategic path to respond. Let's get started.

CHAPTER ONE

A World of Risk

O n the twelfth anniversary of the 9/11 attacks on America, Osama bin Laden's successor, Ayman al-Zawahiri, outlined al Qaeda's current strategy. The London *Daily Telegraph* reported the terrorist commander's message:

> "We should bleed America economically by provoking it to continue in its massive expenditure on its security, for the weak point of America is its economy, which has already begun to stagger due to the military and security expenditure," he said, according to SITE, a jihadist monitoring group. "America is not a mythic power and the Americans, after all, are humans who can be defeated, felled and punished."

Zawahiri urged the Islamic world to "abandon the dollar and replace it with a currency of other countries that are not taking part in the aggression against us." He also said that Muslims should refuse to buy goods from America and its allies, as such spending only helped to fund U.S. military action in Muslim lands.[1]

This strategy should come as no surprise. It was bin Laden's strategy as well.[2] And despite the U.S. government's declaration after bin Laden's death that al Qaeda was all but defeated, its threat to our economy continues.[3] Al Qaeda has been deliberate. As early as 2005, Fouad Hussein, a remarkably well-connected Jordanian journalist, disclosed its strategic timeline.[4] The ultimate goal is the restoration of the caliphate by 2020.[5] But al Qaeda understands that to accomplish that feat, it must destroy the U.S. economy, attacking America's infrastructure through cyberwarfare and other means and ultimately collapsing the dollar. As Robert Martinage of the Center for Strategic and Budgetary Assessments (now an undersecretary of the navy) explained in 2008, "This stage 'will focus on overthrowing regimes by means of direct and fierce clashes with them' and 'when the regimes gradually disintegrate, Al-Qa'ida and the Islamic jihad trend will grow persistently.' Economic warfare will be waged against the United States and the West more broadly—including burning 'Arab oil' and conducting electronic attacks against critical infrastructures. Gold is restored as the 'standard exchange value in international markets,' leading to the 'collapse' of the US dollar."[6]

The threat of economic warfare is concerning because it is the next step after overthrowing critical Arab regimes, another long-held al Qaeda goal. In 2005 the plan was to start this political upheaval between 2010 and 2013.[7] That schedule lines up almost precisely with the Arab Spring, which began in December 2010, toppling governments in Tunisia, Egypt, Libya, and Yemen and spawning uprisings or protests in Syria,

Bahrain, Algeria, Iraq, Jordan, Kuwait, Morocco, and Sudan.[8] The conventional view is that these events were democratic uprisings and a repudiation of al Qaeda. To the contrary, each of these uprisings has furthered al Qaeda's goals,[9] and there is clear evidence of al Qaeda's involvement among the so-called "freedom" fighters.[10] Make no mistake—the Arab Spring is an important part of al Qaeda's plan. But it's halfway around the world, and most Americans don't seem to care. The next step, however, suggests cyberattacks on our economy and an attempt to destroy the dollar. Such blows, if successful, would destroy American power and cripple our way of life.

Al Qaeda is not alone in recognizing America's economic vulnerabilities. Russia, China, Iran, North Korea, Venezuela, and a host of other regimes have at one time or another suggested that America could be taken down by economic warfare. We can actually point to cases in which they were willing to test the proposition.

In the middle of the afternoon on April 23, 2013, the Standard & Poor's 500 index mysteriously fell sharply, wiping out $121 billion of value in about one minute. There were no economic announcements, and nothing was fundamentally wrong. Instead, the Syrian Electronic Army hacked the Associated Press's Twitter account and tweeted a false rumor of damage to the White House. The hoax, fortunately, was revealed quickly, and the market rebounded in minutes.[11] There are dozens of "flash crashes" each day, actually, though usually limited to a single stock.[12] Despite these mysterious drops, the stock market has recovered after hitting a post–financial crisis low in March 2009, reaching record highs in 2013. So no harm, no foul?

The fact is that our global markets are highly vulnerable. They have been for years. That vulnerability allowed the market's collapse in 2008 and the economic decline from which we still suffer. And it could lead to something far worse if we do nothing. In my first book, *Secret Weapon*, I warned, "America stands on the brink. It stands on the brink because of government overspending and our colossal national debt. It stands on the brink because of manipulation, failed regulations, and predatory trading on our financial markets. It stands on the brink because of terrorism threats and covert moves against us by hostile foreign powers."[13]

Unless America took corrective action, I warned, we would be leaving ourselves open. "This is a national security issue, not a partisan one—and we have our work cut out for us. As a nation, we must acknowledge the risks of economic warfare and financial terrorism and seriously address them. The future of our currency, our economy, and our way of life may depend on it."[14]

We haven't acknowledged those risks. We haven't done the work. And we remain open to being hit.

The War We Are Fighting

A new world war—an economic war—is under way, but America's arrogance has kept us from realizing it. Like the Cold War, it isn't fought with guns and bombs. And despite having the largest economy in the world, we remain woefully vulnerable.

I spent five years after the 2008 financial crisis educating policymakers, the defense establishment, and the intelligence community about the economic war. After dozens of high-level meetings, some disconcerting realities became clear. First, few in our government had even considered the risks I was describing. The political elite can't imagine that anyone would want to harm the American economy. They assume that everyone in the world shares their basic motivation—the acquisition of material wealth—and sees the American economy as the goose that lays the golden egg. No rational person would try to harm it, because doing so would impoverish everyone. While that may have been the case in the rebuilding years after World War II and again following the collapse of the Soviet Union, it is certainly not true today. Most of the world now sees America as a failing but arrogant superpower creating more risk than reward for the world as a whole. America's collapse seems inevitable, and they are positioning themselves to profit from it, or at least to avoid the damage.

Second, most of the people in our national leadership with whom I shared the evidence were convinced, but they shared with me the sad reality that not a single American agency was responsible for addressing this threat, let alone prepared to do so. The Department of Defense isn't prepared, and neither is the Treasury, the Securities and Exchange Commission, the FBI, the CIA, or the Defense Intelligence Agency.

Finally, it became obvious that at the highest levels of the chain of command, there is an unwillingness to admit even the existence of the threat, let alone deal with it. This too is based on arrogance and cowardice. The political implications of acknowledging that a global economic war is under way are a threat to both Democrats and Republicans. So the nation remains in a state of agitated ignorance, unaware of the emerging storm, yet sensing that something is wrong.

This is not to say that I made no progress in my attempt to rouse our slumbering defenders. My team persisted until the House Armed Services Committee invited us to provide language for the Defense Authorization Act requiring the DOD's Office of Net Assessment to review my 2009 Pentagon report and respond by a specified date.[15] This was a considerable accomplishment, as Net Assessment and its director, Andy Marshall, have long been considered the top strategists in the Pentagon.[16] I met several times with Mr. Marshall and his top lieutenants.

We had hoped that the findings of this report would awaken America to a very serious danger. The law required that the report be released in late 2011, allowing the voters to assess the information before the national elections in 2012. Unfortunately, the report was held up for months. When I asked the reason for the unusual delay, I was told that there were fears that the findings might be used as "a political weapon."

The report was not released until early 2013, and even then, it was classified and kept from the public. Now the respected Office of Net Assessment itself is on the chopping block.[17]

I later learned from a *For the Record* investigative report that another
division in the Pentagon, U.S. Special Operations Command (SOCOM),
also hired a respected defense contractor to look at my 2009 report and
either validate or disprove it: "As *For the Record* was preparing to file this
story, our investigative Producer was contacted by a Naval Officer serving in Special Operations, one day before he was resigning his commission. He said he ordered a forensic investigation into the 2008 crash. It
was conducted by a military contractor with expertise in global finance
and data solutions. It was done independently of Kevin Freeman's study.
That report concluded 'There is overwhelming evidence that China and
Russia launched economic attacks against the United States in 2008.'"[18]

The report for SOCOM was also withheld from the public, but
however much our political and military leadership might wish the
subject of financial terrorism would go away, the threat is too serious
for the intelligence community to ignore. In the 2012 edition of its qua-
drennial *Global Trends* report, the National Intelligence Council (which
provides long-term strategic analysis to the director of national intelligence) devotes a section to "lethal technologies," where it warns of
economic and financial terrorism:

> Potential cyberwarfare scenarios include coordinated cyber-
> weapon attacks that sabotage multiple infrastructure assets
> simultaneously. One scenario involves a case where power,
> the Internet, cash machines, broadcast media, traffic lights,
> financial systems, and air traffic software simultaneously
> failed for a period of weeks. The trends in cyberattacks so far
> suggest that although some computer systems are more
> secure than others, few, if any, systems can claim to be

completely secure against a determined attack. For some attackers, cyberwarfare offers other advantages that have seldom been the case for most warfare: anonymity and low buy-in costs. These attributes favor the employment by disaffected groups and individuals who want to sow mayhem.[19]

In October 2012 the *Washington Times* reported that the undersecretary of defense for intelligence commissioned another study on weapons of mass destruction, which found that the United States faces serious cyber, electronic, and financial threats from "a vast network of state and non-state actors":

> The new Pentagon report appears to build on one produced for the Pentagon in 2009 by financial consultant Kevin Freeman, who stated that the United States' 2008 financial crash may have been deliberate sabotage by terrorists or foreign states.
>
> That study was criticized by senior Obama administration officials, including the Pentagon's special operations policymaker, Michael Vickers, who is currently undersecretary of defense for intelligence. U.S. officials said Mr. Vickers blocked further study into possible financial warfare behind the economic crisis. Mr. Freeman wrote a book on the issue called "Secret Weapon."
>
> The new Pentagon report said the May 6, 2010, "flash crash" when markets fell by 10 percent "may have been caused by an economic attack by one or a combination of methods," including the manipulation of computer algorithms that control trading or exchange traded funds that allow traders to short sell mass quantities of stock quickly and anonymously. It also could have been the result of covert

currency-manipulation by the holder of a significant U.S.
debt—such as China—designed to intentionally weaken the
value of the dollar by preventing the United States from selling its debt to others.[20]

Our work may have prompted, in part, a joint simulation exercise
between the financial securities industry and key government agencies.
Known as Quantum Dawn 2, the exercise was designed to throw a variety of threats at Wall Street to see what would happen.[21] The sobering
results, reported in the *Wall Street Journal*, demonstrated the vulnerability of our markets: "Hackers were able to force a shutdown of U.S. equity
markets in a simulated cyber attack on the U.S. financial sector, suggesting industry and government could do more to harden the financial
system against external threats."[22]

Juan Zarate, a former deputy national security advisor and assistant
secretary of the treasury, reveals much about the twenty-first-century
economic war in *Treasury's War: The Unleashing of a New Era of Financial Warfare*. He documents the efforts of a variety of enemies of the
United States to harm our economy and destroy the U.S. dollar:

> The United States must begin to play a new and distinctly
> financial game of geopolitical competition to ensure its secu-
> rity and to seize emerging opportunities. Just as the mistakes
> leading to 9/11 were deemed a failure of imagination, the
> inability of the U.S. government to recognize the changed
> landscape could be considered a collective failure of compre-
> hension.
>
> The financial wars are coming. It is time to redesign a
> national economic security model to prepare for them. If we
> fail to do so, the United States risks being left vulnerable and
> left behind as other competitors race toward the future.[23]

The reality is that we have been in a financial war for more than a dozen years. It has seriously degraded our economy. Its reality has been documented in numerous studies by experts and former high-ranking officials. And yet, despite our best efforts, current American leadership seems intent on ignoring this real, dangerous, and growing threat.

A History of Financial Warfare

September 11 was first and foremost an attack on America's financial center. *The 9/11 Commission Report* acknowledged as much, stating that al Qaeda terrorists Khalid Sheikh Mohammed and Ramzi Yousef "reportedly brainstormed together about what drove the U.S. economy. New York, which KSM considered the economic capital of the United States, therefore became the primary target."[24] September 11 was "designed to be a serious attack intended to produce massive casualties and serious damage to the economy, but it was also very much designed to be a symbolic assault—one that would strike the symbols of U.S. economic, political, and military power."[25] Shortly before his death, bin Laden released a tape urging the world to "refrain from dealing in the U.S. dollar" and said that good people across the world "should try to get rid of this currency as early as possible."

Belligerents have been resorting to economic warfare for centuries. During the Seven Years' War, British jurists declared that international law permitted blockades. Napoleon blockaded the importation of British goods into French-controlled territory, a policy that boomeranged on him when the French were forced to pay extra money for their own goods. The Confederacy refused to supply cotton to the North, while a Union blockade kept the South from selling its cotton to anyone else. When the United States embargoed oil exports to Japan and froze all Japanese assets in the United States, Japan responded by attacking Pearl Harbor.

Economic warfare can also be a potent weapon during a war already under way. The Germans attempted to undermine the British pound in World War II by counterfeiting. If they had succeeded, they might have knocked Britain out of the war entirely by inflating its currency. Jan Sejna, the highest-ranking Soviet officer ever to defect to the West, revealed the USSR's elaborate plans to sabotage the American economy during the Cold War.[26] And North Korea, with only limited success so far, conducts its own economic warfare enterprise: its Office 39 steals between $500 million and $1 billion per year through counterfeiting.

The United States has been the most successful modern practitioner of economic warfare, weakening the Soviet Union by lowering oil prices and imposing a massive embargo on the sinking Evil Empire. In the 1956 Suez crisis, the United States succeeded in knocking Great Britain out of the Middle East by threatening to sink the pound. But economic warfare is a double-edged sword. The 1973 Arab oil embargo seriously damaged the U.S. economy.

Today it is not only states that have the capacity to shape international affairs through economic warfare. One of the world's richest men, George Soros, prompted a run on the pound by short selling in 1992; he made $950 million. In 1997, the Malaysian prime minister accused Soros of doing the same thing to his currency. Officers in the Chinese army have even branded him a "financial terrorist."

America's Enemies

America's enemies range from loosely affiliated terrorist groups to countries vying for global dominance. Al Qaeda still has the capacity to launch sophisticated attacks—using not only airplanes or improvised explosive devices but complex financial instruments. Charles Duelfer, former director of the Iraq Survey Group, and Jim Rickards, former general counsel to Long-Term Capital Management, write, "Al Qaeda has declared that damage to the American economy is the second most important goal after mass casualties. Presently, who would warn the White House if foreign entities made a concerted attack on our financial system? Who is charged with detecting such activity?"[27] The real answer: no one is.

Yusuf al-Qaradawi, a leader of the Muslim Brotherhood and host of his own show on Al Gore's favorite network, Al Jazeera, insists that true Muslims must harm the U.S. economy wherever possible. He suggests that Muslims send "money for the *mujahideen*." He also helps run Islamic financial institutions. "I like to call it Jihad with money," he told the BBC in July 2006.[28] A favorite al Qaeda book agrees: "Money is the lifeline of jihad."[29]

The goal of these terrorist groups is not merely the destruction of Western classical liberalism and personal freedom. It is the evisceration of capitalism itself and its replacement with sharia-compliant finance (SCF), which bars interest. No wonder bin Laden explained right after 9/11, "The key pillars of the enemy should be struck, God willing. They shook America's throne and struck at the U.S. economy in the heart.... This is a clear proof that this international usurious, damnable economy—which America uses along with its military power to impose infidelity and humiliation on weak people—can easily collapse. Thanks to Almighty God, those blessed attacks, as they themselves admitted, have inflicted on the New York and other markets more than a trillion dollars in losses.... It is very important to concentrate on hitting the U.S. economy through all possible means."[30]

Saudi Arabia and other Muslim states have been energetically pushing SCF for a while, portraying it as an innocent and private financial code for Muslims. But SCF is part of the global sharia agenda. Dr. Mahathir Mohamad, a former prime minister of Malaysia, has articulated the goal of developing a "universal Islamic banking system." In 2001 he said, "In the old days you needed to conquer a country with military force, and then you could control that country. Today it's not necessary at all. You can destabilize a country, make it poor, and then make it request help. And [in exchange] for the help that is given, you gain control over the policies of the country, and when you gain control over the policies of a country, effectively you have colonized that country."[31]

Iran also supports global sharia, both in finance and in the broader legal system. All of its banking is SCF compliant, and investments are overseen by Islamic clerics who ensure that cash goes to the right terrorists. In 2011 the then president Mahmoud Ahmadinejad declared a "year of economic jihad," and Iran refuses to trade in dollars with regard to oil.

Sudan, Egypt, Libya, and Pakistan are all either SCF compliant or moving in that direction. Islamic nations have begun to create sovereign wealth funds, pooling cash into huge investment vehicles that have the power to turn markets.

Islamic states are not the only economic threat. China is a rising global power and an economic rival to the United States. The Chinese have repeatedly stated, albeit quietly, that they wish to replace the American dollar as the global currency, and they have started working with Russia to set up a non-dollar alternative.

The call to replace the dollar is a cornerstone strategy in developing what an official Chinese news agency editorial described as a desirable effort to create a "de-Americanized world."[32] That's a strong statement from an official news agency.

Russia likewise sees the United States as a rival. Russia is trading currencies with China, and its quasi-dictator, Vladimir Putin, says, "The ruble must become a more widespread means of international transactions."

After the death of Hugo Chavez, Venezuela looked momentarily as though it might move away from its virulently anti-American stance, but so far hopes of moderation have been disappointed. Venezuelan defectors have revealed that Chavez financed al Qaeda's activities for years. Chavez said in 2009 during a visit to Iran, "Capitalism needs to go down. It has to end. And we must take a transitional road to a new model that we call socialism."

While many of those who minimize the threat of economic warfare see our enemies as unsophisticated, the blowhard Chavez proved that rhetorical excess does not mean economic incompetence. He died with $2 billion in his bank account and connections to another hundred billion. Other international adversaries have amassed similar fortunes. Muammar Gaddafi of Libya had a personal fortune of $200 billion. Saudi prince Alwaleed bin Talal has said he was insulted by assertions that he was worth only $20 billion (claiming almost ten billion more than that). Vladimir Putin's net worth is upward of $70 billion if we analyze his holdings in various corporations, and possibly much higher than that. When you add it all up, there's quite a bit of money outside our government's control or even awareness— hundreds of billions of dollars, and even trillions when you include sovereign wealth funds and holdings of Communist governments.[33]

Criminal groups like the mafia and drug cartels also have the potential to become economic warriors. Even some American unions have been interested in pursuing relationships with enemies of the U.S. economic system. The former director of the Service Employees International Union's Banking and Finance Campaign, Stephen Lerner, was caught on tape in March 2011 talking about destabilizing the American economy. "We have a very simple strategy," said Lerner. "How do we bring down the stock market? How do we bring down the bonuses? How do we interfere with their ability to be rich?"

America has plenty of enemies. And those enemies have plenty of means.

The Last Collapse

In 2008, America's financial markets melted down with some $13 trillion lost in a matter of weeks. It began with the oil run-up of 2007–2008, during which prices spiked from $50 per barrel to $150, helping to pierce the real estate and derivatives bubble. When the price of a commodity triples, there are usually winners and losers. The run-up of oil prices, however, hurt nearly all Americans. The beneficiaries were our enemies. The oil-producing countries at the time were, by and large, our geopolitical foes.

In late 2007, while oil prices were rising, massive bear raids targeted several of America's important financial institutions. A bear raid is an illegal manipulation of a target company's stock price. The purpose can be the raider's profit, but it can also be subversion. Citigroup was hit by short selling in November. Analysts who studied the transactions later concluded that this had been an illegal bear raid:

> The study authors at the New England Complex Systems Institute (NECSI) retraced events to show that at a critical point in the financial crisis, the stock of Citigroup was attacked by traders by selling borrowed stock (short-selling) which may have caused others to sell in panic. The subsequent price drop enabled the attackers to buy the stock back at a much lower price.
>
> This kind of illegal market manipulation is called a bear raid and the new study supports earlier suspicions that the raids played a role in the market crash.
>
> The study has direct evidence. Through its analysis of stock market data not generally available to the public, namely the borrowing of shares, NECSI reconstructs the chain of events.[34]

The NECSI analysts estimated that the odds of this kind of trading activity's taking place without malicious coordination were infinitesimally remote: "Professor Yaneer Bar-Yam, president of NECSI, maintains this was no 'freak' or coincidental event. 'When 100 million shares are borrowed on a single day and then returned on a single day, the evidence that this is a concerted action is hard to refute. The likelihood of such an event happening by coincidence is one in a trillion.'"[35]

A few months later, in March 2008, Bear Stearns, America's fifth-largest investment bank, was in the crosshairs. According to *Rolling Stone*'s Matt Taibbi, the Bear Stearns bankruptcy included an unnamed person making "one of the craziest bets Wall Street has ever seen. The mystery figure spent $1.7 million on a series of options, gambling that shares in the venerable investment bank Bear Stearns would lose more than half their value in nine days or less. It was madness." The next day, Bear collapsed. The $1.7 million investment was suddenly worth $270 million. It was, Taibbi concludes, "one of the most blatant cases of stock manipulation in Wall Street history." But authorities couldn't trace it.

That summer Fannie Mae and Freddie Mac, the government-sponsored entities at the heart of the U.S. mortgage business, came under attack from short-sellers. Their stock plunged in value. Treasury Secretary Henry Paulson believed that the Russians and Chinese had attempted to force our government into a costly bailout—economic warfare, in short. Paulson says the Chinese told him they refused to cooperate with the Russians, but the Russians went ahead.

In September, the tactic was repeated. The first target was Lehman Brothers, which experienced a massive spike in short selling. More than one-fifth of trades in Lehman on September 17 were failed trades, a sign of short selling. George Soros spelled out the problem: "It's clear that AIG, Bear Stearns, Lehman Brothers and others were destroyed by bear raids in which the shorting of stocks and buying CDS [credit default swaps] mutually amplified and reinforced each other."

Lehman's collapse led to the collapses of Merrill Lynch, Washington Mutual, Citigroup, Bank of America, and even Goldman Sachs. AIG was soon on the brink. On September 15, Congressman Paul Kanjorski announced that over half a trillion dollars had disappeared from U.S. money-market accounts. The stock market dropped more than 50 percent, the worst decline since the Great Depression. Even though the market has since revived with the help of the Federal Reserve, the nation's economy continues to suffer. Wall Street has recovered, but Main Street is far from healthy. Worse still, our vulnerabilities have been exposed, our nation is weakened, and yet virtually nothing has been done to prevent a next attack.

What Comes Next

Unfortunately, the American government appears to have learned little. In January 2013 the secretary of homeland security, Janet Napolitano, warned that a cyberattack from abroad could cripple the United States. She mentioned the possibility of a "cyber 9/11," which she said could happen "imminently" and threaten water, electricity, and gas for Americans. Napolitano explained, "We shouldn't wait until there is a 9/11 in the cyberworld. There are things we can and should be doing right now that, if not prevent, would mitigate the extent of damage." She added, "The clarion call is here and we need to be dealing with this very urgently. Attacks are coming all the time. They are coming from different sources, they take different forms. But they are increasing in seriousness and sophistication."[36]

Sure enough, in February 2013, even the Federal Reserve admitted that its computer systems had been hacked. The hacker group Anonymous claimed that it stole details on over four thousand top banking executives. "The Federal Reserve system," said a Fed spokesman, "is aware that information was obtained by exploiting a temporary vulnerability in a website vendor product. Exposure was fixed shortly after discovery and is no longer an issue. This incident did not affect critical operations of the Federal Reserve system." But the central bank would not say which website had been hacked or what specific information had been leaked.[37]

It was a low-level attack, but it was a sign of what is to come. Technology around the world is simply very vulnerable. In April 2013 the German government raised the possibility of a flash crash in Europe. Less than one week later, it occurred. *Der Spiegel* reported, "within minutes, the Dax rushed around 180 points down—and also in the afternoon deep in the red. The European Stock Index also lost a flash in value."[38]

Meanwhile, our enemies are not sitting on the sidelines. Al Qaeda now has a Twitter account. Somalia's al Qaeda affiliate, al-Shabab, is pushing its message 140 characters at a time: "Our war against the West is a war for the sovereignty and dominance of Allah's Law above all creation. No to democracy and #Kafir laws!" it tweeted in February.[39]

Our more powerful enemies are doing more than tweeting. The Chinese have launched a series of hard-hitting cyberattacks on America's security and financial infrastructure. In February 2013, Americans were shocked—shocked!—to learn that the Chinese government had been hacking corporations to steal trade secrets, learn negotiating strategies, and otherwise engage in activity that can only be called economic warfare.

Cybertheft has long been a part of China's global security strategy. In 1995, Major General Wang Pufeng, a former director of the Strategy Department at the Academy of Military Science in Beijing, wrote, "The large-scale importation of information technology deep into the field of warfare will inevitably bring about a military revolution. This revolution has actually already started.... The issue of how to adapt to and achieve victory in the information warfare which we will face from now on is an important question which we need to study carefully." A few years later, the Chinese were already thinking offensively rather than defensively. The authors of the widely noticed work of modern strategy *Unrestricted Warfare*, Colonels Qiao Liang and Wang Xiangsui, wrote, "a single man-made stock market crash, a single computer virus invasion, or a single rumor or scandal that results in a fluctuation in the enemy country's exchange rates or exposes the leaders of an enemy country on the Internet, all can be included in the ranks of new-concept weapons." They added menacingly, "Some morning people will awake to discover with surprise that quite a few gentle and kind things have begun to have offensive and lethal characteristics."[40]

It took several major Chinese hack attacks to awaken the U.S. government, however. On March 11, 2013, then national security advisor Tom Donilon warned China that the United States could not tolerate hack attacks. Businesses, he said, are worried about "sophisticated, targeted theft of confidential business information, and proprietary technologies through cyber intrusions emanating from China on an unprecedented scale." He warned, "As the president said in the State of the Union, we will take action to protect our economy against cyber-threats."

But what took so long? For two years the Obama administration flatly rejected any strong measures to curb Chinese cyberattacks. Several options were dismissed out of hand, including economic sanctions and counter-cyberattacks.[41]

While China has aggressively probed our vulnerabilities, it is not the only threat. There are rumors that al Qaeda will work with anyone to hack America's electronic economy. According to a spring 2013 report from Bill Gertz, a journalist and national security expert, "An al-Qaida website recently posted a notice calling for major attacks on vital U.S. infrastructure. Basically [they are] calling on jihadists hackers to join together in this attack. They called it 'Operation Black Summer.' So, presumably, it's going to unfold in the coming weeks."[42]

In the aftermath of the Benghazi terrorist attack of September 11, 2012, Islamic hackers openly threatened to target financial institutions. In October, Izz ad-Din al-Qassam Cyber Fighters posted, "We have selected the banks because we should have done something proportional to what has happened against us. In the system where … religion and sacred things are not honorable, and only material, money and finance have value, this seems a suitable and effective … act[ion] and can influence governors and decision makers." When asked why they would target specifically financial institutions, the group replied, "Money is everything for you."[43]

Iran, too, has been attempting to hack U.S. financial institutions. The *New York Times* reported in January 2013 that Iran has been hacking American banks: "The attackers hit one American bank after the next. As in so many previous attacks, dozens of online banking sites slowed, hiccuped or ground to a halt before recovering several minutes later.… Security researchers say that instead of exploiting individual computers, the attackers engineered networks of computers in data centers, transforming the online equivalent of a few yapping Chihuahuas into a pack of fire-breathing Godzillas."[44]

Russian officials have observed our vulnerability to economic warfare. "[I]t is impossible to undermine such a big country like the U.S. through trade," said the Russian intelligence expert and former KGB officer Konstantin Georgiyevich Preobrazhenskiy. "But it is possible through espionage, sabotage and other types of covert operations. Both Russia and China know the weaknesses of America and they use it as best they can."[45]

And yet nothing has been done.

And while we wait, the enemy acts.

London has become ground zero for economic warfare. Great Britain is not as financially powerful as the United States, and its Muslim population is more militant and more influenced by Middle Eastern potentates. That makes British markets even more vulnerable than America's. London has played a major role in nearly every aspect of the financial terrorism we have identified. During the 2008 financial collapse, the lion's share of shorting was coming from overseas sources such as London and Dubai. In 2013, emails were leaked from a major investment group based in London, Standard Chartered. One of them disclosed that a U.S. regulator had been told by a New York branch officer, "You f---ing Americans. Who are you to tell us, the rest of the world, that we're not going to deal with Iranians?" Standard Chartered has also been accused of hiding some $250 billion in sixty thousand transactions with Iran that could have been used to fund nuclear development or even terrorist activities.

The Chinese, too, are making massive inroads in London. In February 2013 the *Telegraph* reported that the Bank of England was closing in on a deal to make a currency swap with China, with the yuan emerging as a reserve currency. Some U.S. officials are actually encouraging this arrangement in the hope that it will strengthen the yuan against the dollar and improve our exports. But this approach assumes that the dollar will always be a highly sought-after reserve currency. This strategy represents a failure to appreciate that we could "win" a currency war of devaluation only to discover that we had destroyed the dollar in the process.[46]

Monetary issues, it appears, are trumping all other considerations.

Oil is once again a weapon against us. Iraq, abandoned by the United States, has largely become an Iranian proxy state. In November 2012 a high-ranking Iraqi urged other Muslim countries to "use the weapon of oil" against the United States in retaliation for our support for Israel. "The economic weapon is the strongest one to be put into effect now, to assure of standing by the Palestinian people, in light of there being no military power that can stand in the face of Israel at the present time," the diplomat stated.[47] Just as Russia aspires to become the world's top oil producer, the United States is inflicting on itself ever more restrictive environmental regulations.

The ultimate economic weapon—one that makes all the others seem like child's play—is an electromagnetic pulse (EMP) attack designed to take America back to a pre-industrial age in a matter of seconds. This isn't science fiction. It's real, and a number of nations have been developing capabilities to carry out such an attack. And we have admitted to having no real ability to combat such a weapon.[48]

So what is the United States doing about these threats? Plunging its head deeper into the sand. In 2010, Bill Gertz reported, "The Pentagon's intelligence directorate is killing off one of its most strategically important mission areas: monitoring efforts by foreign governments to buy U.S. firms and technology.... The officials said that the move will kill one of the Pentagon's most important and successful financial-threat monitoring programs, designed to track illicit and legal acquisition efforts by China and other foreign nations."[49]

While we are reducing our efforts to monitor and combat foreign influence, potential enemies such as China have actually stepped up efforts of political warfare. Bill Gertz reports:

> The activities of the People's Liberation Army (PLA) General Political Department (GPD) include funding pro-China activities abroad, recruiting intelligence sources, spreading propaganda, engaging in media activities, funding front groups that promote Chinese strategy and goals and supporting perceived "friends" of China.
>
> The report is the first public study of Chinese military political warfare and was produced by the Project 2049 Institute, an Arlington, Va., think tank focused on bringing democracy to China and other Asian countries by 2049....

Among the targets are "international elites" who are used to undermine the integrity of groups and people Beijing views as anti-China.

"At the strategic level, a core PLA political warfare mission is countering perceived political challenges that liberal democratic systems, universal values, and Western culture pose to the [Chinese Communist party's] legitimacy within China itself and the broader international community."[50]

This means that the Chinese PLA has been funding American groups such as think tanks to deny that China is any sort of threat to America, even as the PLA has been actively pushing warlike preparations at home.

It is no wonder, then, that in April 2012, President Obama did virtually nothing to help the Chinese dissident Chen Guangcheng when he escaped from house arrest and fled to the U.S. embassy. China holds hundreds of billions of dollars of U.S. debt, and we aren't doing anything to stop them from buying our institutions. We are in a compromised position. They know it, and we are unprepared to deal with it.

If America is to face down financial ruin, however, it will start with the dollar. It is to the dollar that we turn next.

CHAPTER TWO

This Time Is Different

B ack in summer of 2007, Jim Cramer of *Mad Money* on CNBC
went on a rant about the lack of knowledge at the Federal
Reserve:

I have talked to the heads of almost every one of these firms
in the last seventy-two hours and he has *no idea* what it's like
out there. *None!* And Bill Poole [then the president of the
Federal Reserve Bank of St. Louis], he has *no idea* what it's
like out there. My people have been in this game for twenty-
five years, and they're *losing their jobs* and these firms are
gonna *go out of business* and it's nuts. They're *nuts!* They
know *nothing!* This is a different kinda market. And the Fed

is *asleep*. Bill Poole is a shame, he's *shameful*! He oughta go
and *read* the Accredited Home document, at least I *read* the
darn thing.

Cramer was mocked. But he was right, as the release of Fed transcripts
later proved.[1] In 2008 he was mocked again when he claimed that a spate
of short selling targeting the financial markets could be the work of
financial terrorists.[2]

He's still right. They still know nothing. Only this time it could be
much worse.

Central bankers, including the Fed, seem convinced of their course
once again while ignoring what should be obvious warning signs. The
Fed is leading a global charge among central bankers to devalue their
currencies. As Randall W. Forsyth of *Barron's* writes, "Everybody's racing
to the bottom these days, including the central bankers." He quotes Joan
McCullough, a financial researcher, who says of both Japan and the
United States, "'They did it. And it didn't work. Then we did it. And it
didn't work. Now they're gonna do it again because they're sure that it
works.... It is at the same time shocking and disheartening that these
goobers have not yet figured out that printing money does little beyond
goosing stock and commodities prices.'"[3]

Many observers, including our enemies, predicted that Western
central banks would respond by devaluing their currencies. It was clear
that bin Laden and others intended to "bleed us to death" not by their
terrorist attacks but by what they knew would be our response.[4] It is the
predicted response that creates the opportunity for the kill. In my 2009
Pentagon report, I warned,

> The concern is that the response to the recent collapse *by itself*
> will strain available economic resources for some time with
> large budget deficits and high inflation risks. The situation

would be made significantly worse in the event of further economic attack. It is in this vein that a potential Phase Three must be considered.

Based on the assumed nature of Phase One and Phase Two, a Phase Three attack would likely involve dumping of U.S. Treasuries and a trashing of the dollar, removing it from reserve currency status. This is clearly foreseeable as a risk....[5]

When I wrote that report, our officials were convinced of the dollar's permanent strength and appeal. When Treasury Secretary Timothy Geithner spoke at Peking University in June 2009, he reassured the audience of students that China's dollar investments were safe. They broke out laughing.[6]

No one in the government is listening. Our officials can't imagine that we are at risk, even as our enemies are strategizing our demise.

Parties in Russia and China as well as in the Middle East and Latin America are planning to launch an all-out assault on the dollar's reserve status in an effort to destroy our economy. In my work for the Pentagon, I described "Phase Three" of the offensive against the American economy—a devastating attack on our currency. It may sound far fetched, but the evidence is there, and it is well documented. We can be certain that such plots exist, whether or not they ultimately become successful. Yet the Federal Reserve and the Obama administration seem hell-bent on the very policies that make us most vulnerable.

The risk of a Phase Three has quickly emerged, suggesting a potential direct economic attack on the U.S. Treasury and U.S. dollar. Such an event has already been discussed by finance ministers in major emerging market nations such as China and Russia, as well as Iran and the Arab states. A focused effort to collapse the dollar by dumping Treasury bonds has grave implications, including the possibility of a downgrading of U.S. debt, forcing rapidly rising interest rates and an ultimate collapse of the American economy. In short, a bear raid against the U.S. financial system remains possible and may even be likely.

The Inflation Threat

In February 2013 the Dow Jones Industrial Average hit 14,000 for the first time since October 2007. While Wall Street celebrated, others noticed that the American economy had actually *contracted* in the fourth quarter of 2012. The economist Arthur Laffer expressed dismay at the "catastrophic" conditions, pointing out that the "whole output of the economy" was on the downslope. "It's amazing, isn't it?" he said. "We spent $5.8 trillion in the last couple of years, and this is what we get for it. Have you ever heard of a poor man spending himself into prosperity? It's just dumb on the outset.... Government doesn't create resources, it redistributes resources. And this government spending stuff is why we have the great recession."[7]

How then to explain the return of good times on Wall Street? It's all fake. It takes a lot of monetary printing that hasn't yet affected the real economy but has gone into Wall Street's financial markets, first in bonds and now into stocks. Dylan Grice of Societe Generale's Global Strategy Team sums up the issue well: "When you devalue money, you devalue trust.... If we print a trillion dollars, we can now spend a trillion dollars. We have absolutely benefitted from this. We have a trillion dollars that otherwise we wouldn't have had. But the question is: Who pays for that trillion dollars?" Monetary inflation leads to social breakdown. It is the ultimate economic warfare weapon. Looking at stock prices in isolation might cause you to believe a recovery is under way. Looking at the bigger picture, however, brings you to the conclusion that the currency collapse leading to the end of America may well be at hand.[8]

While the government continues to maintain that it is not inflating the currency—after all, prices have not yet skyrocketed—the truth is that the currency bubble is enormous at this point. Jeff Clark of Casey Research points out that there are two kinds of inflation: price inflation and inflation in the quantity of cash. Clark, citing the researchers Carmen Reinhart and Kenneth Rogoff, points out that debt levels amounting to more than 90 percent of GDP are highly correlated with inflation. Historically, when U.S. debt levels have gone above that benchmark, inflation has risen to around 6 percent. But there is a delayed effect— inflation and debt do not happen at exactly the same time. Low inflation can quickly escalate. From 1915 to 1917, the inflation rate jumped from 1 percent to 17 percent. From 1945 to 1947, inflation jumped from 2 percent to 14 percent, and from 1972 to 1974, it skyrocketed from 3.2 percent to 11 percent.[9]

Keep in mind that even though inflation hasn't spiked yet, we can't assume that it won't. As Michael Snyder observes, Weimar Germany had its own brand of "quantitative easing" to pump its economy:

> The Federal Reserve is recklessly printing money out of thin air, and in the short-term some positive things have come out of it. But quantitative easing worked for the Weimar Republic for a little while too. At first, more money caused economic activity to increase and unemployment was low. But all of that money printing destroyed faith in German currency and in the German financial system and ultimately Germany experienced an economic meltdown that the world is still talking about today. This is the path that the Federal Reserve is taking America down, but most Americans have absolutely no idea what is happening.
>
> It is really easy to start printing money, but it is incredibly hard to stop. Like any addict, the Fed is promising that they can quit at any time, but this month [September 2013] they refused to even start tapering their money printing a little bit.

The behavior of the Fed is so shameful that even CNBC is comparing it to a drug addict at this point....[10]

Of course, despite the appearance of economic progress in Germany, a hyperinflationary collapse became inevitable. I have a German bank note labeled "ein Million Mark," printed in 1923, that came from my grandmother. It is printed on only one side—the currency literally wasn't worth the paper it was printed on.[11] I keep it as a souvenir and reminder of how a government can unwittingly destroy its currency.

The columnist Doug Hagmann actually theorizes that the Obama administration intends to "kill" the U.S. dollar: "An alliance is being forged between Russia and China to replace the USD as the reserve currency, already severely weakened by the policies of those in power, with a gold backed currency. Russia and China are hoarding gold to levels never before seen, while the U.S. issues worthless paper and digital currency backed by ... nothing, save for the 'oil-backed' scenario." Whatever Obama's intentions may be, the fact remains that Hagmann's take on what our enemies are up to is correct. They are out in force, and we have not even come close to responding correctly.[12]

The Federal Reserve, in an attempt to prop up the failing economy, has announced that it will continue to engage in quantitative easing—buying long-term U.S. government securities—until the economy is healed. Which, in effect, may mean forever. "Surprise unconventional policy easing has pushed down the value of the dollar roughly as much as similar surprise downward moves in the federal funds rate did before the crisis," said Reuven Glick and Sylvain Leduc, vice presidents of research at the San Francisco Federal Reserve.[13] There is only one problem: buying up long-term securities means printing money. The only other option is to sell the debt to foreigners. And that means that those who own our debt can harm us if they are determined to do so.

Welcome to Debt Hell

In 2012, Terence Jeffrey reported in his book *Completely Predictable* that "the combined spending of federal, state and local governments per American household [$50,000] actually exceeded the median household income for 2010," which was just under $50,000. Spending on that scale is utterly unsustainable; the only way to make it work is to borrow piles upon piles of cash. Because we are the reserve currency—because people need U.S. dollars—we can get away with it. But that won't last forever.[14]

As I write, the reported federal debt is about $17 trillion, with the debt held outside the U.S. government totaling almost $12 trillion, amounting to over three-quarters of our annual GDP.[15] If we don't raise taxes *and* cut spending, we're in serious trouble—even conservative estimates show national debt rising to a whopping 153 percent of GDP by 2035. Greece's ratio is currently 153 percent. The unemployment rate here would climb to over 20 percent, as it has done in Greece. Taxing the rich won't work, whatever President Obama tells you—if the marginal tax rate were to skyrocket 50 percent on the top 1 percent of earners, by the end of the decade the national debt would nevertheless exceed $20 trillion.[16]

America's unfunded liabilities amount to up to $115 trillion by some estimates (and that is before Obamacare kicks in).[17] And the situation might be far worse. Laurence J. Kotlikoff, an economics professor at Boston University, estimates that our true debt might be on the order of $211 trillion.[18]

So how are we financing that debt? Other than creating it at the Fed, we're financing it by relying on one of our greatest geopolitical adversaries: China owns over 7 percent of all outstanding federal debt. If China were to sell that debt, it would destroy the market for U.S. debt, undermining our ability to raise money to pay off our short-term debt.[19] But our government is not taking that threat seriously. The Defense Department dismissed the threat in July 2012, as reported by Bill Gertz in the *Washington Times*: "'Attempting to use U.S. Treasury securities as a coercive tool would have limited effect and likely would do more harm to China than to the United States,' says the five-page report entitled, 'Assessment of the National Security Risks Posed to the United States as a Result of the U.S. Federal Debt Owed to China as a Creditor of the U.S. Government.'" The same article mentioned my disagreement with this assessment.[20]

This report came out at the same time as a broader Defense Department report about potential weapons of mass destruction, which Gertz covered in the same article:

> A Pentagon-sponsored report warns that the United States faces new threats from mass destruction weapons in the form of cyber, electronic and financial attacks, in addition to more well-known dangers from nuclear, chemical and biological WMD arms.
>
> "In addition to the prolific conventional [weapons of mass destruction] threats posed by a vast network of state and non-state actors, the U.S. must also contend with emerging threats that are not conventionally recognized as WMD," said the report produced last month for the office of the Undersecretary of Defense for Intelligence.
>
> "Very few of America's adversaries will attempt to challenge the unmatched strength of the U.S. military in a traditional conflict, but they may employ alternative asymmetric approaches.
>
> "It is therefore necessary to consider emergent, nontraditional threats, such as cyber, electromagnetic pulse (EMP), and economic attacks, in a comprehensive discussion of WMD threats."

On financial warfare, the report mentions the 1999 Chinese military book, "Unrestricted Warfare," which advocates that China's military utilize stock market crashes, computer viruses and currency manipulations.

"Essentially, any threat to the U.S. economy is a threat to the country as a whole, and the potential impact of an economic attack is considered increasingly significant," the report said.[21]

Bottom line? We are naively betting our nation's future on the notion that China would never purposefully harm its own holdings by dumping U.S. debt. But we are assuming that China's interest is economic growth rather than destruction of the economy of its largest geopolitical foe. That may not be the case.[22]

Even without a direct assault on the dollar, we still have huge problems.

Former Federal Reserve governor Frederic Mishkin, along with David Greenlaw of Morgan Stanley, James Hamilton of the University of California at San Diego, and Peter Hooper of Deutsche Bank, wrote in the *Wall Street Journal* that the United States' massive debt could create "a fiscal crunch [that] would force a central bank to pursue inflationary policies, a situation that's called fiscal dominance." If the United States did not print money to pay off its debt, interest rates would have to rise, since private lenders are nervous about earning back their money. Those higher rates would make borrowing tougher, and the economy would contract. To enable continued borrowing, the Fed would have to print more cash. And that would lead to "a surge in inflation." In order to prevent that catastrophe, the four economists wrote, the government would have to start by "gradually reining in spending on entitlement programs such as Medicare, Medicaid and Social Security, while increasing tax revenue by broadening the base." But the chances of such cutbacks are slim. In fact, some commentators say that the government has already passed the threshold in printing cash. Steve Forbes said, "Like steroids in baseball, it ultimately wrecks the player. The government is making it easier to borrow money for mortgage-backed securities and the like, and small businesses, households have a hard time getting credit."[23]

Former Florida governor Jeb Bush said in March 2013, "No one argues that we can keep doing what we're doing. So either we have it collapse or we change it to protect it.... [We must raise] the retirement age to reflect the life expectancy increase that's been dramatic, means testing some of the entitlement programs over time. We have to reform healthcare underneath the entitlement system as well so that the cost curve is dealt with, which means we should move toward catastrophic coverage as the form of insurance and reward healthy lifestyle decisions and focus on prevention to lessen cost by improving healthcare outcomes."[24] The chances of that happening: close to zero. With America's demographic pyramid completely upside down, older voters now dictate how benefits are distributed. They will not vote to cut their own benefits, and any party that suggests they do will meet electoral defeat.

Gene Epstein of *Barron's* sums up the problem: "Despite media coverage to the contrary, the updated 10-year projections of the Congressional Budget Office ... confirm that the long-term debt crisis faced by the federal government is as much a threat as ever."[25]

That could spell the end of our way of life as we know it, much sooner than anyone expects.

The End of the Dollar as Reserve Currency?

In February 2013, CNBC reported that the dollar was dying: "The U.S. dollar is shrinking as a percentage of the world's currency supply, raising concerns that the greenback is about to see its long run as the world's premier denomination come to an end." Michael Pento, president of Pento Portfolio Strategies, told CNBC, "The No. 1 security issue we have as a nation is the preservation of the U.S. dollar as the world's reserve currency. It's a thousand times more important that we keep the dollar as the world's reserve currency, and yet we are doing everything to abuse that status." He estimated that the United States could lose reserve currency status as early as 2015.[26]

Americans don't want to believe that the dollar could be overthrown. "But it will be," Dick Bove of Rafferty Capital Markets wrote in February 2013, "and this defrocking may occur in as short a period as five to ten years." Bove points out that the U.S. dollar is dropping precipitously as a percentage of the global money supply, down to a fifteen-year low. That's not because of a shortage of dollars in circulation. It's because fewer people want to use it.[27]

The dollar still represents 62 percent of the foreign exchange holdings by central banks around the globe, but that number is rapidly dropping as more and more nations begin trading in the Chinese yuan, the Swiss franc, and the Japanese yen.[28]

Russia announced that it would be avoiding the U.S. dollar by converting its oil revenues into gold bullion—adding 570 metric tons of gold in the past decade, according to the International Monetary Fund. That would weigh more than three Statues of Liberty.[29] Of course, Russia has also long predicted a collapse of the dollar that would destroy the United States. Igor Panarin, a former KGB friend of Putin's and the dean of the Russian foreign ministry's academy for future diplomats, has predicted the collapse of the U.S.-led monetary system and the consequent fragmentation of the United States into six separate countries. Russia and China, he says, will together assume leadership of the global economy when America disappears. What is startling is that he first made this prediction in 1998, repeating it in 2008.[30] Panarin's prediction, Putin's repeated calls for the end of the dollar, and the 2008 "disruptive scheme" that Treasury Secretary Paulson revealed, in which Russia tried to have China join in collapsing the American economy, all make it clear that the leadership of Russia not only expects America's economic demise but is willing to work to make it happen.[31]

In March 2013 the Australian government announced that it would not be using the U.S. dollar for its reserve currency in dealings with China. Instead, Australian cash will be swapped for yuan. "The value of such a deal would be substantial for exporters to China, especially those that import a lot from China like mining companies, as it would remove business constraints including exchange-rate risks and transaction costs," said Geoff Raby, Australia's former ambassador to China.[32]

It's not just Australia. That same month, Brazil and China agreed to a direct exchange of currencies. The exchange will amount to approximately $30 billion per year. "Our interest is not to establish new relations with China, but to expand relations to be used in the case of turbulence in financial markets," said the governor of the Brazilian central bank, Alexandre Tombini. Zhou Zhiwei, a researcher with the Chinese Academy of Social Sciences, agreed: "Trade ties between China and Brazil are of great importance to the two countries' economies amid global woes and the member states' economic stability is vital for the BRICS mechanism." (BRICS is a cooperative organization made up of Brazil, Russia, India, China, and South Africa.) India called this development "the new axis of global development," with Anand Sharma, India's minister of commerce, industry, and textiles, stating, "The global economic order created several decades ago is now undergoing change and we believe for the better to make it more representative."[33]

By late March the BRICS nations were planning the establishment of a development bank to avoid the American-controlled World Bank and International Monetary Fund. Martyn Davies, chief executive officer of Johannesburg-based Frontier Advisory, told Bloomberg News, "The deepest rationale for the BRICS is almost certainly the creation of new Bretton Woods–type institutions that are inclined toward the developing world. There's a shift in power from the traditional to the emerging world. There is a lot of geo-political concern about this shift in the western world." The BRICS nations had a combined foreign currency reserve of $4.4 trillion in 2013. Trade between the BRICS nations could hit $500 billion by 2015.[34]

In February 2013 the Bank of England struck a deal with China to set up a yuan-sterling swap for three years. Direct trading of the yuan jumped 400 percent from 2010 to 2013. "In the unlikely event that a generalized shortage of offshore renminbi* liquidity emerges," said Sir Mervyn King, governor of the bank, "the Bank of England will have the capability to provide renminbi liquidity to eligible institutions in the U.K." In other words, the British are worried about the stability of the yuan but want to make sure they have enough yuan to trade because they don't trust the dollar.[35]

Turkey has been trading gold for oil with Iran to get around economic sanctions.[36] India is reportedly doing so as well, and China is expected to follow suit. The price of gold is therefore expected to rise, and the dollar's value will therefore be depressed.[37]

Other Asian economies, too, are moving away from the American dollar, with a so-called renminbi bloc forming in East Asia. The Peterson Institute for International Economics says that China has now moved closer than ever to the renminbi's becoming a global reserve currency. Seven of ten regional economies are now more closely tied to the renminbi than to the dollar.[38]

China is the greatest threat in the disestablishment of the dollar as the reserve currency. The group that manages China's currency reserves is diversifying from the U.S. government bonds it had been buying in

---

* Renminbi ("People's Currency"), abbreviated RMB, is the formal term for Chinese currency. The yuan is the basic unit of the currency, as the pound is the basic unit of sterling. There is no term for American currency analogous to renminbi; we speak in terms only of the unit of currency, the dollar.

bulk. In June 2013, "[f]oreign holders dumped a whopping $40.8 billion in long-term Treasuries, the biggest exodus from bonds in the history of the U.S.," reports the financial researcher Mike Larson. China alone accounted for half of those sales, which followed a string of monthly selling going back to earlier in the year.[39] Holding up the bond market is the Fed, buying billions in treasuries each month.[40]

So where is China putting its money if not in dollars? We suspect that the Chinese have been quietly adding to their gold holdings. While many American economists would question the wisdom of that approach, leaked cables from the American embassy in Beijing have provided insight into their thinking:

> "China increases its gold reserves in order to kill two birds with one stone."
>
> The China Radio International sponsored newspaper World News Journal (Shijie Xinwenbao) (04/28): "According to China's National Foreign Exchanges Administration China's gold reserves have recently increased. Currently, the majority of its gold reserves have been located in the U.S. and European countries. The U.S. and Europe have always suppressed the rising price of gold. They intend to weaken gold's function as an international reserve currency. They don't want to see other countries turning to gold reserves instead of the U.S. dollar or Euro. Therefore, suppressing the price of gold is very beneficial for the U.S. in maintaining the U.S. dollar's role as the international reserve currency. China's increased gold reserves will thus act as a model and lead other countries towards reserving more gold. Large gold reserves are also beneficial in promoting the internationalization of the RMB."[41]

China is moving full speed ahead to substitute its own currency for the United States' dollar. CNBC reported in September 2011 that the yuan would be fully convertible—that is, Chinese businesses and investors could freely convert yuan to other currencies, a step toward becoming a basis currency—within five years.[42] It might happen even sooner. In September 2013, Gordon Chang, a well-known China analyst, predicted that full convertibility for China's currency would happen "in months."[43] According to Russian media, the stage would be set for a gold-backed yuan to displace the dollar: "Recent media reports suggest that Beijing is considering backing the yuan with gold. This decision, if taken, will likely affect China's economy and may trigger a new wave of the global economic crisis. For Russia, however, such a scenario may have its benefits.... Beijing's possible move to back the yuan with gold ... would be a flaunt aimed at demonstrating to the world (and to the USA in particular) that China is capable of taking the risks associated with a departure from the dollar standard."[44]

The desire to enhance the yuan's status was made clear in a 2010 article published in *Qiushi*, an official journal of the Chinese Communist party: "The fact that the U.S. dollar is the world's reserve currency makes the U.S. a financial superpower. Currently, China's increased share in the International Monetary Fund and its increased voting rights are a very big step forward. The problem is not that the value of this share is expressed in U.S. dollars, but that it would be best if the share could be expressed in RMB. Therefore, for China to challenge the position of the U.S. dollar, it needs to take a path of internationalization and directly confront the U.S. dollar."[45]

It is important to note that such a move has been backed by none other than Russian president Vladimir Putin.[46] Russian state-sponsored media, undoubtedly at his direction, have become major cheerleaders for the yuan to displace the dollar:

The "people's currency" of China is redefining the global economic monetary system. The closed-capital pariah is blossoming into a reserve standard and is hedging appeal against the indebted dollar and the untested euro, piquing foreign interest.

Degenerating credit quality across the board has prompted asset managers to shy away from the dollar, euro, Japanese yen, British pound, and Swiss franc. And some are turning to the yuan, a currency that 10 years ago was completely off limits to foreign investors.

An HSBC forecast projected that by 2015, the yuan will become one of the three most used currencies in global trade, in league with the dollar and euro.[47]

Putin has long desired for Russia and China to join forces against America.[48] Middle Eastern interests also want to see the dollar fail and be replaced by the yuan. The supposedly moderate Al Jazeera, based in Qatar, has explored the question "Why China Might Be a Better Superpower":

Unlike the U.S., China does not have a substantial history of invading and subjugating the inhabitants of far-flung lands.

While China is far less free domestically, in international affairs the country continues to ascend both economically and in terms of international influence. It is thus worth asking, is this a positive development for the world at large? Could China be a more responsible, less violent and more constructive superpower than the U.S.?

The contrast between China's culturally sensitive approach and the contemptuous and violent attitude taken by the U.S. in Iraq cannot be overstated. In fact, these

contrasts are in many ways a reflection of the differing world-
views and historical backgrounds of the two countries.

 While the U.S. seems committed to exert imperial hegemony over the Middle East using brute military force and
punitive economic blockades against civilians, China has
publically committed to a policy of "peacefully rising" and
has built mutually beneficial and respectful relationships
throughout the region.[49]

Such rumblings from the Middle East call into question one of the few
remaining pillars of the dollar—its exclusive use in the oil trade. The
arrangement dates from the early 1970s and allowed the United States
to abandon the gold standard under Nixon and yet strengthen the dollar's reserve currency status. The United States offered Saudi Arabia
military protection and access to weapons and technology. In exchange,
the Saudis agreed, informally, to price oil sales only in dollars ("petrodol-
lars") and to invest the proceeds in U.S. Treasury bonds. By 1975 all
major oil exporters were demanding dollars for oil under a similar
arrangement.[50] This exchange guaranteed a global demand for dollars,
as anyone buying oil would have to have them. At the same time, it also
guaranteed a growing market for U.S. government debt.

 Of course, the situation in the Middle East has changed drastically
since the 1970s. America is no longer Saudi Arabia's preferred customer
for oil. China has taken that role.[51] The Arab Spring has toppled or
weakened several dictators who once supported the petrodollar system.[52]
And popular sentiment in the Arab world has turned decidedly anti-
American.[53] So when Al Jazeera opines that China is the better superpower, we should take notice. If the petrodollar system collapses, the
dollar crashes.[54] The preferred replacement is a gold-backed yuan.[55]

 Most American economists dismiss the notion of the yuan's displac-
ing the dollar as far fetched. They are wrong, suffering from a type of

"normalcy bias," assuming that what has been will always be. Arvind Subramanian, senior fellow at the Peterson Institute for International Economics, has a different view. Within this decade, he says, the yuan could do more than just challenge the dollar for reserve status. "Chinese economic dominance is more imminent and more broad-based—encompassing output, trade, and currency—than is currently recognized," he wrote. "By 2030, this dominance could resemble that of the United States in the 1970s and the United Kingdom around 1870. And this economic dominance will in turn elevate the renminbi to premier reserve currency status much sooner than currently expected."[56]

If the yuan becomes a reserve currency, there is little doubt that China will use its power for political advantage. In September 2012 a senior advisor to the Chinese government called for an attack on the Japanese bond market. Jin Baisong of the Chinese Academy of International Trade, which works for the commerce ministry, said China should use the "security exception" rule under the World Trade Organization to harm Japan. "It's clear that China can deal a heavy blow to the Japanese economy without hurting itself too much," he said. Secretary of Defense Leon Panetta could only call for calm.[57]

Make no mistake—there are plenty of nations that resent the hegemony of the dollar in the world economy. We should understand that no paper currency has ever been permanent. In fact, a recent study demonstrated that most currencies barely make it past age twenty-five: "The average life expectancy for a fiat currency is 27 years, with the shortest life span being one month. Founded in 1694, the British pound Sterling is the oldest fiat currency in existence. At a ripe old age of 317 years it must be considered a highly successful fiat currency. However, success is relative. The British pound was defined as 12 ounces of silver, so it's worth less than 1/200 or 0.5 percent of its original value. In other words, the most successful long standing currency in existence has lost 99.5 percent of its value."[58]

We shouldn't bet our future and our children's future on the U.S. dollar's surviving a $17 trillion debt that is growing by $1 trillion or more every year—especially since we are facing an unprecedented global economic war.

The Currency War

The United States' debt is on a collision course with reality, yet we keep digging ourselves deeper into the hole of inflation and borrowing. Bill Gross, founder and co–chief investment officer of Pacific Investment Management Company (PIMCO), said in February 2013 that the U.S. economy is on the pathway to extinction. "Our current monetary system," he said, "seems to require perpetual expansion to maintain its existence. The advancing entropy in the physical universe may in fact portend a similar decline of 'energy' and 'heat' within the credit markets." Noting that total government, corporate, household, and personal debt in the United States amounts to a stunning $56 trillion, Gross said that the credit needs of the American economy constitute a "supernova star that expands and expands, yet, in the process begins to consume itself." It now takes twenty dollars of credit to generate one dollar of GDP, according to Gross.[59]

The American debt problem is so horrible that Republicans have tried to use the debt ceiling as leverage to stop government spending. But new and creative solutions are being found to avoid spending cuts, including one incredible proposal to mint platinum trillion-dollar coins, which would not require congressional approval.[60] The proposal was for the Treasury to take a small amount of platinum, shape it into a coin, and stamp "one trillion dollars" on it. The Treasury has the right to mint coins of various denominations. In this case, however, they would be telling the world that the coins were "worth" $1 trillion each and use them to pay off debts. Fortunately, despite support from several economists and members of the administration, the outrageous scheme sort of fizzled. If it had been implemented, the dollar would have collapsed immediately.[61]

So let's assume we're not minting trillion-dollar coins, but we also aren't interested in cutting our spending. That means we will have to devalue our currency as another way to pay off our debts by printing money the old-fashioned way. The dollar would be a "sitting duck" for others to destroy, as we have already discussed. Then again, some nations may choose to join us in devaluing their currencies and paying down their debt by inflation also. This situation is known as a currency war, one of the most dangerous developments in international economics, says the investment banker and researcher James Rickards. He warns there are abundant signs of a coming currency war, which would threaten the dollar with collapse.[62]

If there is a currency war, will the United States win? The economist Peter Schiff says yes—but that if we do, our currency will then implode, making things much, much worse. "There is a currency war going on," Schiff says. "The irony of a currency war which makes it different from other wars is the object is to kill itself. Unfortunately, I think the U.S. is going to win the currency war."

"Anybody who believes there is no inflation isn't shopping." Schiff's point is simple: the only way to win a currency war is by devaluing your currency. But if we do that, we run the risk of inflating prices for everything, destroying our economy, and making it impossible for us to pay off our long-term debts.[63] Schiff points out that both in the eurozone and in the United States so much focus has been placed on full employment that devaluing the currency appears to be the only option: "The problem is that economists now believe that the goal of an economy is to provide employment, not goods and services. They see a job as an end in and of itself, rather than as a means for people to get the things they really want. But if we can get all that we want without having to work, who needs to bother?"[64]

China is already thinking about a currency war and how to use it to its advantage. The same article from the *Qiushi* journal quoted earlier states, "Of course, to fight the U.S., we have to come up with key weapons. What is the most powerful weapon China has today? It is our economic power, especially our foreign exchange reserves (USD 2.8 trillion). The key is to use it well. If we use it well, it is a weapon; otherwise it may become a burden.... China, Japan, the U.K., India, and Saudi Arabia are all countries with high foreign exchange reserves." The article continues, "Of course, the most important condition is still that China must have enough courage to challenge the U.S. currency. China can act in one of two ways. One is to sell U.S. dollar reserves, and the second is not to buy U.S. dollars for a certain period of time."[65]

It's not unusual for fiat currencies—currencies not based on tangible holdings like gold, but on a value set by the government that backs that currency—to collapse. Aside from the pound sterling, major fiat currencies have all collapsed by age forty-two. The American dollar in 2013 was in year forty-two of its fiat existence. And even the British pound is worth merely a small fraction of what it once was.[66]

According to Lawrence Goodman, a former Treasury official and the current president of the Center for Financial Stability, the Federal Reserve has been buying a stunning and unsustainable 61 percent of all government debt issued by the Treasury Department. Before the 2008 economic collapse, the Fed was buying "negligible amounts." If those conditions are not corrected, Goodman warns, the U.S. economy and markets are "at risk for a sharp correction." The current policy, he says, "not only creates the false appearance of limitless demand for U.S. debt but also blunts any sense of urgency to reduce supersized deficits."[67] No wonder when Federal Reserve chairman Ben Bernanke announced in the summer of 2013 that a tapering of the Fed's debt-buying program might be on the horizon, the stock market quickly dropped two hundred points.[68]

We're devaluing our currency. If we stop, the economy drops. If we don't, our economy could be murdered by our enemies.

The Coming Attack

Now, with all that in mind, let's review my team's Department of Defense report conclusions concerning economic warfare. In June 2009 we posited that the response to the collapse could

> strain available economic resources for some time with large budget deficits and high inflation risks. The situation would be made significantly worse in the event of further economic attack. It is in this vein that a potential Phase Three must be considered. Based on the assumed nature of Phase One and Phase Two, a Phase Three attack would likely involve dumping of U.S. Treasuries and a trashing of the dollar, removing it from reserve currency status. This is clearly foreseeable as a risk and even could float under the cover of a natural outcome in much the same way that Phases One and Two potentially have been hidden. The implications are extremely serious. If the dollar were not the reserve currency, there would be a mass dumping of Treasury instruments by foreign holders. Treasury interest rates would skyrocket, further worsening the annual deficits due to sharply higher interest payments on expanding debts. The Treasury would have to raise taxes dramatically, further dampening growth or the Federal Reserve would be forced to monetize the debt, worsening inflation concerns. Pushed to the limit, the U.S. dollar

would follow the path of the German currency in Weimar
Germany following defeat in World War I.

Despite that warning, the United States is right on schedule.

In recent years, we have seen economic attacks used to take down
regimes. In the 2011 uprising in Egypt that displaced Hosni Mubarak,
for example, the final trigger to the unrest was food prices, not anger
about human rights per se. It has been widely reported that food inflation was a primary factor behind the initial unrest. Egyptian households
spend about 40 percent of their budget on food, and food prices had
jumped 20 percent prior to the Egyptian revolution. Corn prices shot
up 90 percent, and wheat slightly less.[69] Speculation played a role in
higher food prices.[70] Certainly the global monetary inflation made this
possible.

There should be no doubt that there was a serious economic component behind the revolution in Egypt.[71] The question then arises
whether additional speculation on food prices could have been a geopolitical lever. Based on our research, the answer is an unequivocal yes.
Rapidly rising food prices can destabilize a society, and our enemies
know how to drive prices higher through speculative market activity.
We will see more destabilization caused by inflation-based riots.[72]

I am not saying that the Muslim Brotherhood speculated on food
prices as a weapon to topple Mubarak, although some sources say it did.
I am saying that it is obvious that such a weapon could have been
employed profitably, if imprecisely. The cost is certainly less than a major
arms program, but the results are more dramatic.

Now, attacking America with food-price inflation would be difficult
because we produce our own food.[73] But energy, especially oil, is another
matter. Could a huge oil price shock destroy our economy? Many think
so.[74] As long as the Arab nations, Russia, Iran, and Venezuela are the
major producers, a supply shock is always possible, and it is even called

for by liberated Iraq.[75] And, as with food, speculation can push prices higher even in the face of ample supply.[76]

That's an oblique attack. A currency war, a selling of U.S. bonds, or an attempt to set another currency as the reserve currency would be far more direct and just as damaging. Whether from China or Russia or from rogue states like North Korea counterfeiting currency, America has left herself wide open to all sorts of economic attacks.

Could It Happen?

A common objection to my warning is that the Chinese are so connected to our economy that "they" would never harm us. The idea that "the Chinese" would never harm us is ridiculous on its face; there are Chinese who continually hack our systems and who manipulate and undermine our markets. But don't the Chinese hold so much in dollar debt that they couldn't afford to see the dollar go down? China's military doesn't care. It has a much longer view of things than the next quarter's export sales. The smug response of those who believe China needs us so much that it must remain our friend is another example of American arrogance.

There is further evidence of the danger from China. We have no idea how much dollar debt the Chinese really hold. They have so many ways to obscure their holdings that we can't ever be certain.[77] In March 2012, Treasury Secretary Timothy Geithner said he didn't see any risk to the dollar from China's attempts to establish the yuan as reserve currency with its trading partners. "What you're seeing China do," Geithner explained, "is gradually dismantle what were a comprehensive set of very, very tight controls on the ability of countries to use their currency," Geithner said. "Over time that will mean—and this is a good thing for the United States—more use of that currency and it will mean the currency will have to reflect market forces ... So, I see no risk to the dollar in those reforms." Geithner added that it was virtually impossible for the Chinese currency to become a global reserve currency. "I don't think so," he said. "I don't know, maybe in some long time after we're all gone, it would be possible."[78] Of course, Geithner also insisted that the United States would not lose its AAA credit rating in 2011. Three months later, we were downgraded.[79]

While there are a number of naive analysts who view our codependence as a force that will preserve the dollar forever, a more objective view is provided by Juan Zarate in his book *Treasury's War*. Zarate was one of the top Bush administration officials charged with using financial weapons to fight terrorism. He writes:

> Economic historian Niall Ferguson has dubbed this presently symbiotic yet ultimately dysfunctional relationship "Chimerica…." Chimerica is, for Ferguson, highly unstable. A sudden deterioration in political relations, perhaps stemming from a clash over natural resources or Taiwan, could trigger a major war and a corresponding collapse of the international financial system.
>
> A small but systemically critical event—such as the collapse of the Spanish bond market—could ignite a widespread loss of confidence in paper currencies and a massive transition to hard assets (gold) led by a shrewd and forward-leaning competitor state such as Russia or China.
>
> Even if one doubts the likelihood of such a crisis, China is nonetheless taking steps to internationalize the renminbi and thereby enhance its power relative to the dollar.
>
> Though the dollar remains predominant for now and seems to be the currency of choice amid economic turmoil in Europe, it—along with American financial predominance—is coming under direct assault.[80]

Here is the sad truth: while it once was in China's interest to preserve the dollar's unique status as primary reserve currency, that time is passing rapidly. The Chinese understand that the U.S. debt situation will preclude us from continuing to binge on their products. Without export growth, China must focus on domestic consumption.[81] This favors a stronger, not weaker, yuan.[82] To survive economically, they have to adapt and use their economic weapons, even at our expense. There are several key factions in China. There is the business community, which had long supported a weak yuan to enhance exports but now needs a strong domestic consumer. There is the ruling Communist party, which has put forward five-year plans for global dominance.[83] And there is the People's Liberation Army, which has promoted unrestricted warfare.[84] For the first time in decades, the interests of all three are beginning to align against the dollar.

In discussing the implications of a currency collapse, George Soros told *Der Spiegel* in 2011, "The euro exists, and if it were to break apart, all hell would break loose."[85] Now imagine that happening to the dollar.

It doesn't take much to imagine. We are already on the brink.

CHAPTER THREE

Making It Personal

L et's say America experiences an economic attack. How will it affect
you personally? What will it mean for your job, your real estate
values, your 401(k), your savings? What will it mean for your
children's future?

In this chapter, we'll examine the broad economic issues and show
how they have direct, personal, and potentially devastating effects on
everything each of us holds dear. We'll detail the effects on workers,
entrepreneurs, business people, consumers, investors, families, and
taxpayers. This is not an academic exercise. We are anticipating an attack
that is very much a possibility.

And most people won't see it coming until they feel their wallets get
lighter.

In 2008 only a small percentage of Americans had even heard of credit default swaps, let alone invested in them. Unfortunately, ignorance is no protection. Most Americans were paying their mortgages, unaware that a housing crisis would sink the economy. Yet because the housing bubble burst and the stock market crashed, millions of Americans lost their jobs. Since the 2008 collapse, reliance on food stamps has risen 70 percent. Almost fifty million Americans—one in five—receive them.[1] Put another way, the number of persons on food stamps exceeds the population of twenty-four states plus the District of Columbia.[2] Even though the federal government spends $1 trillion a year on anti-poverty programs—more than on Social Security or defense[3]—poverty is increasing, with almost fifty million citizens at or below the poverty line.[4]

Then there's unemployment. According to a study from the Center for American Studies, *fewer* native-born Americans have jobs now than had jobs in the year 2000; the entire net job creation of the country has gone to immigrants, including illegal immigrants. Nonetheless, our leaders are seriously talking about the legalization of another twelve million immigrants. "The economic problem facing America right now is not too few workers, but too many unemployed workers," lamented Senator Jeff Sessions, a Republican from Alabama. "The Senate immigration bill [proposed in 2013] massively increases the supply of lower-skilled foreign workers, which would produce lower wages and higher unemployment.... [P]olls clearly show the American people don't support such an approach."[5]

The unemployment rate more than doubled over the course of the crisis. According to the Bureau of Labor Statistics, from December 2007 to October 2009, the unemployment rate jumped from 5 percent to 10 percent. BLS reported, "The employment decline experienced during the December 2007–June 2009 recession was greater than that of any recession of recent decades. Forty-seven months after the start of the recession that began in November 1973, for example, employment was more than 7 percent higher than it had been when the recession started. In contrast, 47 months after the start of the most recent recession (November 2011), employment was still over 4 percent lower than when the recession began."[6]

With a miserable job market, millions of Americans have dropped out of the labor force. In the ten recessions prior to 2007, it took an average of twenty-five months to recover all of the lost jobs. Peter Ferrara writes for *Forbes*, "[U]nder President Obama, by April 2013, *64 months after the prior jobs peak, almost 5 1/2 years,* we still have not recovered all of the recession's job losses. In April 2013, there were an estimated 135.474 million American workers employed, still down about 2.6 million jobs from the prior peak of 138.056 million in January 2008 [emphasis in original]."[7]

Worse still, the official unemployment rate understates how bad the jobs situation really is. In the summer of 2013, the real unemployment rate—counting those who are underemployed or who have dropped out of the labor force entirely—was near 18 percent.[8] The U.S. labor force participation rate remains the lowest it has been in over three decades. As the Associated Press reported in April 2013, "Even Americans of prime working age—25 to 54 years old—are dropping out of the workforce."[9]

The recession of 2007–2009 hit just when the economy seemed robust. Shortly before the financial crisis, both the IMF and World Bank were celebrating tremendous gains and predicting further strong growth. The IMF's *World Economic Outlook* published in April 2007 predicted an average world growth rate of 4.9 percent, to continue for two years as the global economy enjoyed its largest boom since 1970. The Global Economics Prospects Report predicted something similar, with the World Bank suggesting future "strong global performance" and "very rapid expansion in developing countries, which grew more than twice as fast as the advanced economies."[10]

Nobody is predicting robust economic growth now. The economy remains weak. So what happens if we suffer an economic attack in a down economy? That's the prospect we face today.

Panic

In *Unrestricted Warfare*, Colonels Qiao and Wang aim at producing "social panic, street riots, and a political crisis." There are those who have downplayed such risks, but the threat of Chinese hacking remains grave. Retired Lieutenant Colonel Timothy Thomas, a student of Chinese strategy, cites *Unrestricted Warfare* and asks,

> If I had access to your bank account, would you worry? If I had access to your home security system, would you worry? If I have access to the pipes coming into your house? Not just your security system but your gas, your electric...?
>
> Maybe nobody's been killed yet, but I don't want you having the ability to hold me hostage. I don't want that. I don't want you to be able to blackmail me at any point in time that you want.... I wonder what would happen if none of us could withdraw money out of our banks. I watched the Russians when the crash came and they stood in line and ... they had nothing.[11]

Of course, there are many who attempt to argue that China's rise is not merely harmless but beneficial. China, they assert, wants to be a cooperative player on the world stage. Unfortunately, this view doesn't square with the facts. It reflects the success of Chinese propaganda rather than China's actual intentions. The Chinese have two stories—one for international consumption and one for their own planning. Their military literature "give[s] you both versions," says Colonel Thomas. "They give you a model that says, 'There will be no way we'll ever fight [the U.S.], we'll work on cooperation.' A chapter later, 'There could be a time where if pushed hard enough, we'll have to do something and there will be a battle.'"[12]

Lest you imagine that the aggressive stance of *Unrestricted Warfare* is somehow out of the Chinese mainstream, the same views were expressed in the Communist party journal *Qiushi* in 2011: "Of course, the most important condition [for economic warfare] is still that China must have enough courage to challenge the U.S. currency. China can act in one of two ways. One is to sell U.S. dollar reserves, and the second is not to buy U.S. dollars for a certain period of time, which will weaken the currency and cause deep economic crisis for Washington."[13]

The threat is not a matter of Chinese bluster. Our own Congressional Research Service published a paper on the danger of China's suddenly reducing its holdings of our debt:

A potentially serious short-term problem would emerge if China decided to suddenly reduce their liquid U.S. financial assets significantly. The effect could be compounded if this action triggered a more general financial reaction (or panic), in which all foreigners responded by reducing their holdings of U.S. assets. The initial effect could be a sudden and large depreciation in the value of the dollar, as the supply of dollars on the foreign exchange market increased, and a sudden and large increase in U.S. interest rates, as an important funding source for investment and the budget deficit was withdrawn from the financial markets.... However, a sudden increase in interest rates could swamp the trade effects and cause (or worsen) a recession. Large increases in interest rates could cause problems for the U.S. economy, as these increases reduce the market value of debt securities, causing prices on

the stock market to fall, undermining efficient financial inter-
mediation, and jeopardizing the solvency of various debtors
and creditors. Resources may not be able to shift quickly
enough from interest-sensitive sectors to export sectors to
make this transition fluid. The Federal Reserve could mitigate the interest rate spike by reducing short-term interest
rates, although this reduction would influence long-term
rates only indirectly, and could worsen the dollar depreciation and increase inflation.[14]

There would be a "deep economic crisis" for Washington, producing
considerable turmoil on the streets of America. George Soros predicts
that the next financial crisis will produce "riots, a police state and class
war for America." He adds, "It will be an excuse for cracking down and
using strong arm tactics to maintain law and order, which, carried to an
extreme, could bring about a repressive political system, a society where
individual liberty is much more constrained."[15] His words echo those of
the People's Liberation Army. "I am not here to cheer you up," Soros says.
"The situation is about as serious and difficult as I've experienced in my
career. We are facing an extremely difficult time, comparable in many
ways to the 1930s, the Great Depression. We are facing now a general
retrenchment in the developed world, which threatens to put us in a
decade of more stagnation, or worse. The best-case scenario is a deflationary environment. The worst-case scenario is a collapse of the financial system."[16]

Soros, in the view of Colonels Qiao and Wang, understands financial
warfare better than anyone else. In the history book about twenty-first-
century financial warfare, they say, Soros will be the "main protagonist."
He is undoubtedly right about one thing: the next wave of attacks could
result in a deflation, hyperinflation, or total collapse, depending on how
events play out. And, the vulnerability is greater than ever before.

Could Deflation Destroy Us?

George Soros says that deflation might be the best of the bad outcomes. What would that feel like?

The Great Depression is an example of severe deflation. According to a report published by the Federal Reserve Bank of San Francisco, "Between 1929 and 1933, real gross domestic product per capita plummeted by nearly 30 percent and the unemployment rate soared from about 3 percent to over 25 percent. The consumer price index (CPI) plunged by nearly 25 percent, with the rate of deflation exceeding 10 percent in 1932." But that's not the end of the story: when the CPI turned around, unemployment remained extraordinarily high, a "surprising" combination.[17] The cycle seemed impossible to break.

The same report cites a more recent example—Japan after the boom of the 1980s. "Japan provides recent evidence of what can cause sustained deflation. Core consumer price inflation in Japan averaged a little over 2 percent during the 1980s and the first half of the 1990s. Following the bursting of the Japanese housing and stock market bubbles, the economy tumbled into a lengthy recession, with the unemployment rate rising to nearly 5.5 percent, about three percentage points above its prior long-run average. Nine straight years of core CPI deflation followed."[18]

Some economists, including Gary Shilling, believe that deflation is inevitable. Slowing birth rates, increased saving, and deleveraging, Shilling states, will contribute to the problem. "In recent years, monetary and fiscal stimulus across the world have led to the assumption that serious inflation, if not hyperinflation, is on its way. I believe chronic deflation is more likely."[19] A cycle of falling prices could devastate the economy, leading to cash hoarding, less investment, and less innovation. Rick Newman of *U.S. News & World Report* points out that deflationary cycles are emotionally driven and difficult to break. They can destroy the lending and credit system that underlies the jobs market. Newman concludes, "Since credit is the lifeblood of capitalism, a sharp cutback in lending and investing is a sure way to torpedo growth or make a recession worse."[20] The biggest problem is that we have already exhausted our bag of tricks—normally, we'd try to inflate the currency by placing the Fed short-term rates near zero. Unfortunately, we're there already.

Why is deflation bad? After all, if prices drop and you're financially responsible, you should be able to buy more. But when deflation continues and people hold out for ever-lower prices, profits drop dramatically. Companies begin to fire employees. You have to rely on your savings. And when those are gone and you can't get a new job, you're in serious trouble. People start selling investments and move into anything that might hold value, including bonds that pay little or no interest. Stocks prices drop. The economy plummets.

And the worst part is that the government typically responds to deflation with enormously increased spending. That means greater debts and deficits. And when people begin to fear that debts won't be paid back, a new deflationary cycle begins, since people call in their debts and save to prevent new debts from accruing. Cash becomes king, at least for a while. Nothing else seems to hold value.

The new deflationary cycle will prompt even *more* government spending—only this time, the government won't be able to borrow the cash. It will either sell assets, further depressing prices; default on its debt; or print money. At this point, the greenback could be disestablished as the global currency, ultimately destroying savings across America. The price of everything falls first when cash is king. When things get really bad, even the dollar becomes worthless.

That scenario is becoming more likely each day. The Fed has committed all of its resources to preventing deflation. It has been engaged in quantitative easing for so long that it's stuck. When it announced the possible tapering of the program, markets freaked out and the Fed backed off.[21]

If things got really bad, the Fed would likely become even more aggressive, following the policies of "Abenomics," named after Shinzo Abe, who began a second term as prime minister of Japan in December 2012. He has made a 2-percent inflation target a top political priority. His directive: "Everything possible" must be done to achieve the goal within two years.

Abenomics is a response to nearly a quarter century of Japanese economic malaise and deflation. Society has held together primarily because the Japanese people have historically funneled their high personal savings into government debt. It is estimated that the Japanese people have savings of roughly $19 trillion, which they have used to purchase about 90 percent of Japanese government debt. Now Abe wants to get those savings out of the banks and into the system. The central bank is already working on it, vowing to get it done at the "earliest possible time." Abe's strategy is stimulus,[22] and the Japanese economy has remained stable in the face of deflation and massive increases in Japanese government debt.

Unfortunately, we do not enjoy similar conditions in the United States. Our savings rate is abysmal by comparison with Japan's. They are up to their eyeballs in debt as we are, but Japanese debt is held mostly by Japanese. So much of our debt is held by foreigners that deflation would prove more painful, triggering a more rapid government response. The United States simply cannot afford to wait as the Japanese did. We can expect that Ben Bernanke and his successors will follow a massive liquidity strategy when facing signs of deflation. In fact, Bernanke is called "Helicopter Ben" because it is said he would drop money from helicopters if needed to avoid deflation. Bernanke is clear in describing the problem: "The sources of deflation are not a mystery. Deflation is in almost all cases a side effect of a collapse of aggregate demand—a drop in spending so severe that producers must cut prices on an ongoing basis in order to find buyers. Likewise, the economic effects of a deflationary episode, for the most part, are similar to those of any other sharp decline in aggregate spending—namely, recession, rising unemployment, and financial stress." He is also clear about his solution: make more money available. Bernanke will be gone in 2014, but the Fed is likely to continue his prescription of "easy money" for a deflating economy.[23]

So even if deflation is the best of the bad outcomes, it could nevertheless lead to the worst of both worlds. The government's response to massive deflation could cause hyperinflation or currency collapse or both, two serious threats.

The Top-Down Approach

Now, George Soros may not be right. In the event of an economic attack, we might be able to avoid outright deflation. But that's not necessarily good news. It could be that our creditors get together and dictate terms for maintaining our debt. These creditors would impose austerity, much as the IMF and World Bank have done in Latin America, Asia, and parts of Europe. That scenario has been playing out recently in Cyprus and Greece. And there are many who think that this imposed austerity is continuing to destroy already downtrodden economies. The IMF itself said that it suffered "notable failures" in the Greek bailout because of its strict austerity requirements.

But the IMF may have no choice, just as the international community may have no choice. A nation that spends too much, borrows too much, and can't repay its debts will eventually be called to account. Unlike Japan, our nation is unable to finance its needs internally and routinely turns to other sources like China. One option to prevent debt default is to print money. This is, in fact, what several leading economists as well as Warren Buffett have suggested. Buffett says that we will never "have a debt crisis of any kind as long as we keep issuing our notes in our own currency," because we have a printing press with which to pay back that debt.[24]

Still, twenty-three countries have actually defaulted on their debts since 1975. And default, as Martin Fridson of *Forbes* says, may be more politically palatable than running printing presses to produce inflation: "In America's case, setting off severe inflation would bring down upon politicians the wrath of savers, many of whom are elderly and conscientious about showing up on Election Day. On the other hand, the Chinese, who would be left holding a large portion of the bag in a U.S. default, are an ocean away and not entitled to vote."[25]

The downside? We depend on foreign nations for so many things like energy, raw materials, manufactured goods, food, and so forth that we would cut ourselves off from the rest of the world if we failed at least to work out our debts. Even then, we still need money to cover the current deficit, which has been running up to $1 trillion per year. We lose superpower status instantly and become vulnerable to all sorts of other attacks. So direct default is a bad deal all around.

If we're not going to default on our debts, then we are left with few other options. We could print money excessively, leading to massive inflation and loss of reserve currency status; we could confiscate private wealth from citizens, causing massive economic dislocations; or we could turn, hat in hand, to outside funding sources.

The idea of confiscating private holdings, at least retirement accounts, has been discussed before and is a tempting idea for cash-strapped governments. Of course, it wouldn't be called confiscation; it would be a type of "forced investment." The National Seniors Council has warned, "A recent hearing sponsored by the Treasury and Labor Departments marked the beginning of the Obama administration's effort to nationalize the nation's pension system and to eliminate private retirement accounts including IRA's and 401(k) plans." Deputy Treasury Secretary J. Mark Iwry reportedly would preside over such a program, destroying 401(k) plans on which millions of Americans rely and in which millions of Americans have invested.[26] The Treasury and the Labor Departments have been exploring proposals for government-mandated retirement plans in which the investments would be primarily U.S. Treasury debt.[27]

Such schemes have been tried in Argentina and Cyprus. More recently, the Polish government seized a large portion of private pension assets for the government's use. Reuters reported: "Poland said on Wednesday [September 4, 2013,] it will transfer to the state many of the assets held by private pension funds, slashing public debt but putting in doubt the future of the multi-billion-euro funds, many of them foreign-owned. The changes went deeper than many in the market expected and could fuel investor concerns that the government is ditching some business-friendly policies to try to improve its flagging popularity with voters. The Polish pension funds' organisation said the changes may be unconstitutional because the government is taking private assets away from them without offering any compensation."[28]

Some German economists want something similar in their country, too. "The rich must give up part of their wealth over the next ten years," said Professor Peter Bofinger of the German Council of Economic Experts, one of the so-called Five Wise Men advising the chancellor on economics.[29]

But such schemes have never resulted in widespread economic growth or in the fiscal security of a broader segment of a population. In the end, there is only so much money to go around, and confiscating wealth depresses the economic activity of those most likely to invest in the new products and services that improve quality of life for everyone.

Economic realities, however, might not deter the Obama administration. The president's proposed 2014 budget included provisions to "tax" private IRAs larger than a certain amount.[30] The government would declare that self-directed investing is too risky and mandate that a large portion of all investments be placed in government bonds for safety. That is essentially the argument made by those who oppose privatizing Social Security. The government could require a portion of every IRA and 401(k) to be kept in government debt. Or the government could simply rule that accounts over a certain size should be confiscated to save the system. That's pretty much what happened in Cyprus, and experts believe the approach could spread. Lars Christensen, head of Saxo Bank, explained, "There will be future bail-ins [loss of deposits] and other types of confiscation in the eurozone, without a doubt. There's no other realistic way forward if politicians continue to fail to deal with the basic indebtedness problem across Europe. They will either have to raise taxes and cut spending, or politicians will take the easier route and take money from the rich."[31]

And it's coming to America. Jim Rogers, a former partner of George Soros, says confiscation will happen—it's just a question of when.

> It's been condoned [now] by the IMF, the European Union, and everybody else in sight; that a government in need, can take assets. We all knew they could tax us … but this is the first time that I'm aware of, that they've gone in and taken bank accounts. They took gold from people in the U.S. in the 1930s … but I've never heard of them taking bank accounts. [Now] they're doing it. So be careful [because], now they can take your bank account under this precedent…. [T]hey can do anything they want to now. I for one am worried and I'm taking preparations. Who knows if I'm right or not, but I'd rather be safe than sorry as all of those people who had money in Cyprus have learned. They thought they had a normal bank account … but now it's been [taken] with the sanctions of many governments and institutions.

Rogers continues, "If people have money in any account, anywhere in the world … cut it down to under the guaranteed amount. They might take that too someday when things get desperate, because the precedent has been set, but that's where I would start if I had money in the bank anywhere in the world." He suggests that 401(k) plans, IRAs, and pension plans would probably be first on the government hit parade.[32]

Of course, the easiest way to seize wealth is under the guise of taxation. Just to balance the budget (assuming limited spending cuts), tax rates would have to double—even for people in the lowest tax brackets. That would not come close to paying off the national debt that we've already accrued.[33] And higher tax rates would necessarily slow economic activity, requiring even more taxes to make up for the slowdown.

If printing, confiscating, or taxing can't produce enough money, external sources will have to be developed. At various points, the Federal Reserve has purchased nearly two-thirds of all U.S. debt issuance.[34] But the Fed can buy that debt only by essentially printing money. Such money printing will devalue the currency and make it even less likely that other nations would buy our debt.

What about the IMF and World Bank?

Won't the IMF and World Bank step in and support America's debt at some point? Well, no. The IMF and World Bank receive more funding from the United States than from any other nation. In fact, it isn't even close. Our share of the total IMF and World Bank budget is almost 18 percent. The next closest is Japan, at less than 7 percent.[35] Much of the other major sources of funding for the IMF and World Bank are from Western nations directly tied to American prosperity. Should we go down in flames, the IMF would not be in a position to bail out the American economy.

In the case of a U.S. failure, those who held America's debt would be the ones handing down terms. They would likely structure an alternative to the IMF, as Vladimir Putin and representatives of other BRICS nations have been attempting to do. Such a new financial world order would result in the economic colonization of our nation. Those with capital and those who hold our debt would take control of critical resources, manufacturing capacity, technology, land, and intellectual property. There would be a "fire sale" to extinguish or reduce American debts. The foreign countries recently under duress have accused the United States of doing the same thing to them. The international "human rights organization" Global Exchange, for example, complains about the "structural adjustment policies" (SAPs) that the IMF imposes on the countries it bails out, calling them "an immoral system of modern day colonialism."[36] This would be their "payback" time.

We are not seeing this happen—yet. But we are seeing an increasing interest in acquiring U.S. properties. In May 2013, China's Shuanghui International tried to buy the pork company Smithfield in a deal worth up to $7 billion. In 2005, China tried to take over Unocal with its oil and gas conglomerate CNOOC. The deal, which would have been worth $18.5 billion, was stopped by U.S. lawmakers, enraging the Chinese. China also tried to buy Maytag in 2005 and Hawker Beechcraft in 2012. In 2013, Chinese companies bought ten American companies worth an aggregate of $10.5 billion.[37]

Forbes notes, "Foreign firms are moving in and buying up household names from sea to shining sea, and then some." Nirmalya Kumar, professor of marketing at the London Business School, warns us, "The Chinese are using American money from its trade deficit with you and putting it to use to acquire American brands. Every sector in China has a company Beijing wants to develop into a market leader. They have an acquisition agenda. It is hard to predict which one will break out."[38]

China already owns AMC Theaters, which is now a division of Dalian Wanda. Chinese investment in the United States topped $6.5 billion in 2013. "We are in the midst of a structural growth story that will transform the China-U.S. investment relationship from a one-way street into a two-way street," Thilo Hanemann of Rhodium Group told CNBC.[39]

The Chinese appreciate America's weak economic position. And they understand that debtors can't say much when creditors come asking for payback. Foreign nations, acting separately or together, are prepared to hand down terms. The American employer, employee, and consumer would all be losers.

The Dangers of Inflation

For a lot of reasons, inflation may be the most likely outcome of our precarious economic position. Inflation is in many ways a natural result of any serious crisis, short of total collapse. That's because, as we've noted, the central banks of the world are trying to create it. They just don't want it to get out of hand. But that's the problem: inflation feeds on itself.

So why haven't we seen the fallout from inflation yet?

The reason we have had so much Fed stimulus with so little inflation is because the velocity of money has fallen sharply. Money has been coming from the Fed into the banking system, but the banks haven't loaned the money out. Instead, they have put it back on deposit at the Fed. Michael Snyder has pointed out that U.S. banks "have more than $1.8 trillion parked at the Federal Reserve.... [T]he truth is that the vast majority of the money that the Fed has created through quantitative easing has not even gotten into the system." That's because in 2008, Fed chair Ben Bernanke stated that the Fed would pay interest on reserves kept at the Fed. "[N]ow that big pile of money is sitting out there, and at some point it is going to come pouring in to the U.S. economy. When that happens, we could very well see an absolutely massive tsunami of inflation," Snyder points out.[40]

At a certain point, such extraordinary stimulus will eventually find its way into the real economy, and that's the problem. Such a tsunami would end one of two ways, says Martin Hutchinson, a global investing specialist: "Eventually—like it did in 1929, the volume of malinvestment becomes so great that a crash occurs, in which all the bad investments have to be written off, huge losses are taken and a wave of bankruptcies sweeps across the economy." Or, we could follow the Japanese example: "This didn't happen in Japan. The banks went on lending to bad companies, creating a collection of zombies which sapped the vitality from the Japanese economy and has produced more than 20 years of economic stagnation."[41]

Hyperinflation is not guaranteed, but it remains a risk. High inflation hurts savers, investors, and consumers. Hyperinflation is much worse. In Greece in October 1944, just before the end of World War II, monthly inflation was 13,800 percent, with prices doubling every 4.3 days. That means that no one could keep up with wages. Thanks to military expenditures rising quickly and tax revenues dropping dramatically, Greek finances fell apart. The Bank of Greece simply printed money to cover all the spending.

Greece isn't even the top of the list of inflationary disasters. In October 1923 the monthly inflation rate in Germany was 29,500 percent, with prices doubling every 3.7 days. In January 1994 the Yugoslavian currency saw an inflation rate of 313 million percent, with prices doubling every day and a half. Zimbabwe infamously saw a monthly inflation rate of nearly 80 billion percent, with prices doubling every twenty-four hours.[42] In 1998, a Zimbabwe hundred-dollar bill was worth about twenty U.S. dollars. Ten years later, Zimbabwe was producing bills marked $100 trillion, and they weren't worth a penny.

Some argue that hyperinflation is not possible in the United States, but they assume that we will always have the reserve currency of the world. Matthew O'Brien of the *Atlantic*, for example, writes, "U.S. government finances might look Zimbabwe-esque, but a look back at some of history's worst hyperinflation episodes show why goldbugs' fears are completely unfounded now." O'Brien says that hyperinflation in the United States is impossible because "(1) we don't have any problems selling our debt; (2) we aren't actually printing money; and (3) the United States is a highly productive economy that is nothing like bombed-out Budapest."[43] This is only half true. We don't have problems selling our debt *right now* thanks to other economies' problems—but that won't remain true for long. As for the notion that the United States isn't printing money, that may be technically true, but only technically—the Fed is buying longer-term bonds from banks for cash and injecting money into the economy. At a certain point, there will be no more long-term bonds to buy. As for our functioning economy, that won't last long with the current attempt to spend our way out of every problem we've ever had, and tax and regulate ourselves in order to do so.

Higher inflation is inevitable, and even without true Zimbabwe-style hyperinflation, consistently rising prices can be a problem. Carmen Reinhart and Kenneth Rogoff, authors of *This Time Is Different*, suggest that debt levels above 90 percent of GDP lead to much higher inflation; when that number is reached, inflation jumps to 6 percent. Bud Conrad, chief economist of Casey Research, said that we're currently at 110 percent.[44]

We don't suffer from hyperinflation, but we don't need hyperinflation to devastate the economy, as we learned during the Jimmy Carter years. In Britain, for example, inflation rates reached almost 25 percent per year in the 1970s. Not hyperinflation, but terribly destructive nonetheless.

The Worst-Case Scenario

Finally, there's the worst-case scenario: complete financial collapse.

What would it look like? A complete financial collapse could happen in several ways: a full currency collapse, a shutdown of the financial transaction network from hacking, an EMP, a complete collapse in the rule of law. While these scenarios may seem far fetched to Americans fed a steady diet of "normalcy bias," they remain reasonable possibilities of which we must be aware.

Whatever the cause, however, financial collapse would be devastating. Society would become lawless. Barter would be the only way to buy and sell. Think of a bad Kevin Costner movie about the end of days (*Waterworld*, *The Postman*). Or maybe a *Mad Max* movie with Mel Gibson.

The problem is that we live in a "just in time" society. There is only enough food on the shelves to last a few days with our inventory systems and dependence on regular trucking supplies. According to a report from the American Trucking Associations, "Significant shortages will occur in as little as three days, especially for perishable items following a national emergency and a ban on truck traffic. Consumer fear and panic will exacerbate shortages. News of a truck stoppage—whether on the local level, state or regional level, or nationwide—will spur hoarding and drastic increases in consumer purchases of essential goods." Water will run dry within a month. Healthcare will be jeopardized. Gas stations will run out of fuel within two days. Sewage will pile up.[45]

Congress established a blue-ribbon commission to evaluate the threat of an electromagnetic pulse attack on America's electrical

infrastructure. The commission's 2004 report addressed the consequences of a failure of the country's food infrastructure (by EMP or
any other cause):

> Even today, according to the USDA, 33.6 million Americans,
> almost 12 percent of the national population, live in "food-
> insecure households." Food-insecure households, as defined
> by the USDA, are households that are uncertain of having or
> are unable to acquire enough food to meet the nutritional
> needs of all their members because they have insufficient
> money or other resources.
>
> A natural disaster or deliberate attack that makes food
> less available, or more expensive, would place at least Amer-
> ica's poor, 33.6 million people, at grave risk. They would have
> the least food stockpiled at home and be the first to need food
> supplies. A work force preoccupied with finding food would
> be unable to perform its normal jobs. Social order likely
> would decay if a food shortage were protracted. A govern-
> ment that cannot supply the population with enough food to
> preserve health and life could face anarchy.
>
> In the event of a crisis, often merely in the event of bad
> weather, supermarket shelves are quickly stripped as some
> people begin to hoard food. Hoarding deprives government
> of the opportunity to ration local food supplies to ensure that
> all people are adequately fed in the event of a food shortage.
> The ability to promptly replenish supermarket food supplies
> becomes imperative in order to avoid mass hunger....
>
> Federal, state, and local agencies combined would find it
> difficult to cope immediately or even over a protracted period
> of days or weeks following an EMP attack that causes the food

infrastructure to fail across a broad geographic area encompassing one or more states. Infrastructure failure at the level of food
distribution because of disruption of the transportation system,
as is likely during an EMP attack, could bring on food shortages
affecting the general population in as little as 24 hours.[46]

Similarly, any economic collapse that destroyed the water infrastructure would be catastrophic, according to the EMP Commission:

> Denial of water can cause death in 3 to 4 days, depending on
> the climate and level of activity. Stores typically stock enough
> consumable liquids to supply the normal demands of the
> local population for 1 to 3 days, although the demand for
> water and other consumable liquids would greatly increase
> if tap water were no longer available. Local water supplies
> would quickly disappear. Resupplying local stores with water
> would be difficult in the aftermath of an EMP attack that
> disrupts transportation systems, a likely condition if all crit-
> ical infrastructures were disrupted.
>
> People are likely to resort to drinking from lakes, streams,
> ponds, and other sources of surface water. Most surface water,
> especially in urban areas, is contaminated with wastes and
> pathogens and could cause serious illness if consumed. If
> water treatment and sewage plants cease operating, the con-
> centration of wastes in surface water will certainly increase
> dramatically and make the risks of consuming surface water
> more hazardous.[47]

Now, we do not see total collapse as a likely outcome, although it should
be noted as a risk with extreme consequences. To address this one, you

will have to take some disaster-preparedness measures, as we will outline in chapter eleven, "A Sane Strategy for an Insane World."

We face a number of serious vulnerabilities and risks. The threats may be more or less remote, but they exist because of our own economic policies. The potential damage is *huge*. In the next chapter, we'll look at how some attacks might take place and how you can respond if they do.

CHAPTER FOUR

What to Do When Crisis Strikes

t should be clear by now that, when it comes to the economy, things are not as they seem and certainly not what we would call "normal." Our enemies have targeted our very way of life, and our government's response adds to the uncertainty. The next crisis might be Chinese computer hacking, an undermining of our infrastructure, Wall Street panic, dumping of bonds, a currency collapse, or a rapid loss of confidence—but each form of attack will have unique consequences, and we have to be flexible enough to respond appropriately. Understanding the law of unintended consequences, or at least unexpected consequences, could make the difference between survival and ruin. Yet while it is obvious that our economic situation is not normal, the vast majority of investment plans are predicated on traditional thinking.

The possibility of economic terrorism is quite real. Whether our geopolitical enemies sell off U.S. bonds or simply decide to remove the dollar as the reserve currency, whether they inflate their own currencies in a currency war or engage in a short-selling orgy as they may have during the 2008 stock market collapse, Americans' financial futures are in serious peril. There are many threats, and each requires a different response. The economy is far too fluid and the means of attack too diverse to offer a simple solution. You may hear some encourage you to put all your dollars in gold; others may recommend stock; still others may push bonds or real estate. But there is no "one size fits all" solution.

The biblical monition "Sufficient unto the day is the evil thereof" is truer than ever in our modern world. In this chapter, let's walk through a variety of possible troubles and discuss their causes and effects. In the chapters that follow, we will explain how to respond to the threats and protect your investments.

Electromagnetic Pulse

One of the most frightening possibilities of economic warfare is an electromagnetic pulse (EMP) attack, which is within the means of many of our enemies and could completely wipe out the American economy. The science of such an attack is fairly basic, and a number of potential perpetrators have discussed it. What's worse, we currently have no defense against it.

First, some basics. Our society is dependent on electricity, which is delivered through complex interconnected technology systems. If these fail catastrophically, modern life comes to a halt. If the failure is widespread, it would probably take years to restore the systems. Without power, there is no way to distribute water, food, medicine, or other necessities. The EMP Commission described a doomsday scenario of widespread disease and starvation with an estimated 90-percent loss of life.

What could cause such a catastrophic failure? A relatively low-yield nuclear device detonated above the atmosphere of the continental United States would send a pulse wave across the nation that would overwhelm power generation and render nearly all electronic devices useless. We know this happens based on our own nuclear testing.

We also know that solar activity could generate a catastrophic electromagnetic pulse. From a Center for Security Policy report: "To make matters worse, as Michael Del Rosso, the former chairman of the Institute of Electrical and Electronics Engineers' Critical Infrastructure Protection Committee, added—even if no hostile power responds catastrophically to our vulnerability to EMP, a similar level of devastation can be caused by natural phenomena."[1]

Del Rosso is a friend of mine and was one of the first people to recognize the financial terrorism that was taking place in 2008. In fact, he called me that September as Lehman was failing, and on hearing my concerns he made the initial introductions to the FBI and the Pentagon. He has been warning about the risks of EMP for years after serving on the blue-ribbon congressional commission that identified the risks.

How would a natural EMP occur? Perhaps the best example was observed in 1859:

> On the morning of September 1, 1859, amateur astronomer Richard Carrington ascended into the private observatory attached to his country estate outside of London. After cranking open the dome's shutter to reveal the clear blue sky, he pointed his brass telescope toward the sun and began to sketch a cluster of enormous dark spots that freckled its surface. Suddenly, Carrington spotted what he described as "two patches of intensely bright and white light" erupting from the sunspots. Five minutes later the fireballs vanished, but within hours their impact would be felt across the globe.

That night, telegraph communications around the world began to fail; there were reports of sparks showering from telegraph machines, shocking operators and setting papers ablaze. All over the planet, colorful auroras illuminated the nighttime skies, glowing so brightly that birds began to chirp and laborers started their daily chores, believing the sun had begun rising. Some thought the end of the world was at hand, but Carrington's naked eyes had spotted the true cause for the bizarre happenings: a massive solar flare with the energy of 10 billion atomic bombs. The flare spewed electrified gas and subatomic particles toward Earth, and the resulting geomagnetic storm—dubbed the "Carrington Event"—was the largest on record to have struck the planet.[2]

Solar events like the one that Carrington observed occur on a fairly regular basis. In 1989 a minor version wiped out Quebec's electric transmission system. We barely averted a catastrophe in July 2013 when solar flares just passed the earth:

> "There had been a near miss about two weeks ago, a Carrington-class coronal mass ejection crossed the orbit of the Earth and basically just missed us," added Peter Vincent Pry, who served on the Congressional EMP Threat Commission.
> "Basically this is a Russian roulette thing," he said. "We narrowly escape from a Carrington-class disaster."[3]

We are overdue. Lloyds of London made this clear in a recent report to the insurance industry. They suggested that a full-scale Carrington event happens about every 150 years. It has been 154 years since the last one over the United States.[4] Estimates are that there is a "one in eight" chance of a major natural EMP event happening by the year 2020.[5]

We face a few major problems in dealing with the EMP risk, whether natural or intentional. First, we lack the supply of transformers and other equipment needed to restore power quickly. We simply don't keep enough of the thousands of large power transformers (LPTs) required to replace all we could lose. A loss of just twenty to thirty major transformers would black out a substantial part of the United States, according to James Woolsey, the director of the CIA under President Clinton.[6] Unfortunately, we don't even manufacture them in the United States, and there is a long lead time to order them, even under normal circumstances. They are manufactured, at least in part, by hand.[7]

Secretary of Defense Donald Rumsfeld used to keep on his desk a satellite image of North and South Korea at night. He would comment that there were virtually no lights in North Korea, while South Korea was abuzz with light and life.[8] While that was a telling image showing the benefits of a free versus closed society, it also serves as an ominous warning of our dependence on modern systems. An EMP over the Koreas would take South Korea back more than a century in development but perhaps have limited effect on its northern neighbor. That is what makes an EMP so appealing as an economic weapon. It can level the playing field between superpower and failed state in less than a second.

The bad news is that we don't have any real defense against a planned EMP. We have not pursued missile defense.[9] We have not hardened the grid.[10] The good news is that we can still do so. Protection against a natural EMP might cost billions of dollars, and protection against a planned EMP attack might require tens of billions of dollars,[11] but a successful EMP attack would wipe out trillions of dollars and could result in the death of millions of Americans.[12] When you realize the stakes and that even rogue nations likely have the capability to launch an EMP, you quickly recognize that this is a mighty weapon of economic warfare. Ambassador Henry Cooper, the director of the Strategic Defense Initiative Organization under President George H. W. Bush, warns:

An EMP catastrophe also can be created by rogue states armed with nuclear weapons. North Korea already has nuclear missiles and nuclear weapons; Iran nearly so—and these two rogue states actively collaborate on both nuclear and ballistic missile development. It is also plausible that Jihadi terrorists might get their hands on a nuclear weapon—especially if Iran can get such a nuclear capability, mate it to a short range ballistic missile they can easily buy and launch it from a vessel off our coasts and detonate it over the U.S. to create a lethal EMP. A single nuclear weapon detonated at high-altitude over the center of this country could collapse the electric grid, leading to the collapse of other critical infrastructure and within a year lead to the death of several hundred million Americans. Based on extensive Department of Defense efforts during the Cold War, we (specifically, the Defense Nuclear Agency and the Services) understand EMP effects and how to protect against them, and we have applied these protective measures to harden our strategic systems—but not to harden our critical civil infrastructure. A high altitude nuclear explosion creates an EMP with three wavelength components, a mid-range one that is essentially the same as lightning, a short wavelength one that can cause severe damage to solid state electronics, and a long wavelength one that is essentially the same as that from a solar storm which would couple into the electric power grid that would transmit a massive energy pulse through the grid to focus on a few thousand large transformers, which when severely damaged would require many months to repair—if ever.[13]

I have been working with the EMP Coalition co-chaired by James Woolsey and former Speaker of the House Newt Gingrich. The coalition includes important experts and is addressing this serious threat.[14] Concern about the EMP threat is by no means a partisan issue.[15]

What can you do? First, make certain that you have more than a week's worth of food, water, and basics on hand. I will address some things you might want to have available in chapter eleven. Second, make your voice heard and demand that our government and utilities take action to defend us. Hardening the grid would add at most a few dollars a month to our electric bills. Having a defense would itself deter an attack. Investors should look for opportunities to invest in grid protection. As the public becomes aware of the threat, there will be some free-market efforts to address the problem. These could include investments in response mechanisms like food and water, emergency response, or hardening the utilities. While Y2K did not end in disaster, in part because of extensive protection measures, wise investors who took positions in solutions to the problem made an enormous amount of money.[16]

Network Heart Attack

An attack on computer networks is the final step outlined in *Unrestricted Warfare* for destroying a superpower. First, build up capital. Next, launch a sneak attack. Third, carry out a network attack:

> [B]y using the combination method, a completely different scenario and game can occur: if the attacking side secretly (or quietly) musters large amounts of capital without the enemy nation being aware of this at all and launches a sneak attack against its financial markets, then after causing a financial crisis, buries a computer virus and hacker detachment in the opponent's computer system in advance, while at the same time carrying out a network attack against the enemy so that the civilian electricity network, traffic dispatching

network, financial transaction network, telephone communications network, and mass media network are completely paralyzed, this will cause the enemy nation to fall into social panic, street riots, and a political crisis.[17]

A cyberattack on financial markets, even if isolated, would shut down trading, preventing anyone from getting his money out of the market or putting his money in. As early as November 2010, Doug Kass, the head of Seabreeze Partners, predicted such an attack. "The Internet," he said on CNBC, "becomes the tactical nuke of the digital age. I believe cybercrime is going to explode exponentially next year as the web is invaded by hackers." More specifically, he predicted an attack on the New York Stock Exchange. "The aftermath will have a profound impact and cause a weeklong hiatus in trading as well as a slowdown in travel," he continued.[18]

A catastrophic attack isn't just possible, or even likely. It is inevitable, according to the best security experts in the world. Admiral J. Michael McConnell, who served as director of national intelligence under Presidents Bush and Obama, said that financial terrorists could take advantage of our reliance on technology: "What they will finally figure out is that crashing an airplane into a building gets them a lot of publicity, [but] at some point, they're going to move to different means. They will eventually, in my view, move to the soft underbelly of the country, which is the digital infrastructure and digital dependence. And when they figure that out, a relatively small group could do strategic damage.... They'll eventually figure it out." Asked whether it is a question of when rather than if, McConnell answered in the affirmative.[19] The director of the National Security Agency and U.S. Cyber Command, General Keith Alexander, confirmed that report, stating, "Securing our nation's networks is a team sport. We need your help."[20]

In fact, we've already had a variety of hacking attempts on NASDAQ, the system that runs the markets. Federal investigators said in February 2011 that hackers had repeatedly broken into the NASDAQ over the previous year. While the exchange's trading platform wasn't damaged or compromised, investigators said they didn't know what had been accessed. As the *Wall Street Journal* reported, "The Nasdaq situation has set off alarms within the government because of the exchange's critical role, which officials put right up with power companies and air-traffic-control operations, all part of the nation's basic infrastructure. Other infrastructure components have been compromised in the past, including a case in which hackers planted potentially disruptive software programs in the U.S. electrical grid, according to current and former national-security officials." That might have been a preliminary move by hackers in preparation for a larger strike. Tom Kellermann, a former computer security official at the World Bank, said, "Many sophisticated hackers don't immediately try to monetize the situation; they oftentimes do what's called local information gathering, almost like collecting intelligence, to ascertain what would be the best way in the long term to monetize their presence."[21]

The attack reported by the *Wall Street Journal* did not, fortunately, inflict substantial damage. But such attacks are cause for alarm because they are probably state-sponsored probes of our weakness. That's why the National Security Agency got involved. Joel Brenner, a former head of U.S. counterintelligence under Bush and Obama, said as much: "By bringing in the NSA, that means they think they're either dealing with a state-sponsored attack or it's an extraordinarily capable criminal organization." Bloomberg News suggested that the NSA's involvement could hint at a national threat to the financial infrastructure. It would not take a full-scale hack to throw the financial system into turmoil. Even the appearance of impropriety could destroy faith in the market. Brenner said that manipulating trading could cast doubt about validity of any trade throughout the system.[22]

FBI director Robert Mueller said in March 2012 that the top threat to national security is cyberattacks. "We are losing data, we are losing money, we are losing ideas and we are losing innovation," he said. "Together we must find a way to stop the bleeding." Unfortunately, he said, America's companies and financial system are completely unprepared for such an attack. "There are only two types of companies," he concluded, "[t]hose that have been hacked, and those that will be."[23] Leon Panetta, a former director of the CIA and former secretary of defense, has made the same point, warning of a massive disaster that he dubbed a "cyber–Pearl Harbor." He said, "An aggressor nation or extremist group could use these kinds of cyber tools to gain control of critical switches.... They could derail passenger trains loaded with lethal chemicals. They could contaminate the water supply in major cities, or shut down the power grid across large parts of the country." Were terrorists to launch "several attacks on our critical infrastructure at one time, in combination with a physical attack ... that would cause physical destruction and the loss of life, an attack that would paralyze and shock the nation and create a profound new sense of vulnerability."[24]

The possibility of cyber–financial warfare is not merely the product of the worried imaginations of American security officials. It comes from our enemies. Al Qaeda has called on its minions to wage "electronic jihad" against us and has suggested that America's cybersecurity is just as weak as its physical security was prior to September 11, 2001. "This is the clearest evidence we've seen that al Qaeda and other terrorist groups want to attack the cyber systems of our critical infrastructure," said a stunned Senator Joseph Lieberman in response to al Qaeda's statement. "Congress needs to act now to protect the American public from a possible devastating attack on our electric grid, water delivery systems, or financial networks."[25]

Were a cyberattack to occur, we probably wouldn't be able to do anything about it until after it ended. For example, on May 6, 2013, the media announced the possibility of a cyberattack titled "OpUSA." The Department of Homeland Security even released a statement explaining, "The attacks will likely result in limited disruptions and mostly consistent of nuisance-level attacks against publicly accessible web pages and possibly data exploitation." But as the *Weekly Standard* reported,

> the OpUSA threat was made on the Web weeks ago. The threat statement online listed 140 banks as targets and rambled on about U.S. war crimes in Iraq, Afghanistan, and Pakistan. The government said that the attack would come from "Anonymous-linked hactivists in the Middle East and North Africa."
>
> This government action should strike one as comical. What kind of cyber defense is the announcement that there is going to be an attack that no one can keep from happening?[26]

How will an attack affect you? It could affect you directly—your money could disappear from the bank. In December 2012 the U.S. financial services industry warned that Russian cybercriminals were planning to hack into and rob American banks; at the same time, the computer security firm McAfee said that a cybercriminal calling himself "Thief-in-Law" had broken into thousands of computers across the country in an operation called "Project Blitzkrieg." According to the McAfee report, "McAfee Labs believes that Project Blitzkrieg is a credible threat to the financial industry and appears to be moving forward as planned." In September 2012, Thief-in-Law claimed to have already stolen some $5 million.[27]

Beyond a direct hit on the markets, cyberattacks could destroy media, utilities, and other infrastructure, unleashing general chaos. Imagine if all ATMs stopped working and people could not get into their bank accounts. Or if the lights and television stopped. How about the traffic-dispatching network? Or just basic internet access? We are now a technology-dependent society that requires these conveniences just to survive. How could we possibly service our massive debt if any or all of these cyberareas were attacked?

Mutually assured destruction doesn't work as a deterrent unless we can be completely certain about the source of the attack. The risk, therefore, is even higher than during the Cold War. In March 2012 the White House invited senators to a classified simulation of the effects of a hacking attack directed toward the electricity in New York City. As David Sanger of the *New York Times* reported, "The city was plunged into darkness; no one could find the problem, much less fix it. Chaos, and deaths, followed.... The real lesson of the simulation was never discussed: Cyberoffense has outpaced the search for a deterrent, something roughly equivalent to the cold-war-era concept of mutually assured destruction. There was something simple to that concept: If you take out New York, I take out Moscow. But there is nothing so simple about cyberattacks. Usually it is unclear where they come from. That makes deterrence extraordinarily difficult."[28]

So what can we do?

Depending on what happens—what gets hit and how—you will need a strategy. If ATMs cease to operate, it will be good to have a certain amount of cash on hand. Yet, if the dollar were to collapse in value, even wheelbarrows full of paper dollars would be useless. That is why we will repeatedly stress diversification. And you should keep paper copies of your most recent statements showing what you own and where to access it.

Depending on how long the cyberattack lasts and the damage it inflicts, there may be a place for precious metals in addition to cash. Most of the money supply is electronic, so in a massive network outage, people would have to resort to paper money, which would become scarce. A devastating network attack would cripple the stock markets.

Since most stock certificates are held electronically, it would be virtually impossible to buy or sell. The result would be mass chaos.

Other items of value, including food, water, fuel, and ammunition—anything you can use or barter—will be valuable in the case of a prolonged network outage. It is reasonable to keep at least a small supply of these items. Be sure to rotate your stock.

Flash Crash

A flash crash would initially look similar to a network attack, but it would focus more specifically on crashing the market, as opposed to an attack designed to take down an entire system. This version of attack is designed to cause the markets to purposely implode. On May 6, 2010, the Dow Jones Industrial Average dropped and then regained six hundred points in minutes. The causes of the crash are still unknown, although experts attributed the crash to high-frequency trading—as we've explained, high-frequency traders dump stock to avoid losses and to even out market transactions.[29]

In 2006, less than 10 percent of stock market trading was conducted by high-frequency computers. By 2010, high-frequency trading constituted over 60 percent of all U.S. equity volume. From 2008 to 2011, two-thirds of all stock trades made in the United States were made by high-frequency trading firms.[30]

That's not the end of HFT influence. It's not so much the trading as the quoting. For every actual trade, there are hundreds if not thousands of quotes designed to overwhelm the system and create opportunities for profitable trades.[31] About 95 percent of all high-frequency trades are later canceled. And as David Zeiler, associate editor of *Money Morning*, writes, "The threat of another flash crash caused by high-frequency trading is as great as ever. And the next flash crash could be much worse than the one that shocked investors in May 2010." Current Securities and Exchange Commission rules will do little or nothing to stop a flash crash. "You can't stop a flash crash unless you stop the computers from doing what they're programmed to do," said *Money Morning*'s "Capital Waves" strategist Shah Gilani. "And that's not being addressed. The SEC is looking at keeping the ship from sinking, not stopping it from hitting icebergs." Professor James Angel of Georgetown University said of smaller flash crashes, "It's like seeing cracks in a dam. One day, I don't know when, there will be another earthquake."[32]

Dave Lauer, a previous high-frequency trader turned whistleblower, explains that the only solution for many investors is to wait out the market, since day-to-day problems are bound to occur and are almost impossible to police.

> It's hard to have any confidence and I understand it having seen it from the other side. One of the main problems is … the police aren't on the beat, the regulators aren't able to keep up technologically. I've spent a lot of time talking to regulators and Congress about what I think needs to be done for them to, not compete with high frequency and their technology skills, but at least be there and be able to monitor what's going on. And I know they don't have those capabilities and, until they do … until they have the ability to monitor and enforce existing regulation and stop relying on individual exchanges to do surveillance and, again, nothing happens on a single exchange basis from the perspective of a high frequency trader—it's 13 exchanges and many dark pools, and that's how they see the world and that's how regulators need to see the world as well.[33]

There are other techniques for manipulating the market using hacking, including "spoofing" and "layering," in which orders are placed and then canceled, moving the market up and down based on false demand. In September 2012 a major New York brokerage and its top executives agreed to pay a $5.9 million fine for such manipulation in a settlement with the Securities and Exchange Commission. The SEC had accused the brokerage of orders that "intended to deceive and did deceive certain algorithms into buying (or selling) stocks." Brokerages are now being set up to trade largely overseas—most are located in China. After the flash crash of 2010, the SEC tried to increase the responsibility of brokerage firms for offering direct access to the markets for those who would manipulate it. Obviously, that didn't work.[34]

The truth is that the markets endure flash crashes daily in one sector or another. In fact, traders estimate that there are, on average, about one dozen such targeted crashes every trading day.[35] This is not normal for properly functioning markets but is symptomatic of manipulation. Traders manipulate the market to make a profit. What happens if someone manipulates the system to harm it rather than profit from it? We remain vulnerable. In September 2010 the House Committee on Homeland Security held a hearing at which virtually all witnesses agreed "the nation's 10 or so stock exchanges and 50-plus related trading venues are vulnerable to attacks from traders overseas."[36]

There are a variety of ways for enemies to flash crash the market, or at least systemic stocks. The question is whether a flash crash can do permanent damage. Some high-frequency traders use social media to trigger activity. They scour the news for stories that might indicate movements and attempt to react ahead of the market. As John Bates, chief technology officer for Progress Software, writes, "According to an August 2011 infographic from media agency We Are Social, there are 138,888 Tweets per minute, 180 million posted each day and 1.6 billion search queries per day. There are 200 million Twitter users with 450,000 new accounts created daily.... With the high frequency-obsessed trading community, speed is essential. And social media, particularly Twitter, is becoming a key source of high-speed information for feeding trading algorithms." Bates notes that manipulating the news is not that difficult—in fact, the stocks for Berkshire Hathaway rose routinely last year whenever the actress Anne Hathaway was hot on Twitter or in the news, thanks to algorithms mixing up the actress with the trading firm.[37]

The Syrian Electronic Army appreciates the power of social media. In April 2013 it hacked the Associated Press's Twitter feed, planted a false story, and briefly caused a $136 billion market drop. The planted story suggested that the White House had been bombed twice and that the president of the United States was injured. The tweet was corrected within seconds, but not before the Dow plunged 143 points. Sal Arnuk, the coauthor of *Broken Markets*, lamented, "When I realized it was a fake tweet, I was outraged and ashamed that the market was able to be manipulated so easily." The market is not completely rational. There are still people making trades and reacting emotionally. And beyond that, algorithms pick up what's happening on the social media front.[38] The *New York Times* reported, "The markets recovered in minutes, but the episode has heightened concern among regulators about the combination of social media and high-frequency trading.... The vulnerability, in part, stems from the Securities and Exchange Commission's decision to let companies and executives use social media sites like Twitter and Facebook to broadcast market-moving news."[39]

A flash crash can destroy traders who use stop-loss orders—orders that automatically sell when the price hits a certain low. "You talk about $200 billion being erased [in the Twitter flash crash], but how much was folks with stops in the market?" Jeff Kilburg of KKM Financial asks. "These [algorithms] really ran the gauntlet and they cleaned out a lot of people. I don't know the percentages, but definitely there was damage done to the ma and pas."[40] Richard Miniter points out that even as flash crashes increase, so do settlement failures: "Despite 2008 regulatory reforms, settlement failures are rising again. A settlement failure is what traders call it when buyers or sellers fail to provide the agreed-upon stock or cash to complete a transaction." In a world of high-frequency trading, settlement failures pervert the market. Miniter concludes, "Imagine a computer virus designed to wipe out your retirement savings and sink our economy. The flash crash may have been a test run."[41]

So far, such attacks have had only temporary effects, mostly because they happened with time left in the trading day for recovery. Also, the markets were rising, and investors were looking for buying opportunities. The damage would be much greater if such activity took place with nervous markets near the end of a trading day.

Financial terrorists could also crash markets by stealing or altering trading algorithms, either by theft or by coopting an insider. In 2009, Sergey Aleynikov allegedly stole some thirty-two megabytes of Goldman Sachs technology, including algorithmic information on which the company's high-frequency trading was based. As Rob Iati of the TABB Group wrote, "There's no doubt that Goldman Sachs, or any other proprietary trading firm, could indeed lose tens of millions of dollars from its proprietary trading if their strategies are stolen—and that is very serious. The competitors that obtain access to these trading secrets could (and would) use it to front-run or trade against it, ruining even the most well-planned tactics."[42] While the alleged thief of the Goldman Sachs trading code was later released, charges were refiled.[43] Whether Aleynikov is guilty or innocent, the financial system is vulnerable to the kind of crime with which he is charged.

If the threat is a "flash crash," the answer is cash. Flash crashes cause stock prices to drop below their intrinsic values. Having cash to pick up shares could be very rewarding, assuming the markets bounce back as they have so far.

The Domino Effect

The real risk is that a chain reaction of systemic failures overwhelms the financial system. That is what happened in the crash of 2008, as even the strongest institutions found themselves interdependent on weaker ones. Few people realize how close the whole economy came to absolute catastrophe. Representative Paul Kanjorski, a Democrat from Pennsylvania, explained on C-SPAN how dire the situation was when Congress stepped in:

> [There was a] tremendous draw-down of money market accounts in the United States, to the tune of $550 billion.... The Treasury opened its window to help. They pumped a hundred and five billion dollars into the system and quickly realized that they could not stem the tide. We were having an electronic run on the banks. They decided to close the operation, close down the money accounts, and announce a guarantee of $250,000 per account so there wouldn't be further panic out there. And that's what actually happened. If they had not done that their estimation was that by two o'clock that afternoon, five-and-a-half trillion dollars would have been drawn out of the money market system of the United States, which would have collapsed the entire economy of the United States, and within 24 hours the world economy would have collapsed.... It would have been the end of our political system and our economic systems as we know it.[44]

In hindsight, it is obvious that Lehman's failure was the fall of the first domino. That risk has not abated. "Too big to fail," warns Ben Bernanke, is "still here." Richard Fisher, the president of the Federal Reserve Bank of Dallas, wants the entire financial system restructured to prevent another too-big-to-fail scenario. The giant banks, he says, "represent not only a threat to financial stability but to fair and open competition, … they are the practitioners of crony capitalism and not the agents of democratic capitalism that makes our country great."[45] He suggests that "the largest financial holding companies be restructured so that every one of their corporate entities is subject to a speedy bankruptcy process, and in the case of the banking entities themselves, that they be of a size that is 'too small to save….' The downsized, formerly too-big-to-fail banks would then be just like the other 99.8 percent [of banks], failing with finality when necessary—closed on Friday and reopened on Monday under new ownership and management in the customary process administered by the FDIC."[46] The editors of USA Today write, "Perhaps the best way to view the world's largest banks is not as companies, but as nations unto themselves. Like rogue states, they profit from their ability to wreak havoc on the world, borrowing for less because lenders know that governments wouldn't dare let them collapse. And like opportunistic governments, they are brilliant at playing nation against nation."[47]

Although the risk persists, politics stands in the way of a solution without another crisis. The problem now, however, is that we may not have the firepower to stop another systemic collapse as we did in 2008. The federal debt is already almost twice as large as it was in early 2007.[48] The unemployment rate is substantially higher than the 5-percent level of December 2007, and the number of food-stamp recipients has more than doubled, with well over forty-five million Americans receiving such assistance. We have barely recovered from 2008–2009, and we might not recover at all the next time. The risk is another Great Depression. Depending on the policy response, we could see massive deflation or hyperinflation. We could even see confiscation. There is no simple way to address this risk in advance. It would require a great deal of flexibility and willingness to adjust as circumstances unfold.

If the government were unable to borrow to provide additional stimulus, the Federal Reserve could be left as the only buyer of government debt. Inflation would soar, leading to currency collapse. Almost any investment would then be better than cash. On the other hand, the government might pursue a policy of austerity and raise taxes. We would then face deflation, and cash would be king.

One complication is that the government could restrict access to cash in money-market or other accounts, as the government of Cyprus did in 2013. Americans might think that such a policy is impossible here, but in June 2013 the SEC proposed a new rule that would make it difficult for investors to pull cash from money-market investment vehicles "during times of financial distress." Bernanke backs the proposal.[49] If that happens, cash on hand becomes king, and assets lose value.

Bear Market Redux

One way to set off the domino effect is a "bear raid" targeting one or more systemic companies. This is what George Soros says started the 2008 crisis, as we've discussed.[50] While some argue that bear raids do not exist, most on Wall Street realize they can and do occur.

Unfortunately, none of the safeguards necessary to prevent future bear raids has been implemented. The so-called price test rule or uptick rule, as we've discussed, has been rejected. The only rule in place, an "alternative" rule that applies only when the price of a share drops by more than 10 percent, "would not have stopped the bear raid on Citigroup on November 1, 2007," says Professor Yaneer Bar-Yam of the New England Complex Systems Institute. "This is only one example of the deleterious effects of the weakened rule. The overall effect of unregulated selling of borrowed shares is surely much larger and continues today."[51]

Most assume that bear raids are carried out for profit. But as I demonstrated in my Pentagon report, they could also be used as weapons of financial terrorism or economic warfare. A bear raid targeting a systemic company has the potential to destroy the entire economy. That was true in 2008 and is perhaps even truer today. The initial effect would be deflation.

In the case of a bear raid, you want to be out of stocks initially and look for bargains among companies that can survive any short-term collapse. These would be fiscally sound companies with strong earnings power even in the event of extreme economic weakness.

No Longer Solvent

An entirely different form of collapse could occur if the banking system suddenly became technically insolvent because of loan defaults on a massive scale. Systemic bank insolvency may sound unlikely, but there are persons who would like to see it happen. Stephen Lerner, the ferociously anti-capitalist head of the Service Employees International Union, has called on state and local governments to cut off all business with banks that don't pay confiscatory tax rates, don't slash interest rates, or refuse to forgive homeowners' mortgages. What he is encouraging amounts to a countrywide strike against the banks.[52]

The effect of such a run on the banks would be insolvency. Bank account balances over the FDIC guarantee level could be confiscated. More troubling still, the FDIC has enough money to cover only a small portion of the nation's banking deposits. As Peter Schiff says, "While the FDIC currently has about $25 billion available to bail out failing banks in the event of isolated events (mainly held in U.S. treasuries that would need to be sold), it insures more than $10 trillion in deposits. Clearly it lacks the resources to cover major losses in a systemic failure. A failure of just one of the nation's forty largest banks could swamp the resources of the FDIC."[53]

As with a network collapse, a major banking failure would make it nearly impossible to get cash out in a timely fashion. It would also hit stocks and bonds. This type of calamity would be deflationary at the onset.

Interest-Rate Jump

Since the 2008 crash, the Federal Reserve has kept interest rates artificially low, making it easier for the government to finance its massive debt. At one point, Treasury rates were as low as 1.6 percent.[54] Over the past hundred years, ten-year Treasury rates have averaged 4.9 percent. If rates simply went back to their hundred-year average, the federal government's costs would increase dramatically. While not all federal debt is funded by ten-year Treasuries, as an illustration, an increase of 3.3 percent in the interest rate on almost $17 trillion in debt would cost an additional $561 billion. That is about 20 percent of the total federal tax collections expected in 2013.[55] And if rates ever approached their peak of 15 percent from the early 1980s, the added cost would roughly equal 85 percent of all expected taxes in 2013. And that is not even considering the effect of higher rates on the economy, which would undoubtedly depress tax collections. The reality is that higher interest rates would dramatically hurt bond prices. That is because bond prices fall as interest rates rise.

Most stocks perform poorly when interest rates are rising. But others can do well. Cash becomes more valuable when rates are rising. The prices of gold and other precious metals can either rise or fall, depending on what else is happening. Real estate may be more difficult to purchase when rates increase, hurting prices. Initially, of course, people may try to buy as soon as possible when they see rates rising, but at some point the higher cost of property ownership from higher rates will discourage buyers.

What if Nobody Wants Dollars?

As we have explained in detail, one of the greatest risks we face as a nation is the possibility that the U.S. dollar loses its status as the pre-eminent reserve currency of the world. The problem is that our nation depends on maintaining this status. Without it, it's doubtful that we could sell our debt to anyone other than the Federal Reserve.

According to Dick Bove, one of the top banking analysts, "If the dollar loses status as the world's most reliable currency, the United States will lose the right to print money to pay its debt. It will be forced to pay this debt," Bove said. "The ratings agencies are already arguing that the government's debt may be too highly rated. Plus, the U.S. Congress, in both its houses, as well as the president, are demonstrating a total lack of fiscal credibility."[56]

The implications are huge.

For investors, a loss of reserve status would be deadly to bonds, as the currency would collapse, ushering in massive inflation. On the other hand, the right stocks could do very well, as would hard assets. Cash would lose value rapidly if the dollar lost reserve status, while gold, silver, and foreign currencies would jump higher, at least in dollar terms.

Head for the Hills:
Hoarding and Other Dangers

Financial terrorism or economic warfare could lead to hoarding. Even the fear of an economic problem can cause hoarding, which in turn could trigger a collapse. Historically, nothing destroys an economy as surely as hoarding. The Roman Empire may have fallen because its citizens hoarded bullion while the barbarians looted the treasury. That meant that there was not enough money in circulation to create a functional supply-and-demand economy. Economists of the Chicago school have made this case about the Great Depression as well. Noting Roosevelt's tight-money policy, Milton Friedman and others suggest that the Federal Reserve's failure to inject liquidity into the system drove the economy over the cliff.

Hoarding kills exchange, which is the oxygen required for economic life. Many items can be hoarded—money, food, and ammunition among them. The best thing to own at the start of a hoarding crisis is the item that will be hoarded. Of course, at some point, all hoarding will end. When it does, the price of the hoarded item will collapse.

———————————

Given the variety of risks, it is obvious that there are no simple answers that apply to everyone in every situation. Over the next six chapters, we will review the advantages and disadvantages of major asset classes and the risks each holds. Flexibility is crucial. You have to know when and how to use each of the investment approaches if you are to navigate the coming turbulence safely.

CHAPTER FIVE

The Gold Rush

You've seen all those ads for gold on TV: people telling you that it has never been worth zero, that it's a hedge against inflation. And you've seen those commentators on TV telling you that putting money into gold is a fool's errand, forcing your cash into a physical asset instead of into investments that could bring a return.

Who's right?

Nothing sparks a debate in financial circles like the subject of gold. John Maynard Keynes thought gold was a "barbarous relic" that makes no sense. Fed chairman Ben Bernanke, predictably enough, said that he doesn't think gold is money, and that people only think of it that way because of tradition. Milton Friedman said that gold could be money, of course, but that "money is what money does"—meaning that if it's used for currency, it is currency.

More recently, Warren Buffett has also expressed serious skepticism about gold. "Gold gets dug out of the ground in Africa, or someplace. Then we melt it down, dig another hole, bury it again and pay people to stand around guarding it. It has no utility. Anyone watching from Mars would be scratching their head," he famously said. Buffett thinks that investing in gold works for the short term but fails for the long term since gold has no productive value. "What motivates most gold purchasers is their belief that the ranks of the fearful will grow. During the past decade that belief has proved correct," he said in 2012. "Beyond that, the rising price has on its own generated additional buying enthusiasm, attracting purchasers who see the rise as validating an investment thesis. As 'bandwagon' investors join any party, they create their own truth—*for a while* [emphasis in original]."[1]

There's only one problem—over the long term, Buffett has been wrong. He said that gold "never interested me ... even when it was at $35," since gold "just sits there, and you hope somebody pays you more for it." But, as Mike Fuljenz of Moneynews.com points out, "Most gold investors are satisfied to hold gold with the hope that the price does not soar too far too fast, since that would represent a world in crisis, hurting most of their other investments. Buffett has been wrong about gold for over 40 years, ever since it was $35 per ounce. Even with the recent price correction, gold is still up 35-fold."[2]

Some very serious economic thinkers—Peter Schiff and former congressman Ron Paul, for instance—disagree with Buffett about gold's utility. Schiff said in early 2008, "Gold is money. And money retains its value, that's the good thing about money. The problem is that what everybody is using that they think is money, dollars, doesn't retain its value because Ben Bernanke is printing it like crazy." Schiff predicted that, without inflation, Fannie Mae and Freddie Mac would go bankrupt, adding that America should go back to the gold standard. "We wouldn't have had a NASDAQ bubble, we wouldn't now be on the verge of an unprecedented collapse of the American standard of living because of years of monetary excess," Schiff said. "If we were on the gold standard, oil would be about $3.50 per barrel."

Former Fed chairman Alan Greenspan eventually strayed from his core beliefs about monetary policy, but he originally believed quite strongly that gold was not just money, but the best basis for any currency. The criteria for currency, he wrote in 1966, were materiality, limited quantity, homogeneity, and wide acceptance, among others. Gold fit the bill. "In the absence of the gold standard," he said, "there is no way to protect savings from confiscation through inflation. There is no safe store of value.... Deficit spending is simply a scheme for the confiscation of wealth. Gold stands in the way of this insidious process. It stands as a protector of property rights. If one grasps this, one has no difficulty in understanding the statists' antagonism toward the gold standard."[3] Unfortunately for all of us, as chairman of the Federal Reserve, Greenspan inflated the currency. That's because he was right: without something backing the currency, the government will do anything it can to keep itself in power.

A Brief History of Gold

Let's take a look at the price history of gold over many centuries, converting values to modern-dollar equivalents. In 1263, gold would have traded at approximately $4.10 per ounce. Gold steadily rose in price to $20.40 per ounce in 1696. During the American Civil War, the price of gold jumped to $45.40 per ounce, but then it returned to its stable prewar value of twenty dollars. It remained at that price until 1932. In other words, for hundreds of years, gold was relatively steady. Then the government decided to inflate the currency by centralizing gold. The price was suddenly raised to nearly thirty-five dollars per ounce—*after* the U.S. government confiscated the supply. It stayed there until the advent of the Bretton Woods system, when gold was unmoored from the dollar. Gold has risen to almost $2,000 per ounce.

So what happened? To understand gold, you have to understand human history. Egyptian goldsmiths first smelted gold in 3600 BC, but it took a thousand years for gold to become common in jewelry in the Mesopotamian empire. From there, it took another two thousand years for the first international gold currency to take shape under King Croesus (hence the phrase "rich as Croesus"); the currency was called the Croesid. For the next two and a half thousand years, gold was the centerpiece of all monetary trading, until "full faith and credit" of governments took its place, unmooring value from a hard asset.

In 1300, Goldsmith's Hall in London established the first hallmarking system, meant to ensure standards of gold purity and prevent counterfeiting. In 1717, Britain moved to the gold standard, fixing the price of gold at seventy-seven shillings, ten and a half pence per ounce of gold. It could do this because of the great scarcity of gold on the planet—the chances of a huge vein of gold being discovered were minute. Naturally, a gold rush began all over the planet to search for more of the mineral. In 1848 thousands Americans went west in search of gold, finding their dreams—and more often, a stake of land—in California during the gold rush. Two years later, California became a state. A gold rush began in South Africa in 1885, drawing thousands of miners. During this period, every major country but China joined the gold standard.

During World War I, the British government, pressed by wartime spending, delinked the pound from gold. Inflation spiked—almost 11 percent in 1919—so Britain returned to the gold standard and pegged the price of gold at seventy-seven shillings, ten and a half pence per ounce. Sound familiar? That's the same price as two hundred years before. Stability in currency matters.[4]

The Founders' View

Historically, money *was* precious metals. The word "dollar" comes from "thaler," a German coin named after the Joachimsthal, the valley in Bohemia where the silver from which it was minted was mined. The Spanish dollar, which circulated widely in the British North American colonies, was likewise minted from silver. In 1792 the fledgling U.S. government adopted the dollar as its unit of currency, defined as twenty-seven grams of silver. In 1834 the United States went to gold as the single monetary standard.

The founding generation recognized the danger of a currency not backed by precious metal. Thomas Paine wrote, "Gold and silver are the emissions of nature: paper is the emission of art. The value of gold and silver is ascertained by the quantity which nature has made in the earth. We cannot make that quantity more or less than it is, and therefore the value being dependent upon the quantity, depends not on man.... Paper, considered as a material whereof to make money, has none of the requisite qualities in it. It is too plentiful, and too easily come at. It can be had anywhere, and for a trifle." The evils of paper money, said Paine, "have no end. Its uncertain and fluctuating value is continually awakening or creating new schemes of deceit. Every principle of justice is put to the rack, and the bond of society dissolved. The suppression, therefore, of paper money might very properly have been put into the act for preventing vice and immorality." Paine called such currency a "presumptuous attempt at arbitrary power" that would undoubtedly remove freedom.[5]

Thomas Jefferson agreed with the evils of paper money: "Paper money is liable to be abused, has been, is, and forever will be abused, in every country in which it is permitted." He warned, "We are now taught to believe that legerdemain tricks upon paper can produce as solid wealth as hard labor in the earth. It is vain for common sense to urge that *nothing* can produce but *nothing*; that it is an idle dream to believe in a philosopher's stone which is to turn everything into gold, and to redeem man from the original sentence of his Maker, 'in the sweat of his brow shall he eat his bread.'"[6]

George Washington held similar views: "Paper money has had the effect in your state that it will ever have, to ruin commerce, oppress the honest, and open the door to every species of fraud and injustice."[7]

Because the Founders distrusted paper fiat cash, the Constitution explicitly addresses gold and silver coinage for the states. It is clear that the Founders wanted the nation and also the states to avoid the pitfalls of fiat currency. Here is Article I, Section 10, of the Constitution: "No State shall ... coin Money; emit Bills of Credit; make any Thing but gold and silver Coin a Tender in Payment of Debts...."

The reason for the Founders' antipathy is that "fiat" money had a spotty history. Paper currencies had a nasty tendency to collapse. As Nathan Lewis writes, "the [American] colonies had a wave of hyperinflation in the 1740s, and again in the 1780s. There was another round of currency devaluation during the Civil War. However, after the smoke cleared, they returned again and again to the stable gold dollar.... Capitalism, as we know it, was based on the foundation of the stable dollar." Lewis predicts that the floating currency system in place since the Nixon administration will eventually be seen as an aberration.[8]

Confiscation

With the advent of the Great Depression, however, governments began to recognize that the presence of gold in the economy was a threat to government spending. At a time when they wanted to spend enormous sums, governments found themselves limited to what they could collect through taxation, since inflation was out of the question. The followers of Keynes who came to power—men like Franklin Delano Roosevelt in the United States and Ramsay MacDonald in Great

Britain—believed that only the confiscation of wealth and an injection of cash into the economy could spur recovery.

The logic went something like this: If average citizens were allowed to hoard gold, they wouldn't spend it. Instead, they would stick it in a mattress for a rainy day, depriving the economy of the cash flow necessary for growth. By grabbing wealth and forcing it to be spent, the government could stimulate economic growth. Deflation was the fear of the day, and they felt that only government-created inflation could combat it.

There is only one problem with this idea—it doesn't work, at least over the long term. It doesn't work when President Obama tries it, just as it didn't work when Franklin Delano Roosevelt tried it. Investors prefer opportunity to gold, especially if there is stability. But massive new government programs and regulations, the seizing of assets, and extravagant federal spending do not inspire confidence. Radical change can bring uncertainty, and uncertainty kills investment.

The economist Harry Veryser sums up the situation:

> It may be hard to imagine today, but only a hundred years ago the Western world had an economic system that was probably the best in history. Inflation was nonexistent, and there was free and open trading throughout the world. There was also price stability: for a full century the price of a loaf of bread remained about the same. At every level of society in America and Europe, people saw their standards of living ratchet up continually. People lived longer, diseases were wiped out, and literacy spread. These were years of monumental technological achievement, unprecedented economic growth, and extraordinary population growth.[9]

Then the government got involved in the game of trying to spur economic growth by tampering with the currency, which required it to seize gold. Few remember or even realize that from FDR's administration until Nixon's, it was illegal for Americans to own gold. "Of two men walking down Main Street, one with a gold coin in his pocket and the other carrying a bottle of booze, the first was now breaking the law and the second was an upstanding citizen," writes Adrian Ash of *Forbes*. "FDR's gold confiscation meant private owners were obliged to take their coins, bars or gold certificates to a bank, and exchange them for dollars at the prevailing rate of $20.67 per ounce. Over the next year, the president then raised his official gold price to $35 per ounce, effectively cutting 40% off the dollar in a bid to stoke inflation and spur the economy.... [S]eizing private gold and then devaluing the currency was in fact a 1930s version of quantitative easing."[10] This analysis is backed up by the Federal Reserve Bank of St. Louis.[11]

FDR knew he was removing the country from the gold standard. "We are now off the gold standard," he told his advisors. Lewis Douglas, an aide, said that it would herald "the end of Western civilization." Roosevelt then told reporters in his first press conference, "As long as nobody asks me whether we are off the gold standard or gold basis, that is all right.... [The United States will have a] managed currency [that] may expand one week and it may contract another week. That part is all off the record."[12]

In order to accomplish this seizure of American wealth, Roosevelt had to ignore the limits on his constitutional power. As Thomas Woods explains, the Emergency Banking Act of 1933 gave Roosevelt powers far beyond anything the executive branch is granted under the Constitution. Congress expanded that power to the point that the president could arbitrarily set the value of cash each day:

> For the next six months President Roosevelt pursued an
> erratic monetary course. Every day a new gold price was

declared, on a basis no one could figure out. Private lending in effect came to a halt, with the value of the dollar in constant flux amid the prospect of ongoing devaluation. As Senator Carter Glass (D-Va.) put it, "No man outside of a lunatic asylum will loan his money today on a farm mortgage." And thus the government could triumphantly announce that since the private sector was cruelly depriving Americans of credit, it would have to step in and provide relief.[13]

Did it work? Of course not. The Great Depression lasted all the way until World War II, and it was truly cured only by tremendous deregulation in the aftermath of the war and by the devastation in Europe, which required American goods and services in order to rebuild.

It is important to understand the confiscation of gold. Governments view gold as a policy tool to be exploited for their purposes. It cannot be viewed as an ultimate safe haven, therefore, as long as governments retain power. In the 1930s, FDR confiscated gold. Today, central banks can use their vast storehouses to drive down the price at will. Of course, over the really long term, gold *has* proved a storehouse of value (assuming the government doesn't take it).

While FDR removed us from the gold standard as a practical matter, Richard Nixon made it official in 1971, about the time he embraced price and wage controls. Unionized labor was driving manufacturing costs up, so the United States' import-export balance was moving in the wrong direction. Foreign governments began showing up demanding to exchange U.S. dollars for gold, and Nixon wanted to address those problems before his reelection campaign. In his history of modern capitalism, *The Commanding Heights*, Daniel Yergin describes how the decision was made: "The climax came on August 13–15, 1971, when Nixon and 15 advisors repaired to the presidential mountain retreat at Camp David.

Out of this conclave came the New Economic Policy, which would tem-porarily—for a 90-day period—freeze wages and prices to check infla-tion. That would, it was thought, solve the inflation-employment dilemma, for such controls would allow the administration to pursue a more expansive fiscal policy—stimulating employment in time for the 1972 presidential election without stoking inflation. The gold window was to be closed." The predictable result was an economy entirely at the behest of the federal government: on wages, on prices, and on currency valuation.[14]

Thanks to the public's hunger for government action—a consistent failure of public understanding about economics that continually under-mines the possibility of growth—gold came to be seen as Keynes's "bar-barous relic" rather than the underpinning of sound money. Even Ben Bernanke has admitted, "Nobody really understands gold prices and I don't pretend to understand them either."[15] With that statement, the Fed chairman denies any real role for gold in backing currency—quite a departure from the early views of his predecessor Greenspan, let alone from those of the Founders.

Nevertheless, it was not that long ago that gold played a central role in thinking about currency. As recently as the creation of the euro in 1999, there were discussions of backing the currency with gold, at least in part. More recently, the "father" of the euro, Professor Robert Mun-dell, a Nobel laureate, even called for putting the currency on a gold standard.[16] Steve Forbes agrees: "The American dollar was linked to gold from the time of George Washington until the early 1970s. If the world's people are to realize their full economic potential, relinking the dollar to gold is essential. Without it we will experience more debilitating financial disasters and economic stagnation."[17]

Since 1913, when the Federal Reserve System was established, the dollar has lost 96 percent of its purchasing power. It has suffered most of this decline since the gold standard was ditched in 1971. The dollar has lost 80 percent of its purchasing power since 1971.[18] We're not alone in destroying our own currency. From 1750 to 2002, the British pound lost more than 99 percent of its purchasing power.[19]

So Who Owns the Gold?

Though our great economic minds inform us regularly that gold is passé, central banks are the largest official holders of gold, with almost thirty-two thousand tons in their vaults. That's almost 20 percent of all the gold in the world, which is estimated at a little over 171,000 tons.[20]

The largest official holder of gold is the United States, with over 8,133 tons. Next in line is Germany, with 3,391 tons. Outside of official holdings, most gold is used for jewelry, which accounts for 78 percent of annual consumption. China led the world in gold production as of 2011. Australia was second, the United States third, Russia fourth, and South Africa fifth.[21]

It should be understood that since central banks control almost 20 percent of the world's gold supply, they are in a position to move prices in any direction they desire. Since those same central banks also control the value of paper money, they have an incentive to keep gold prices, well, reasonable. A rapid run-up in gold prices would indicate a failure of confidence, which central banks want to avoid. That's why in July 2013, when the Indian rupee dropped, Indian government officials told citizens not to buy gold. Jewelers actually pulled gold coins and bars after the Indian finance minister asked people to resist "temptation."[22]

There are many who believe that the central banks' claims about their holdings of gold are a sham. The gold vault of the Federal Reserve, for example, has not been the subject of a full-scale audit. It is not only individuals who are questioning the official accounts of how much gold is in the vault. Foreign countries store some of their gold in the vaults of the Bank of England and the Federal Reserve, and Mexico and Germany have expressed concern about how accurately their reserves are accounted for: "In the case of Mexico, questions have been raised about the country's off-shore storage of precious metals and its ability to take possession if necessary. These concerns have been magnified by Germany's experience. Germany's Bundesbank intends to repatriate a large portion of gold reserves abroad and by 2020 seeks to have at least 50 percent of its total gold reserves at home."[23]

Germany's demand for the return of its gold reserves is a sign of growing distrust among central banks.[24] The Mexican government also appears distrustful, requiring an internal audit of that country's gold holdings:

> The Government Audit Office has concluded that 95% of the gold reserves of the Bank of Mexico are stored abroad and 99% of this gold is stored with the Bank of England. However, the Mexican central bank has never inspected the gold it bought, has not performed purity tests on it and doesn't even have a list of all the gold bars stored in London. In their current state, Mexico's gold reserves are no more than "paper gold" in the meaning that the Bank of Mexico doesn't have any physical gold, but mere "claims" on a certain amount of gold supposedly held by the Bank of England.
>
> Bill Gross, the Chief Investment Officer of PIMCO (the world's largest bond fund) has recently said that "Central banks distrust each other." The pending audit of the Mexican gold reserves is not a singular case of actions that show a high level of mutual distrust among central banks. The latest move of the Bundesbank, which demanded the repatriation of its gold holding from Bank of New York, Bank of England and Banque de France, is another sign of distrust in the world's financial system. It is quite probable that after the audit,

Mexico will decide to repatriate its gold holdings, possibly prompting other countries to follow suit.[25]

The real concern is that while the central banks lay claim to a huge supply of gold, they may have loaned it out or even sold claims on it. This concern grew when the Federal Reserve indicated that it would take years to return the Germans' gold deposits to them: "A particularly interesting aspect of the announcement that has been largely ignored is the extraordinarily lengthy seven year time period in which the Germans expect to receive back their gold. The 300 tons they're repatriating from the New York Fed reflects just five percent of the more than 6,700 tons held there. It strikes many as unusual that the Fed would need so much time to deliver what should be a manageable withdrawal."[26]

If people discovered that central banks do not have the gold they say they have, or have loaned it out or sold rights to it, the price of gold would soar.

It is not yet clear who possesses how much gold in the murky world of central banking holdings. But as these issues are sorted through, the impacts on currency valuations will likely be significant. Issues of gold holdings and repatriation are interlinked with currency valuations, and both bear watching.[27]

The Role of Hedge Funds and the Potential for Manipulation

While the central banks have led us to believe that they have cornered the market on gold, large hedge funds like Soros Fund Management, which got involved in trading gold in the early part of the twenty-first century, also are able to move the market. As Amine Bouchentouf of Seeking Alpha reports, "While it's difficult to quantify the amount that capital hedge funds account for in the gold markets, suffice it to say that gold has become such a prominent asset class for the industry that some of the world's biggest hedge funds have launched dedicated gold funds specifically to trade the yellow metal."[28]

Such concentrated holdings can lead to manipulation. In the 1970s the Hunt brothers proved that if you controlled enough of the supply, you could control the price of a commodity like silver. They began buying enormous quantities of silver, and the price soon doubled. Within four years, they controlled 9 percent of all the silver on the planet, and the price doubled again. With a little subterfuge and the help of the Saudi royal family, the Hunts kept amassing silver, and the price almost tripled again. Jason Tillberg tells how it ended: "The Hunts and their allies controlled 62% of all the silver in the COMEX warehouses and 26% of all the silver held by the Chicago Board of Trade, the CBOT, plus all the silver they held in Switzerland, the 40 million ounces they first bought in 1974." Silver was selling for $1.50 an ounce when the Hunts started buying. By the end of 1979, the price was $34.45. The U.S. government eventually foiled the Hunts' designs by limiting holdings of silver. When it became clear that the Hunts could go bankrupt, the government stepped in to bail them out. That's how it works in the world of big government and manipulative finance.[29]

Silver is not the only commodity susceptible to manipulation. Dr. Paul Craig Roberts, considered the "father of Reaganomics," believes that gold has been manipulated by the government in order to curb demand and prop up the dollar:

> On Friday, April 12, 2013, short sales of gold hit the New York market in an amount estimated to have been somewhere between 124 and 400 tons of gold. This enormous and unprecedented sale implies an illegal conspiracy of sellers intent on rigging the market or action by the Federal Reserve through its agents, the [banks too big to fail] that are the

bullion banks. The enormous sales of naked shorts drove down the gold price, triggering stop-loss orders and margin calls. The attack continued on Monday, April 15, and has continued since.... Who can be unconcerned with losing money in this way? Only a central bank that can print it.[30]

Roberts accuses the government of colluding with hedge funds in order to scare investors out of bullion: "Brokerage houses told their individual clients the word was out that hedge funds and institutional investors were going to be dumping gold and that they should get out in advance. Then, a couple of days ago, Goldman Sachs announced there would be further departures from gold. So what they are trying to do is scare the individual investor out of bullion."[31]

Dr. Roberts may be right, or he may be wrong. But if he's right, then it appears that the Fed is using just a fraction of its reported eight thousand tons of gold to send prices plummeting. It could even sell promises of gold, not backed by the metal itself, and have the same effect. What about the other countries with thousands of tons? In the second quarter of 2013, the price of gold fell 23 percent, more than any previous quarter in history.[32]

Now the point is this: The advice to put all your eggs in the gold basket should give you pause, because gold can be manipulated. It would be too easy to destroy wealth in the short term.

Dollar Failure?

This is not to say that gold has no place in your portfolio. It is very useful in many ways. First, it will always have some value. Over the long term, it is a remarkable hedge against a host of ills. But its short-term performance is spotty. The economist Mark Skousen writes that "stocks are a superior inflation hedge over the long run because they represent a growing economy. U.S. stock indexes have outperformed gold and silver by a long shot.... But precious metals traditionally have held their purchasing power over long periods of time."[33]

So what are the pros and cons?

The fundamental advantage of gold is that it will never go to zero. In all of human history, gold has had a premium value of some sort. The same cannot be said about paper money.

Gold is universal. All societies have a reverence for gold. Therefore it is always liquid. As Greenspan said, gold *is* money.

Most important for investment purposes, gold is not correlated with other asset classes over longer periods—that is, it doesn't perform the same as other major investments. Because it can rise in price while other things are falling, and vice versa, it is an ideal addition to portfolios for the purpose of diversification. As Fidelity says in its "pros' guide to diversification":

> When you put assets together in a portfolio that have low correlations, you may be able to get more return while taking on the same level of risk, or the same returns with less risk. The less correlated the assets are in your portfolio, the more efficient the tradeoff between risk and return.
>
> To build a diversified portfolio, an investor should look for assets whose returns haven't historically moved in the same direction, and ideally, assets whose returns move in the opposite direction. That way, even if a portion of your port-folio is declining, the rest of your portfolio is designed to be growing. Thus, you can potentially dampen the impact of poor market performance on your overall portfolio.[34]

But it's not all sunshine and rainbows with gold. There are important disadvantages. First, you can't eat gold. For all those suggesting gold as the ultimate in survivalism, it's going to hurt your teeth. Second, it costs money to store and keep gold. For investment purposes, far more importantly, it can be manipulated or confiscated, as I have pointed out. It doesn't always perform as expected, since many people sell gold when things go bad as a way to get cash from a liquid asset.

In fact, the price of gold can go down for long stretches of time. Gold fell from $850 an ounce in January 1980 to below $300 in 1984. It traded at $251 an ounce in August 1999, a loss of 70 percent over two decades. Given the choice in January 1980 of gold at $850 an ounce or the Dow Jones Industrial Average at about 850, you would have fared better with the stock market. Over the next thirty-three years, gold went from $850 to over $1900 in 2011, falling to $1200 in 2013. By contrast, the Dow increased from 850 to over 15,000 in early 2013. Meanwhile, holding gold would have entailed insurance and storage fees, while stocks were paying dividends over and above the gains in the index.

On the other hand, when gold traded as low as $250 in 1999, the Dow was closer to 11,000. Over the next twelve years, gold increased almost eightfold, while the Dow was virtually flat. Even accounting for storage costs and dividends, gold trounced stocks in that period. As you can see, one of the problems with gold is that analysts have a poor track record in predicting price movements. For example, just as gold was peaking at $1,900 an ounce, many of the top analysts were predicting a move up to $5,000 or higher.

Gold sometimes fails in the short term to protect against inflation or disaster. James Pethokoukis of the American Enterprise Institute cautions, "Gold returns are surprisingly correlated with stock returns, suggesting gold may not be a reliable safe haven asset during periods of financial stress." He also notes, "In time of crisis, you may not be able to get to your gold." Unless it's literally in your mattress, it's not going to save you from the apocalypse.[35]

While Pethokoukis is right about the short-term high correlation between gold and stocks, over time the correlation falls sharply. The reason is that in a panic, all assets can be sold if cash is needed, and gold is no exception. When the smoke clears, however, people will return to gold as a safe haven. Overall, we view gold as an essential part of long-term portfolios. Sometimes it acts as a hedge. Sometimes it acts as a store of value. Sometimes it acts as an insurance policy. Sometimes it is a drag on performance results. But it is a good thing to hold as part of a portfolio.

Where Is Gold Headed?

I just said that it's very difficult to predict where the price of gold will go. So now let's try to predict where it will go.

If the currency collapses or there is a return to a gold standard, the price per ounce could go to $5,000, or even $7,000. That's the opinion of Jim Rickards, the author of *Currency Wars*, who sees the dropping price of gold as an indicator of the *weakness* of the dollar:

> So today [in the summer of 2013], with the dollar price of gold coming down very sharply in recent months, what that tells me is that if gold is constant, then the dollar is getting stronger. Well, think about it. The Fed wants a weaker dollar to create inflation, but they are getting a stronger dollar, which is deflationary. The Fed is actually getting the opposite of what it wants. It's a pretty scary thing when a central bank wants inflation and they can't get it. That shows you how powerful the deflation is, and that's what the price of gold is telling us.

That leaves the Fed with two options: stop inflating the currency, or blow up the inflation to record proportions. And Rickards thinks he knows which way this one will go: "[I]n the world where the Fed gives up and deflation takes over, gold could go to, let's say, $800 an ounce, but the problem is, the S&P will be at 800 also.... But I don't think the Fed is going to do that. I don't think they are going to throw in the towel. What they will do, as I said, is to try harder." That means inflation, and a real increase in the price of gold again.[36]

Rickards isn't the only one. MacNeil Curry, head of foreign-exchange and interest-rates technical strategy at Bank of America Merrill Lynch, said in September 2012, "We will be focusing on gold. Ultimately we think gold can trade between $3,000 and $5,000 an ounce going forward. Certainly not within the next few months, but on a long-term basis we are on a well-defined uptrend, and we have got more to run before that runs its course."[37]

There is a question, though. If growth and higher interest rates kick in, who needs gold?

The argument here is that we could return to a 1980–1999 style economy, when gold prices fell about 70 percent from their high. Does this mean that gold could fall to just over five hundred dollars an ounce? Absolutely, especially if central banks felt confident enough in the paper moneys of the world to use them as reserve currencies. Some respected analysts believe that this will happen, and they suggest gold has been in a bubble.

Michael Novogratz of Fortress Investment thinks that gold is in a "classic bubble" that could drop to five hundred dollars an ounce. "I personally think gold is toast," he says. "We peaked out at $1,900 two years ago."[38] Interestingly, a drop to five hundred dollars would simply be a return to 2005 price levels. Of course, for gold to drop this sharply, we would expect to see some real positives, including a further run-up in stock prices. Those who hold a portion of their assets in gold would be disappointed in their holdings but likely pleased with their overall portfolio.

There are some fundamental factors that cut in favor of gold owner-ship. The cost of producing gold has risen. In mid-2013 the average cost to produce an ounce of gold ("all in" costs) was approaching a thousand dollars.[39] This cost may provide a floor under the price, as yearly demand for jewelry is substantial and the supply from people "cashing in their gold" will drop with the lower price. Of course, central banks can supply a great deal of gold, as can frustrated investors. Over the longer term, however, we would expect the price to match or exceed the costs of production.

The Untold Risk

One of the problems with a full gold standard is that the money sup-ply needs to grow with the economy. But, the supply of gold doesn't increase or decrease at a set rate. There can be new finds, and old mines can run out. Would our lives be substantially better if someone discov-ered a massive supply of new gold under the ocean or on an asteroid? Or would such a discovery have the same effect as doubling the supply of paper money? What if we suddenly discovered an amount of gold greater than several moons? Some scientists believe that is how much gold was formed with the collision of two exotic stars thousands of years ago, as reported in *USA Today*:

> A team led by Harvard astronomer Edo Berger now reports that gold is likely created as an aftereffect of the collision of two "neutron" stars. Neutron stars are themselves the col-lapsed remains of imploded stars, incredibly dense stellar objects that weigh at least 1.4 times as much as the sun but which are thought to be less than 10 miles wide.
>
> Observation of the cloudy aftereffects of the burst sug-gest that each merger of two neutron stars produces several

moons worth of gold by weight. "At today's prices, that amount of gold would be worth 10 octillion dollars," says Berger. (That's $10,000 trillion-trillion or $10,000,000,000, 000,000,000,000,000,000, for anyone counting.)[40]

So much for the scarcity factor if true. The question is, how much of that gold will we find on earth or in space?

Milton Friedman argued that the ideal rate of growth of the money supply is the rate of economic growth (which includes population growth). It is highly doubtful that the amount of gold above ground would ever grow at exactly the rate of the economy. And, as we have noted, if the United States based its economy exclusively on gold, could foreign governments manipulate the price or supply to affect our economy?

There does appear to be an effort, or at least strong rumors of one, by Russia and China, supported by other BRICS nations, to create an alternative global reserve currency backed by gold, as we've discussed. This effort appears even more ominous as China and Russia have declared their relationship the most strategic ever on the planet.

So it all gets complicated and confusing. When is the ideal time to own gold? Is there ever a time to sell? Is there a time to go short? This will require a very careful reading of global markets, and even then it involves a good deal of short-term insight (or at least luck). If you want to own gold, and we believe it prudent for at least a part of your portfolio, consider owning other precious metals as well. Include silver, which has so many industrial uses and could partially offset the manipulation of gold. There are good reasons, actually, for owning silver *instead of* gold. It's cheaper and easier to monetize. European states can't sell silver, because they don't own it. Other precious metals with substantial industrial uses are also great diversifiers.

How to Own: Diversify

Diversify by owning several precious metals and owning the metals in various forms. Own the bullion, coins, and jewelry. You can also buy mining stocks, ETFs, and a variety of other assets. Each has different pluses and minuses. It's probably worthwhile owning some bullion—physical silver and gold. Unless you know what you're doing, don't mess around in the volatile futures market.

There are tax implications to owning gold, too. Gold can be held as tangible property or intangible property, capital gains, or personal business. Normally applicable property taxes may not apply to gold, since it is movable. Until ownership changes, federal taxes don't kick in. Some U.S. states, however, do tax ownership of precious metals. Proceeds from sales are taxable as capital gains.

In the end, gold is not the only answer, and it can be painful in the short term—but you should own some. It's ideal as a long-term non-correlated asset; it's like an insurance premium that can pay off in disaster. By the same token, too much of it in your portfolio can be a drag on your performance. How much you should own is largely dependent on your investing style, age, and needs. Professionals should help you determine how much gold to own.

In an uncertain world, however, don't hold a portfolio without it.

CHAPTER SIX

What about Stocks?

The 2008–2009 market collapse centered on the stock market. Many who had bought shares during the technology bubble a few years earlier finally threw in the towel in early 2009, when the Dow Jones Industrial Average sank to 6,500. The stock market has become synonymous with financial collapse as a result.

But this does not mean that stocks should be avoided in every financial crisis. In fact, the stock market can be an extremely useful hiding place for wealth under a number of circumstances. To avoid it or ignore it can be a huge mistake.

To understand what role stocks can play, it is important to know what the stock market is. The stock market is an exchange mechanism where investors can buy and sell shares of companies. A share represents ownership with various rights, privileges, assets, and earnings. Being a stockholder, in its simplest terms, is owning a fraction of a company. Those who say they would never invest in stocks are essentially saying that they don't want to own companies.

So why do companies sell shares of themselves? The first reason is to raise money. There are only three ways for companies to raise money: sell a product, issue debt (borrow money), or sell stock. That money is then used for growth … we hope. At least that's how it used to work when ownership of companies was generally united with executive leadership. In the age of widely diversified public companies, however, executives are often separated from ownership, meaning that their interests do not always align with those of the stockholders—hence golden parachutes, bad management decisions, and short-term values overwhelming long-term interests.

So when is it smart to invest in stocks? How can you tell a good stock from a bad stock? Is the stock market the magical money machine that so many seem to think it is? Or is it a rigged casino designed to strip you of your hard-earned wealth?

Benefits of Stock Investment

Most financial planners will tell you that the stock market should form the biggest part of your financial portfolio. They're right for most people. Benefits of investing in the stock market include:

Liquidity: Unlike many hard assets—real estate, for example—stocks are generally tradable immediately and quickly. Stocks trading on the major exchanges, not merely on the over-the-counter market, often have a broad market with thousands or even hundreds of thousands of ready buyers. You aren't going to get trapped in stocks, except in very rare cases. You'll be able to cash out your chips.

Market pricing: The stock market is unusually stable over time. Actually, it's better than stable—given long enough, it has always risen. In

October 1929, when the stock market crashed, the Dow Jones Industrial Average dropped from 381.47 to 198.69, then tumbled all the way down to 41.22 by the end of 1932. Disastrous, right? Only if you sold. Thanks to government interventionism, the stock market remained at about 150 at the end of 1939. But by 1960 it was all the way up to 680. By 1980 it was at 840. And by 2000 it was up to 11,500. That exponential growth is due in part to the growth of corporate earnings with new industries and opportunities emerging, but it's also due to inflation. In general, the stock market benefits from continual addition of information and discovery.

An increasing number of people are investing in the stock market, meaning that every company is owned by a vast network of human beings, all adding information to the system. Many economists therefore subscribe to the efficient markets hypothesis (EMH), which holds that you can't truly beat the stock market, since at any point in time all the relevant information available on a given company has been entered into the system. As we'll see, that's not entirely the case, especially under the current trading rules, which often encourage secrecy from the public. The rise of trading formulas as opposed to human investigation of the inherent worth of particular companies has also undermined the notion of fully efficient markets.

Ability to diversify: Unlike cash or gold, the stock market allows you to offset your own risk. Imagine that you're betting on horses (although in stocks, you hope, you're not betting at all—you're believing that a company's leadership will allow it to separate itself from the market and create profit). You have three horses. Let's call them Apple, Microsoft, and Blackberry. Now, you could bet on one of them to win. Or you could put money on all three horses. You'll have a better shot at risk mitigation if you put money on all of the horses. Stocks are like that, except that you don't have to diversify within a given field. Think that green stocks are hot? Buy a solar energy company ... but then buy Chevron just in case. Diversification will help prevent you from going broke.

Business ownership ... from a distance: You don't have the time to manage somebody else's business. You're not Mitt Romney, a specialist in turnarounds, or Warren Buffett, a specialist in capital maximization. But you know you like a certain company, or your brother-in-law does. Stock ownership allows you the perks of ownership without the headaches of management. That's why executives are paid so much to run companies—they're running those companies not only on behalf of the employees and the customers but also on behalf of thousands of owners. They're legally responsible for the actions of the company, while you aren't. You may feel the pinch when it comes to the price of your stock, but until then, you're happy. And you'll never go to jail unless you traded on inside information.

Potential for high returns and ability to share in profits: This is the biggest reason people buy stock. Most people think of Google when they buy a stock—will it make me a millionaire in a few years? Generally the answer is no. Stocks are for long-term ownership. Unless you were one of the few who got in on the ground floor at Google—meaning, before it went public—you have earned a truly great profit, but you haven't quit your day job. Google stock debuted at one hundred dollars per share and has since traded above nine hundred dollars. Unless you sank $100,000 into the stock in the first place, you're not hiring a decorator for your place in the Caymans. But over the course of your life you might. Imagine the man who bought stock in General Electric in 1979, when it cost about a dollar. GE isn't even doing that well these days, and it still trades at around twenty-five dollars per share. If that man had spent the last thirty-four years investing in other companies like GE, he'd be solid in his retirement plans. That's the principle behind a 401(k) plan—invest now, reap the benefit later. It's the reason that Republicans have proposed opening private accounts for future Social Security beneficiaries rather than continuing to operate the Ponzi scheme that is Social Security, in which Social Security taxes earn near zero return.

Delayed taxation: When you buy a stock, you generally aren't taxed until you sell it. When you lose money on a stock, you can offset gains from other stocks with that loss. That's not true for bonds or a bank account, the interest from which is taxable every year. Were you wondering why Mitt Romney paid an effective tax rate of 14.1 percent on an income of $13.7 million in 2011? The answer is that capital gains are often taxed at a different rate than earned income. Earning makes you comfortable. Investing can make you rich.

What are people talking about when they say that "the stock market" rose or fell? They're usually referring to the Dow Jones Industrial Average, which tracks the stock prices of thirty large companies from a broad range of industries, such as Boeing, Coca-Cola, American Express, and Wal-Mart. It is important to remember that the Dow represents only thirty companies, and makeup of the Dow changes over time. In fact, when Charles Dow created the average in 1885, it comprised fourteen stocks, twelve of which were railroads. In 1896, the average shifted to a broader array of industries. Of the twelve stocks chosen for inclusion at the time, only General Electric remains in the average today. Others, such as U.S. Leather Company, no longer exist.

The changing composition of the Dow reflects an important characteristic of the stock market: it evolves and adapts over time. Today's opportunities are vastly different from those of a hundred, twenty-five, or even ten years ago. A century ago an investor might have chosen the proverbial buggy-whip maker or invested in the emerging, disruptive industry of automobiles. And depending on the buggy-whip maker, you might have done okay for a few decades—the *Saturday Evening Post* profiled one in 1931, reporting that the "oldtime whipmaker, still doing business in an eastern city, is carrying on in a way that contradicts the notion his vocation is a disappearing trade. His yearly production includes not only 10,000 riding crops, but also policemen's billies, polo mallets, fly flickers made of horses' tails, sword loops, and revolver holsters which permit one to shoot from the hip. Constant research aiming at new and better products is the cornerstone of this man's success in a century-old business."[1] Of course, you'd have done a lot better if you'd invested in Ford.

The stock market forces business evolution. And business evolution means better products, more profits, and better stock value.

Today's opportunities are even wider and more diverse. For example, you can buy organic food companies, heart-transplant-device makers, gold miners, electric utilities, biotechnology companies, movie studios, gun makers, space travel providers, and just about anything else you might imagine. You can buy stocks in a variety of industries and countries. For example, you can buy German telecommunications, Singaporean water companies, Brazilian oil producers, or American retailers. Estimates are that there are 112 stock exchanges in the world and close to fifty thousand stocks available. The largest of those exchanges represented some $55 trillion in stocks and over forty-six thousand companies at the end of 2012.

What about Financial Crises?

During a serious financial crisis, many types of companies will suffer, but others may prosper. At the same time, some countries will prosper while others suffer. This is why you cannot exclude investing in stocks in many types of financial crises. There are opportunities to profit regardless of the situation. That's why *Mad Money*'s Jim Cramer says, "There's always a bull market somewhere." He adds, "It might mean that you may have to look further and harder than your time and your inclination allow. That's OK, too. What matters is that you don't simply default to what's in bear mode because you are time-constrained or intellectually lazy.... For 25 years there has always been a sector that works. You just have to find it."[2]

There is an important caveat, however. Stock market opportunities are wide and diverse, but when a crisis hits, all stocks tend to drop together, regardless of industry or country of origin. This is what is known as a spike in correlation. Why? Alan Greenspan once described a stock market bubble as the result of "irrational exuberance." John Maynard Keynes, for all of his mistakes about the benefits of government spending, was right when he said that "animal spirits" help control markets. When people panic, they sell first and ask questions later. Even investments destined to do well in a crisis are often sold indiscriminately. Panic selling can be the result of emotions or investors' desperate need for cash.

In a crisis, buyers tend to pull back from buying even what they want to own. So prices fall across the board, punishing the good and bad alike. The indiscriminate drop in stock prices is short lived, however, and once things stabilize, prices begin to reflect opportunity once again. So in the short run, all stocks may seem to act in unison. A century ago both the buggy-whip maker and the automobile developer would have fallen in a panic. But the automobile maker nevertheless had a brighter future, which eventually would be reflected in its share price.

Passive Investing versus Active Investing

Before making a decision about the stock market, it's worthwhile to investigate the different classes of assets subsumed under the broader term "stock market." Now, there are many different ways of investing in stocks. You can buy a fund that mirrors a market index. The fund rises and falls with the overall market. This is known as passive investing or index investing. It is a low-cost strategy to match the performance of the overall market. You can buy shares of index funds to mimic the Dow Jones or the New York Stock Exchange. The only reason to do this is if you think the economy overall is going to rise, but you don't know anything about the particular companies constituting the index. This is a passive investment strategy.

A passive investor can also select individual sectors or geographies using exchange-traded funds (ETFs). Sector ETFs are great for diversification—they allow you to buy an entire swath of the economy rather than picking a single stock. If you buy a telecommunications ETF, for example, you're not betting on Verizon or AT&T—you're betting on them and all their competitors. In some ways, it's easier to spot profit opportunities in sector ETFs, since all you need to do is see the broad trends in the economy. Sector ETFs are narrower than buying an ETF for the entire S&P 500, for example. Sector ETFs aren't all upside, however—they can be more expensive and more volatile than broader ETFs.

Here's how sector ETFs work. There are two classification systems: the Global Industry Classification Standard (GICS) and the Industry Classification Benchmark (ICB). GICS has ten sectors, which include twenty-four industry groups and sixty-seven industries. The ICB has ten industries and thirty-nine sectors. In the end, they are quite similar.

So how do you pick a sector ETF? You can choose between market-weight sector ETFs, equal-weight sector ETFs, fundamentally weighted sector ETFs, and leveraged sector ETFs. Market-weight sector ETFs are focused on what are called "large cap" stocks—companies with market capitalization of over $10 billion. Equal-weight sector ETFs give equal weight to all companies in a sector, no matter the size. Fundamentally weighted sector ETFs are more sophisticated, selecting companies on the basis of certain fundamental measures of their health. Leveraged sector ETFs multiply gains and losses because they are based on borrowing and selling options and futures contracts.[3]

Studies have shown that sector ETFs can be a reasonable way to manage risk. If you don't like risk, you might pick a utilities ETF; if you want a more volatile sector, you might go toward technology. Here's a recent breakdown of the stock market by sectors: utilities (3 percent), telecommunication services (3 percent), information technology (18 percent), financial (16 percent), industrial (12 percent), energy (12 percent), healthcare (12 percent), consumer discretionary (11 percent), consumer staples (9 percent), basic materials (4 percent). Some advisors recommend that your ETF holdings mirror these market percentages. But you wouldn't want one sector to get too heavy if you're looking broadly to diversify—that's how you could get hurt during a bubble. From most to least volatile, sector ETFs rank as follows: technology, financial, healthcare, consumer discretionary, industrial, materials, energy, consumer staples, and utilities. That makes sense, because you're moving from most sophisticated in terms of inputs to least sophisticated.[4]

If you don't want to just plug your money into an index of stocks, active investment is the way to go. You can pick individual stocks with exactly the exposure you want. Or you can hire a professional to do the picking for you. For active investors, an obvious choice is actively managed mutual funds. Their managers buy and sell as they see fit, rather than maintaining a certain group of stocks. The goal is to make a greater profit than you would by simply investing in the S&P 500, the Dow Jones, or some other index. Jim Cramer is an advocate of active stock picking. Warren Buffett is another guy who tries to outsmart the market, and he has a great track record in doing so. As Mark Riddix of Money Crashers writes, the good news about active investing is that it allows you to take advantage of holes in the market, gives you greater profit availability, and offers the opportunity of day-to-day control over your investments.

But there are downsides. First, if you go on your own, you have to invest a fair amount of time in research. You can have more taxable income since you're buying and selling all the time, and every time you realize a profit, it is taxable. Trading fees can begin to stack up. And if you're a bad investor, you'll lose cash. Riddix recommends a combination strategy of passive and active investment.[5]

Passive investing typically beats active, according to Russell Campbell of *Inside Investing*. Most investors beat themselves by being too quick or too slow on the draw. But if you're good, you can do great: "A check of Morningstar data as of the end of June [2013] shows that the median U.S. equity fund over the last 10 years has reported an annualized return of 7.94%. Funds that landed in the top 25% of the performance survey earned at least 10.00%. That is a difference of 2.06% per year after fees."[6] If you started with a portfolio of $100,000 and received a 7.94-percent return compounded for ten years, you would end with about $215,000. The same amount invested with a 10-percent net return would net slightly less than $260,000—quite an improvement. Over thirty years, the difference is even more remarkable. A 7.94-percent gain on $100,000 compounded over thirty years ends just below $1 million. But, the same amount compounded at 10 percent would rise to over $1.7 million in thirty years. So small performance differences compounded over a long period can make a major difference in wealth. Of course, the same argument can be made in the other direction—if you underperform over a long period because of fees or bad stock picking, you will end up with a lot less over time.

Are there opportunities out there? Some economists say there aren't—they cite the efficient markets hypothesis and figure that it's not worth trying to beat the market. There's an old joke: Two economists are walking down the street. One sees a dollar on the ground and says, "Hey, look, a dollar!" The other says, "That's not true. If a dollar were lying there, someone would have picked it up already." The first economist thinks about it and nods, and they both walk away.

But sometimes the dollar is there. If it weren't, there wouldn't *be* an efficient markets hypothesis. As one columnist writes at Seeking Alpha, "The irony of course is that without market participants seeking the mythological alpha, EMH falls apart. Like economists passing up free money, EMH proponents recognize collective market participation irons out mispricing, but seem to forget it's real individuals who do the ironing."[7] Even Fidelity Investments recognizes that basic truth: "In a free-market economy, financial markets play a key role in generating and distributing information about corporate, private, and sovereign issuers through active management, which in turn fosters independent decision-making and the effective allocation of financial capital. The prevalence of information influences security prices. If an investor has favorable information about a security, it will often lead to the purchase of that security and drive up its price. Conversely, unfavorable information often leads to selling activity and downward pressure on prices. Thus, active strategies can be viewed as 'price makers.'"[8]

An absence of active investors and a reliance on passive investment strategies has actually made the market *more* volatile. Everyone marching in lockstep can destabilize the market.[9]

Thanks to a nasty economy, financial planners like Ted Schwartz suggest that the only way to make true profit in the markets is to go more active:

> Ed Easterling of Crestmont Research talks about two market climates: a positive climate, in which you can just set sail and let kind market winds propel your portfolio vessel in the right direction, and a difficult one that requires you to laboriously row to reach your goals. Because of the current global economy, which includes recession forecasts for Europe, I don't believe Easterling's beneficial climate is on the horizon. If you

disagree, you might want to go heavy on passive investments. But if you agree with me, you should use some active investments to get where you want to go.[10]

Schwartz may well be right. Of course, there are always the investors who make active investing look far superior—people like Warren Buffett, Peter Lynch, and John Templeton, who not only beat the market but beat it with ease. The best way to beat the market is to *know* the market. As Prem Jain writes in the *AAII Journal*,

> Buffett has proposed that investors think of making only a limited number of stock market decisions in their lifetime. Once they have made those decisions, they should not be allowed to make any more decisions. If you keep this in mind, you are unlikely to make many mistakes. To cement this thought, think about the effort you expended before you bought a house or a computer, before you decided to attend a particular college or accept a job offer. Because these decisions are not easy to reverse, most people make good decisions. If you think of buying a stock as a similarly long-term commitment, you will make better decisions.[11]

Even so, other experts favor passive investment. One of them is the investment great John Bogle, who founded Vanguard Funds and has spent his career trying to lead investors away from stock selection. "In the stock market, some investors do better and some worse, but their aggregate returns equal the market's returns, minus the costs of investing. After all, they are the market. So if a fund matches the market's gross return and does so at a cost much lower than the average fund, it will always beat the average fund over time," he theorizes. He has been so successful in convincing people that about a quarter of all investing is done passively.[12]

"Disaster Economics"

What's the best approach? It depends on your personality, the circumstances you are facing, and what's happening in the markets. This is where it helps to have a properly trained professional to guide you through the process. It is also essential that this pro understand the risks of crisis investing. The National Security Investment Consultant Institute is training financial professionals to deal with the risks of financial terrorism, economic warfare, and general investment calamity.

Sadly, most investment pros assume "normal" markets and therefore are unprepared to address the threat of disaster. More and more countries are risking default on their debt, yet the markets are not responding appropriately. According to economists at Fulcrum Asset Management, that's because so few analysts are working in the new global paradigm. They simply don't understand the concept of "disaster economics." People might want to prevent disaster rather than aim for higher profits. If so, analysts would miss that trend.[13]

Not all, though. Merrill Lynch understands that the U.S. economy is a potential risk. To offset the risk, they have recommended dumping gold and U.S. Treasury securities and looking at foreign assets like Australian sovereign debt and Singaporean bank bonds. "Unlike old U.S.-centric portfolios that called for nearly half of bond allocations being dedicated to U.S. Treasurys and municipals, [our] current models consider all bonds 'global,'" the firm said in 2012. "Geopolitical instability is the new status quo.... As political powers shift and the global economy struggles to rebalance itself, investors might consider flexible investment approaches and a more globally diversified approach to their portfolio."[14] Merrill Lynch isn't the only company making this argument. Saker Nusseibeh, chief executive at Hermes Fund Managers, told CNBC in September 2012, "What is different now is that political risk is now a factor in western countries and this risk is becoming more important than it has been before."[15]

What should you do—or what should your fund manager do—if disaster strikes? You can sell stocks short (the legal way). The ability to buy long and sell short is a big advantage of the stock market. You can make money from a declining stock market just as you can from a rising market. In short selling, you borrow shares of a company and sell them. Later, when (as you hope) the price has declined, you buy those shares back at the lower price. You then return the borrowed shares and pocket the difference between what you sold them for and what you paid to buy them back. It can get complicated, but professional assistance can provide you with an important strategy during a crisis.

Above all, though, remember that stocks can perform irrationally in the short run. Don't panic.

Irrationality was clearly to blame for the dot-com bubble, in which the market valued emerging internet companies at billions of dollars without actual revenues or even a business plan. Everybody remembers Pets.com. Thanks to easy credit and easy money, investors poured cash into software and the internet. The result was the growth of the internet—and the massive growth of a bubble that burst in 2000, wiping out tremendous amounts of stock. Hundreds of thousands of people lost jobs and their life savings. Jesse Colombo wrote, "At the peak of the dot-com bubble in 1999, it was said that a new millionaire was created every 60 seconds in Silicon Valley." That couldn't last, and it didn't.[16]

On the other side of the equation, markets can be irrationally pessimistic as well. Rachel Beck of the Associated Press identified widespread irrational pessimism in 2009, and she was right. If you put your money in stocks in March 2009, when she called out the pessimists (and the Dow hit 6,627), you were doing the happy dance in September 2013, when the Dow hit 15,700.

Over time, however, the market adjusts, and the irrational optimism and pessimism average out. This is why stock market investing requires a commitment to the long term. The point is that you can invest in the stock market in a variety of ways, long and short, that can produce profits in nearly any environment. Most want to write off stocks because they fear turmoil when they should be embracing the opportunities there.

Where and How Do Stocks Make Sense?

So, when should you buy?

In a deflationary environment, it would pay to sell, if not short, most stocks. That makes perfect sense, because when prices drop, so do profits. If you're convinced that the economy is going to tank in a deflationary collapse, call your broker right now and tell him to sell short. There is another option: You can buy high-quality, dividend-paying stocks— companies with great balance sheets that can consolidate their gains during the down times. Most strategists recommend cash and bonds (especially government bonds) during deflation.

In a time of inflation, even hyperinflation, stocks can perform well. A 2004 study from Harvard found a correlation between stock earnings and inflation.[17] A personal example comes from my time at the Templeton Private Client Group. I met Sir John Templeton in 1987, when he was active in Latin American markets. Inflation in that region was terrible in the 1980s and 1990s; the regional average peaked at 438 percent in 1990.[18]

Sir John knew that. In 1985 he wanted to invest in Peruvian stocks, knowing that the government was printing cash at record rates. But Peruvian law forbade foreigners from investing. So he set up a local corporation, stashed $2 million in it, and asked Peter Gruber to run the portfolio. Soon President Fujimori came to power, and Gruber made a killing, bringing a 1,000-percent return for Templeton.[19] Sir John bought stocks primarily because the massive inflation rates made them both a hedge and opportunity. And it worked.

The German experience of 1920s proves the point as well. It seems that stocks become one of the investments of choice (along with gold and hard assets) in times of high inflation. Even firms that paid a solid dividend of 20 percent were so overinvested that traders couldn't make a profit. Getting in early during an inflationary cycle is crucial.[20] The most recent example of this comes from Zimbabwe in 2007–2008, when the stock market was gaining hundreds of percentage points per day. "Why leave money in the bank? People are forced to come on the stock market. They believe that after hard currency, the stock market is the only viable option where you can get a bit of a return," explained Emmanuel Munyukwi, chief executive of the Zimbabwe Stock Exchange.[21]

The Austrian school of economics agrees. John Paul Koning of the Ludwig von Mises Institute explains, "As money-supply growth continues and prices become more contorted, more and more ventures are undertaken that would not be undertaken in a regime without money-supply growth. When, for whatever the reason, money supply finally contracts, the artificial strength in prices that encouraged unprofitable ventures is removed, prices collapse, and large numbers of ventures go bankrupt. Thus we have the recession part of the business cycle, the simultaneous failure of many firms at the same time."[22]

Currency collapse is virtually the same as investing in hyperinflation. In Germany of the 1920s, Latin America of the 1980s, and Zimbabwe of 2007–2008, hyperinflation and currency collapse were virtually synonymous. The one difference is that a currency collapse is really hyperinflation limited geographically to either a single country or region. Owning foreign stocks, therefore, can be a good way to protect your investments. As Peter Schiff says, "Getting out of the dollar is a lot easier today than it used to be. Every time you buy a foreign stock, you're buying a foreign currency." In any case, even as the market as a whole may prosper during hyperinflation, the focus should be on specific sectors that have pricing power or that represent inflation hedges (like mining shares or real estate).

Schiff actually goes further. He believes that our economy will collapse but thinks it will be good for the rest of the world: "When the dollar collapses and when the rest of the world stops wasting their resources, propping up our economy, buying our debt, selling us products that we can't pay for, I think you're going to have a global economic boom outside of the United States."[23]

So, what happens if there's a cyberdisruption of the market? If a hacker wiped out all the records of the stock exchanges including backups, the effect would be devastating. Of course, a system that has been properly backed up can be restored.

The Right Temperament

Most stock market investors can find their worst enemy by looking in the mirror. Studies regularly find that investors driven by fear and greed jump in and out of stocks at the worst possible times. For example, if an investor bought the S&P 500 for a $100,000 in 1992 and left the investment alone for twenty years, by 2013 the investment would have grown to over $484,000. This represents a compound average rate of return of 8.21 percent per year. Yet according to a Dalbar study, the average investor jumped in and out of stocks, often at the wrong times, and ended with only about $230,000, or a gain of 4.25 percent.[24] Investors tend to sell at the bottom when they are fearful and buy at the top when they are greedy—precisely the opposite of what they should do. One way to overcome this serious problem is to put a plan in place with professional help and then stick with the plan. Even with a plan, if you lack the proper temperament, you shouldn't own stocks.

The Ups and Downs of Stocks

Stocks can be a great hedge against inflation. If you're scared by the government's printing more and more dollars, putting your money in the market is a smart play. The key is not to be in or out of the *market* but in or out of the *right stocks*. A currency collapse would dramatically increase the value of many foreign shares. That's why diversification is so important.

But when it comes to the possibility of financial terrorism, stocks can be hit hard. Cybersecurity is not nearly where it should be to stop hackers from taking advantage of the market—and if you're not smart about your investments, you could watch your cash dwindle quickly.

A bear market attack would also be bad for stocks. But not all stocks, at least over time.

So how should you invest? The answer is to invest *knowledgeably*. If you know a sector well, active investment may be for you. If not, passive investment may be the best strategy. If you're an entrepreneur or supported by a qualified professional, you may even want to think about finding some small companies to invest in, private-equity style.

Alan Greenspan worried about "irrational exuberance" distorting the stock market. Today's thinkers should worry about financial terrorism destroying it. Make sure that you have the temperament to own stocks and not to panic at the first sign of bad news. After all, in a crisis, the only thing standing between wealth and poverty is you.

CHAPTER SEVEN

What's a Bond Bubble?

I n the investment world, the word bubble conjures images of risky investments bid to outrageous prices in some sort of mania. Think the internet bubble of the late 1990s, when investors shoved billions of dollars into the pockets of twenty-something entrepreneurs who had an idea and a website. Never mind earnings; all you needed were "eyeballs" and "clicks." "That's all anybody had to grab on to," explained Shane Greenstein, professor of management and strategy at Northwestern University's Kellogg School of Business, in 2001, shortly after the internet bubble burst. "Who would have been the skeptic?"[1] The companies that went boom—and then bust—included Webvan, a company that wanted to deliver groceries at home and was once valued at $1.2 billion; Pets.com, which raised $82.5 million in an initial public offering before collapsing just nine months later; and Kozmo.com, which offered delivery of various products for free and raised $280 million before going bust.[2]

Or think of the housing bubble in the late 2000s. People were buying and "flipping" un-built homes in hot markets like Phoenix and Las Vegas, pocketing big profits without ever taking ownership. Thanks to banks' handing out loans like candy to borrowers not worth their salt—and everyone banking on real estate prices going up forever—the bust was enormous. At the bottom, you couldn't buy a stick of chewing gum with a Vegas condo. Researchers with the Federal Reserve Bank of New York actually found that investors who used subprime credit to purchase residential properties for flipping were the biggest wrongdoers in bringing on the recession. Over a third of all mortgages given in 2006 were to people who owned one house already. "This may have allowed the bubble to inflate further, which caused millions of owner-occupants to pay more if they wanted to buy a home for their family," said the Fed. Between November 2010 and November 2011, the median home price in Las Vegas dropped from $134,900 to $125,000.[3] And that decline happened *after* the bubble had burst.

Those American bubbles pale in comparison to Japan's combined real-estate and stock market bubble of the late 1980s. The Nikkei stock index nearly quadrupled in less than five years. At one point, the land surrounding the Imperial Palace in Tokyo was rumored to be more valuable than the entire state of California.

Perhaps the most famous bubble of all time was in Holland, where people speculated on the price of tulip bulbs. From 1634 to 1638, the price multiplied many times over. People mortgaged homes and borrowed against their businesses to buy bulbs. During that time, people traded one thousand pounds of cheese for a single specimen of the rarest tulip bulb. But then people lost faith in the value of the bulbs, and the bottom dropped out. In 1638, in an attempt to stop the bleeding, the government said that tulip contracts could be fulfilled by paying a mere 3.5 percent of the originally agreed purchase price.[4]

Bubbles are usually associated with risky investments and greed. Yet fear has produced a bubble in what has been considered the safest investment in the world, U.S. government bonds.

To understand how the bubble has formed, you must understand bonds and how they operate. Bonds are essentially loans. Those issuing bonds are borrowing money, and those who buy them are lending money. The bond explains the terms of the loan. How is the loan to be repaid? What is the rate of interest? Who is the borrower? How long will the loan last? U.S. government bonds are merely bonds issued by the government. Bonds can be traded, just like mortgages; typically, someone trades a bond when he believes that the bond is not going to be repaid at the rate promised or would rather have cash now than repayment later.

Because bonds represent loans, they are considered safer than stocks. In the event of a company's failure, bondholders are paid first, and if there is anything left over, the shareholders divide the scraps. Companies pay bond interest before issuing dividends. Unlike stockholders, bondholders are assured the face value of the bond when the time expires, as well as a promised rate of return. Over time, bonds are more stable than stocks.

Borrowers with excellent credit ratings can offer lower interest than those with less stellar ratings. This makes sense. Assume that Lindsay Lohan comes to you with a bond offering. You wouldn't trust her to repay the loan, so you'd want her to pay a high rate of interest pretty quickly to ensure you get some money out. But let's assume that Warren Buffett wants to issue you a bond. You'd be willing to accept a far lower interest rate, since it's a pretty solid bet that Buffett will pay you back.

Borrowers can be companies, governments, or foreign nations. Interest rates reflect the perceived riskiness of the borrower, as well as the general level of interest rates in the economy. Essentially, there is an interest-rate premium added to the "risk-free" rate. (The "risk-free" rate represents the interest rate that would be charged to a hypothetical borrower who would be certain to make every payment on time. There would still be an interest rate charged to compensate for inflation even though there would be no risk to the loan.)

Understanding Bonds and Interest Rates

A high-risk borrower will pay a big premium to borrow money, just as Lindsay Lohan would. A lower-risk borrower may pay a small premium. The lowest-risk borrower of U.S. dollars is generally believed to be the U.S. government, and the German government is perhaps seen as the lowest-risk borrower of euros. During the twentieth century, the interest rate on U.S. Treasury bills—loans that are repaid within a year— was just 0.9 percent annually. Because of the short term of the loan, Treasury bills are generally seen as risk free, a perception reinforced by the government's ability to print money if it needs to.[5]

There are some terms that will be useful to know in our discussion of bonds. The *maturity* of a bond is the date on which its term ends— that is, when the principal of the loan is due. *Callability* is the ability of the issuer to pay off the bond before it matures. *Put provisions* allow the bond buyer to sell the bond back to the issuer before the maturity date. *Secured bonds* are bonds backed by collateral; *unsecured bonds* don't have any collateral backing. Government bonds are considered unsecured, since they are not backed by anything physical.[6]

There are some elements of risk that play into the value of government bonds, however. There is *legislative risk*—the possibility that the government will change tax rates to hurt income from bonds; *call risk*—the possibility that the government will exercise a call option early; *liquidity risk*—the possibility that it will become difficult to sell bonds because of low demand; *credit risk* or *default risk*—the possibility that the government won't pay you back; and *event risk*—the possibility that some intervening event interferes with the ability to pay off the bond.[7]

The economic climate is another variable that influences interest rates. If inflation is low, the cost of borrowing will be low—the lender will get his money back without its being devalued by inflation. If inflation is high, rates will be high—you'll want more cash back in order to give a loan in the first place. In addition, investors will look into the future with their expectations and set rates for longer terms. Charting the rates over different time periods for a similar borrower gives us what's known as the yield curve. Imagine a graph with time on the X axis and return on the Y axis. As the time lengthens, the return must go up.

There are many different types of yield curves. A *normal yield curve* slopes upward, just as I have explained—a bond with a longer maturity gives you a higher yield. You're going to demand more money back in order to lend money for a longer time. A *steep yield curve* occurs when there are a lot of borrowers looking for cash. They must compete for loan dollars, and competition drives up the return curve. A *flat yield curve* indicates that the yields for bonds of multiple maturities are close to one another. That usually happens when there's no risk of inflation or when there is deflation—everybody is happy to lend money for long periods of time, knowing he will get his money back with interest. The *humped yield curve* occurs when short- and long-term interest rates are closer together than medium-term rates. That happens when there's a sharp spike in demand in short-term bonds because of a fear of inflation but also faith that the economy will eventually recover. Finally, an *inverted yield curve*, where longer-term interest rates are lower than shorter-term rates, indicates that people are frightened of an economic collapse; they demand high returns for short-term loans and believe that the economy will bottom out, resulting in no demand for long-term bonds.[8]

As you may have noticed from this discussion of yield curves, inflation plays a major role in the market for bonds. When investors expect increased inflation, they will demand higher interest rates to compensate. While it is fairly easy to guess the short-term inflation rate, it can be very difficult to predict the inflation trend over thirty years. As an example, annual inflation rates ranged from -0.34 percent to 13.58 percent in the thirty-year period from 1980 to 2010. That was a relatively stable period, too. The legacy of the Carter economy was high inflation in the early 1980s, forcing the Federal Reserve to raise interest rates on bonds. Higher rates stimulated demand for bonds, encouraging people to put money back into the government. The result was a prolonged period of higher unemployment (money removed from the economy went to the government by way of bond sales) followed by the greatest peacetime boom in American history after inflation had been tamed.

In the last few years, the government has dramatically increased the money supply, yet inflation, strangely enough, has remained low. Though interest rates have been at record lows, the market for bonds has stayed strong because the economy has been so fragile. At some point, though, inflation will return. When it does, the government will have to pay higher interest rates, driving down bond prices, and bond investors will lose money. So much for the so-called safety of bonds.

Bills, Notes, and Bonds

When it comes to government bonds, there are several types. You hear about them on CNBC and in the *Wall Street Journal*, but it's important to know the difference between them.

- **T-bills:** T-bills are bonds issued by the U.S. Treasury Department that mature in no more than one year. They are short-term bonds designed to give short-term injections of cash to the government. Investors buy them in order to hedge against deflation, for example. The T-bill market is very liquid, allowing you to buy and sell easily. You would typically buy a thousand-dollar T-bill at a discount—at $990, for example—and then hope that inflation doesn't outpace the bond.
- **Treasury notes:** These are intermediate-length bonds from the government, sold with maturities of two, three, five, seven, and ten years. You would buy these for long-term expenses, like college tuition or retirement. It's the kind of bond Grandma might have bought you for your First Communion or Bar Mitzvah. Interest is paid every six months.
- **Treasury bonds:** These are long-term securities, over ten years. Right now, they're issued with thirty-year maturities, and interest is paid every six months.[9]

The Role of the Federal Reserve and Monetary Policy

As you noticed in our discussion of gold, the Federal Reserve plays a major role in setting monetary policy. Some believe that the Fed sets interest rates for America, but it is more accurate to say that the Fed is the greatest influence on rates. The Fed influences rates several ways.

Banks don't individually set the interest rates at which they lend money. The Federal Reserve controls the supply of money and therefore controls interest rates. Federal law requires banks to keep a certain amount of money on deposit with their regional Federal Reserve Bank—deposits known as "federal funds." If a bank has extra money in its federal funds account, it can lend that money to other banks that are temporarily short in their accounts at the "federal funds rate" of interest. That rate is negotiated by the banks involved, but the Fed sets the permissible range with its "target federal funds rate." If banks don't comply, the Fed can intervene through what are called open-market operations.[10] The target federal funds rate influences the interest rates for business and consumer loans throughout the economy.

The Fed also influences interest rates with its "discount rate"—the interest rate "charged to commercial banks and other depository institutions on loans they receive from their regional Federal Reserve Bank's lending facility," as the Fed describes it. In other words, when banks come up short on the amount of money in their deposit accounts, they can borrow money directly from the Federal Reserve Bank at a given rate—the discount rate. The Fed's credit programs come in three types: primary credit programs, which are short-term and given to sound financial institutions; secondary credit programs, which are also short-term but for less stable banks; and seasonal credit, given to small institutions that vary in their monetary needs based on the season (for example, banks in tourist or agricultural communities).[11]

The Fed can also take extraordinary measures to move interest rates up or down. In an operation known as "quantitative easing," the Fed increases the money supply—and, in the view of many, risks setting off inflation—by electronically increasing bank reserves and using that money to buy securities, including government and corporate bonds. When banks sell these bonds for cash, the money supply increases, and interest rates go down because banks have more cash on hand to lend, increasing the "supply" of capital and thus lowering its price. Quantitative easing has been a staple of monetary policy during the Obama years.[12]

Another attempt to inject money into the economy has been "Operation Twist," which is designed to alter the yield curve. In this strategy, the Federal Reserve sold off an enormous amount of short-term debt and then used the cash to buy long-term debt. This maneuver injected money into the economy while at the same time lowering the interest rates for longer maturities—an obvious attempt at stimulus. The Fed announced, "The Committee expects economic growth to remain moderate over coming quarters and then to pick up very gradually. Consequently, the Committee anticipates that the unemployment rate will decline only slowly toward levels that it judges to be consistent with its dual mandate. Furthermore, strains in global financial markets continue to pose significant downside risks to the economic outlook."[13]

To summarize, the interest rate charged to any given borrower is determined by (a) the "risk-free" rate (which the Fed determines by buying and selling Treasury bills), (b) the borrower's credit rating, (c) the economic forecast, and (d) Federal Reserve policy.

Other Types of Bonds

Investors can lend money to the federal government, state governments, foreign governments, non-profit organizations, corporations, and a variety of other borrowers. These borrowers offer different forms of bonds, each with its unique attributes. For example, municipal bonds are tax exempt, meaning that the interest they pay is exempt from federal and sometimes state taxation.

Another popular type of bond is the so-called high-yield or "junk" bond. The companies issuing such bonds have low credit ratings. The bonds are speculative, but the returns can be quite high, as though you're buying stock.

What Happens When Interest Rates Rise?

With all bonds, there is an inverse relationship between the price of the bond and its interest rate. If you hold a bond and interest rates rise, the price at which you can sell that bond goes down because it pays a lower interest rate than new bonds. If you bought a thousand-dollar bond with an annual interest rate of 7 percent and interest rates suddenly rise to 8 percent, nobody is now going to pay you face value for your bond that earns only 7 percent.[14]

If there is an economic crisis and interest rates spike, short-term bonds (or bills) are not affected as severely as longer-term bonds. That makes sense because you can quickly roll over a short-term bond into another security paying the new higher rate. But if your money is in a thirty-year bond with a low rate, you have a long time to wait before you can roll over into an investment with a higher rate. So the price of long-term bonds is affected more severely by interest-rate changes than the price of short-term bonds is.

Investment advisors like Rob Williams, the director of income planning for Charles Schwab, see a substantial risk of a crisis in the long term: "We see limited value and higher risks in long-term funds today compared to intermediate-term funds. The benefits of a slightly higher rate aren't well-balanced with the increased interest-rate risk, in our view, for funds with average maturities much greater than 10 years. An exception might be if you're focused on income and income alone and won't need to sell, or if you believe that interest rates will fall. While we believe rates could stay lower longer than many investors expect, they will rise eventually."[15] John Waggoner of *USA Today* agrees: "Nevertheless, it's hard to look at current yields and think that they will stay this low forever. (And, yes, many Japanese probably said the same thing in 1990.) … Long-term bonds get hit harder by rising rates than shorter-term ones. If interest rates rise 1 percentage point, to 3 percent, the value of a 10-year T-note would fall 8.6 percent. A 30-year bond's price would fall nearly 20 percent. But a 3-year bond's price would fall 2.8 percent." Waggoner's conclusion: "If you expect rates to rise, then you should consider funds that keep their duration short."[16] What is "duration"? As PIMCO explains, it is "a measurement of a bond's interest rate risk that considers a bond's maturity, yield, coupon and call features. These many factors are calculated into one number that measures how sensitive a bond's price may be to interest rate changes. Generally, the higher a bond's duration, the more its price will fall as interest rates rise…."[17]

Remember that the value of a bond is realized only when it is sold or cashed out. So if your bond is going through a bad time, there is usually time for it to recover. In other words, just because you have a bond at 7 percent and the current rate is 8 percent, you haven't lost money until you sell, just as you don't lose money on your home unless you sell it in a bad market.

When Do Bonds Make Sense?

In normal times, with low to moderate inflation, bonds can be a flexible store of value and provide opportunity for returns. Most investors should hold bonds as part of a diversified portfolio, depending on their age and risk tolerance. Bonds are designed to hold value. They are not growth oriented unless interest rates are high and expected to fall. Buying bonds in the early 1980s, for example, would have provided tremendous growth for investors.

There are rules of thumb, such as subtracting your age from 100 (more recently 110 or 120) and investing that percentage in stocks with the rest in "safe" bonds. The thinking is that the younger you are, the more you can risk in stocks hoping for higher returns. Of course, the direction of interest rates, inflation levels, risk of default, Fed policy, and a host of other factors will determine whether a bond investment is successful.

This book is not intended to be a primer on all things investing. It is necessary, however, to understand how bonds work so you can understand just how dangerous they can be under the right circumstances.

In a deflationary environment, high-quality bonds, especially government bonds of financially sound countries, work very well. In fact, they are the investment of choice. When interest rates are dropping, bonds with higher interest rates are more valuable. Deflation will actually increase purchasing power over time, enhancing returns. If you lend $100,000 today at 2-percent interest, and if there is deflation of 2 percent, your $100,000 would have increased by the end of the year to $102,000 because of interest, and it would have $104,080 in purchasing power.

In a deflationary environment, credit becomes tight and cash is king. So corporate bonds issued by companies with strong balance sheets will do fine. But high-risk (junk) bonds will struggle as the credit crunch puts many marginal companies out of business. Keith Springer, president of Capital Financial Advisory Services, says, "Short-term you've got a little bit left in stocks. Ultimately in a deflationary environment bonds are the place to be. The pros see deflation. What do you do in a low-interest environment? You buy bonds." And as Americans worry about deflation, they turn increasingly to bonds.[18] "You can tell from the Fed that they're worried," says Ryan Sweet, a senior economist at Moody's. "The Fed has a playbook for dealing with inflation. They don't have a playbook on deflation."[19]

In a major inflation, however, the opposite is true—long-term bonds are a terrible investment. If you buy a bond yielding 2 percent and inflation is 3 percent, you're actually losing 1 percent on your money every year. Inflation destroys purchasing power, and long-term bonds provide a fixed rate of return, regardless of the inflation rate. This is why Warren Buffett believes that bonds may be riskier than stocks, at least if you believe there will be serious inflation: "The riskiness of an investment is *not* measured by beta [a Wall Street measurement of risk] ... but rather by the probability ... of that investment causing its owner a loss of purchasing power over his contemplated holding period. Assets can fluctuate greatly in price and not be risky as long as they are reasonably certain to deliver increased purchasing over the holding period. And ... a non-fluctuating asset can be laden with risk."[20] Buffett's view is supported by academic research. Javier Estrada, a professor of financial management at Barcelona's IESE business school, evaluated bonds along two metrics: the possibility of destroyed purchasing power, and bonds' underperformance of stocks. He found that stocks are unlikely to destroy purchasing power, and that bonds are more likely to do so than stocks. Stocks, he found, aren't as risky as bonds in the long term.[21]

Some investment advisors believe that the bonds known as Treasury inflation-protected securities (TIPS) take much of the risk out of bond buying. These bonds allow principal to increase and decrease with inflation, measured by the consumer price index. They pay twice a year. The Treasury Department promotes TIPS as providing "protection against inflation." But as Charles Wallace warns, "TIPS are a horrible investment when the economy is facing higher inflation." Why? Because interest rates rise during inflation, so bond prices drop. As Jeremy Siegel of the University of Pennsylvania Wharton School of Business writes, "As economic growth recovers and real rates rise, the price of TIPS will fall, leaving TIPS investors with large losses in the face of accelerating inflation."[22]

The worst problem with owning bonds of any kind occurs when inflation suddenly spikes, as when a currency collapses. Bond interest rates jump from low to high quickly, and the old low-yield bonds can lose a great deal. As the Welton Investment Corporation points out, "[S]ince 1919 investors have experienced eight different corporate Aaa rate increase periods of +1.5% or greater, trough-to-peak. From the corresponding drawdown calculations, bond investors would have experienced peak losses between -7% to -24% over each of the eight periods identified. For example, periods like the 1950s were marked by a slow and steady rate rise, with Aaa losses reaching -15.3%. Other periods like the 1970s/early 1980s experienced sharp rate increases and produced deep acute bondholder losses in the -24% range."

Even a slow and steady rise in rates can be very painful for bond investors if the starting interest rate is very low:

> First, it's important to recognize that bondholders are subject to additional interest rate risk when rates are low—in other words, at times like today. The most notable example of this occurred between 1954–1963.... [T]his period had one of the slowest and more moderate rate increases (just +1.8% peak-to-trough), and yet it produced one of the deepest (-15.3%) and longest (8+ years) drawdowns for bondholders. Why? After all, rates rose by a much greater +7.6% from 1977 to 1981. Faster rate increases should mean worse returns, right? In most cases, yes, but a key factor is that the starting yield in 1954 was only 2.85%, and for bondholders, the starting yield is critically important.

When starting yield is low, any change is relatively substantial. But a quick loss of confidence (as might accompany a currency attack) can result in even more dramatic losses. The one-year impact of a sharp loss in confidence suggests that bonds could lose 34.8 percent in nominal value in a year, magnifying the loss of purchasing power inherent in the currency collapse itself.[23]

So if the dollar were to fall quickly by 40 percent in international markets, the corresponding loss of confidence would cause the holdings to fall by another one-third or more. That means so-called "safe" assets could lose 60 percent or more in the course of a year, worse than the worst stock market decline of the past eighty years.

Worries of a Bond Bubble

Now, the United States has not suffered such a currency meltdown, and many believe it unlikely, if not impossible. But when you factor in the risks of financial terrorism and economic warfare, the unthinkable begins to seem possible. The fearful rush of investors into bonds because of their perceived safety only enhances the potential risks.

Normally, investment bubbles are created by irrational greed, but overwhelming fear has its risks as well. Many observers see fear at work in the rush to bonds following the 2008 crash and believe that it has created a bubble in bonds, especially Treasuries. The yield is so low that it can't drop further, meaning that the market is overheated. At some point, the Fed will raise rates, the thinking goes, killing the bond market. People generally think that Treasury yields will be higher in three to five years than they are today, although some experts say that the bubble will deflate gradually instead of bursting. Historically, huge bubble bursts have been relatively rare.[24]

But there is the chance of a nightmare scenario. Michael T. Snyder of Seeking Alpha writes, "[I]f bond investors all over the globe start acting rationally, that is going to cause the largest bond bubble in the history of the planet to burst, and that will create utter devastation in the financial markets."[25] What happens if Snyder is right? If businesses can't borrow cheaply, economic activity will slow down. If local governments can't raise money cheaply with municipal bonds, they will have to resort to higher taxes, and some of them will go bankrupt.[26] "We've intentionally blown the biggest government bond bubble in history," says Andy Haldane, director of financial stability at the Bank of England. "Eventually interest rates have to normalize," says Lloyd Blankfein, the head of Goldman Sachs. "It's not normal to have 2 percent rates."[27]

How much damage would the bursting of a bond bubble inflict? According to the Bank for International Settlements, an organization of sixty of the world's central banks, even a 3-percent rise in rates would cause American bond investors to lose more than $1 trillion, about 8 percent of gross domestic product. And that is not counting what the Federal Reserve would lose. The BIS believes that a return of interest rates to levels seen as historically normal could, "if not executed with great care," undermine the stability of the financial system.[28]

The famous investor and blogger Jim Rogers is certain that the bubble is going to break: "[A]t some point, markets won't take central bank policies anymore, and interest rates go up regardless of how much bond buying they do. Market timing is tough. As for the fixed income market, I'm short junk bonds. In any market, the marginal stuff goes first. This could precede problems with sovereign debt." He said he'd be buying more gold.[29] Doug Casey, chairman of Casey Research, agrees: "Worst possible place to be is in bonds of any type.... This is going to be a bigger catastrophe than real estate when the bond bubble bursts." He predicts inflation, interest rate increases, and default risk.[30] Michael Hartnett, the chief investment strategist for Bank of America Corporation, warns, "Risks of a bond crash are high."[31] In January 2013 the chief operating officer of Goldman Sachs, Gary Cohn, said, "At some point, interest rates will go higher again, and all of the money that has piled into fixed income over the past three years, some of it will come out."[32]

The unstable situation of the bond market makes it a tempting target for financial terrorists. "You can see why the financial sector would be a particularly good target for someone wanting to wreak havoc through the cyber route," says Haldane. "If I were to single out what for me would be [the] biggest risk to global financial stability right now it would be a disorderly reversion in the yields of government bonds globally."[33] And none of these dire forecasts includes the risks of a financial terror attack. Imagine what a force multiplier that would be.

In a severe crisis, government bonds might be a worse investment than corporate bonds. Corporations have assets to sell, but governments rely on their taxing power. If the government is already running massive deficits, this power is limited. All government bonds are unsecured. So as the government incurs more debt, people will grow more wary of buying government bonds—they might not get paid back, except in inflated dollars that destroy the value of the repayment.

The billionaire Wilbur Ross has said that long-term government debt is a ticking time bomb: "I think the greatest bubble that is about to burst is the 10-year and longer Treasury, because the idea that inflation is gone forever and for all time, and therefore these artificially low rates can last, is silly."[34]

Could the U.S. Government Simply Default?

One of the most intense Washington debates in years took place in the autumn of 2013. The Republican party, led by House Speaker John Boehner, faced off against President Barack Obama and Senate Majority Leader Harry Reid over raising the federal debt ceiling. The White House argued that if the debt ceiling were not raised, the U.S. government would default on its debts. The House Republicans were ready to raise the debt ceiling but wanted some changes regarding how the new debt would be spent. All of this took place in the shadow of a "government shutdown" that resulted from the Senate's refusal to pass the continuing resolution that originated in the House.[35]

Partisan brawls over shutdowns and the debt ceiling have been a Washington staple for decades.[36] While President Obama calls the actions by Congress unconscionable and unprecedented, he conveniently forgets that as a senator he actually voted against raising the debt ceiling, even as he was running for president. He now says he regrets that vote.[37]

This is normal politics. It is unlikely that the government would default when in a position to continue to raise the debt ceiling and borrow more. But what happens if the government ever loses that ability? In August 2011 this same basic wrangling resulted in a downgrade in the rating of American government bonds.[38] People panicked and rushed into government bonds. Yep, a downgrade of any other bond on the planet would cause investors to flee and rates to rise. But in the summer of 2011, such a downgrade actually increased the appeal of the very bonds that were questioned,[39] reflecting the residual confidence that America will never default. But with each trillion dollars added to the national debt, that confidence is eroded.

The federal government some day might default on its debt, but it won't be because it refuses to borrow money. It would happen because the government couldn't borrow enough to pay its bills come due.[40] Various governments have defaulted in the past, although never one with the leadership position of the United States. Alex Pollock offered a sobering assessment of the risks in the *Wall Street Journal*:

> Twenty-first century economists, financial actors and regulators blithely talked of the "risk-free debt" of governments, and European bank regulators set a zero-capital requirement on the debt of their governments. The manifold proof of their

error is that banks and other investors are now taking huge credit losses on their Greek government bonds.

The only question is why anybody would be surprised by this. The governments of country after country defaulted on their debt in the 1980s, a mere generation ago. In a longer view, Carmen Reinhart and Kenneth Rogoff count 250 defaults on government debt from 1800 to the early 2000s. As Max Winkler wrote in his instructive 1933 book, "Foreign Bonds: An Autopsy": "The history of government loans is really a history of government defaults."[41]

Another form of default was suggested by Lord Monckton, a former advisor to Prime Minister Margaret Thatcher of Great Britain. He suggested that the U.S. government could simply replace the dollar with another currency.[42] It has been done before. Debts denominated in dollars would become worthless, but other assets could be priced in the new currency. Either direct default or a currency replacement would shake the system to its core. That's why the Chinese, and even the Japanese, so seriously warned America not even to flirt with default.[43]

America's global economic dominance is being called into question. Default may no longer be unthinkable. And the implications for investors are serious.

What Happens if the Fed Loses Control?

Even if the government pays its debts on time and keeps the currency in place, there is another risk. What happens if the Fed can no longer hold everything in place? Jim Rogers believes that this will happen. At some point, he suggests, bondholders might stop caring about what the Federal Reserve is doing. So far, the Fed remains "god" of the markets. A sentence in a press release can move markets up or down. But the Fed's weapons, ultimately, are only paper. They either increase or reduce the supply of dollars. If the dollar loses its value, the Fed loses its weapons. Likewise, if the Fed loses control, the dollar could collapse.

The Federal Reserve has almost single-handedly propped up the global financial system since 2008. The Fed supported banks around the world and has pumped trillions of dollars into economies. The Fed could do that because the world desired and trusted dollars. The Fed could electronically inject dollars into a bank in Italy, making it instantly solvent. If the dollar lost value, however, this intervention would be meaningless. The Fed would not be able to help anyone. The result would be massive inflation, tremendous bond losses, and a knockout of support for everything the Fed has held up—in other words, chaos. Prices would be volatile for almost every asset class, even as the dollar collapsed. In this unprecedented calamity, inflation and deflation would occur almost simultaneously—food and other necessities would skyrocket in price, while other assets could collapse. The economy would be a ship in a sea, rocking from one extreme to another in short order. Some currencies might skyrocket while others failed, so we would see hyperinflation in some areas and deflation in others. Even the strongest metal will ultimately fail from stress if repeatedly bent back and forth at a rapid pace. To quote Zero Hedge: "[I]f and when Bernanke finally loses control, there are simply no words to describe what would ensue, as a situation like that—one where not just the Fed but every single central bank has gone all in on reflating the world's biggest asset bubble—has never been encountered before."[44]

Certain asset classes could survive a Federal Reserve crackup, but maintaining ownership would be challenging. Bonds denominated in dollars would likely be hit the worst.

If the system stabilizes and you are smart about how you allocate capital (based on your age, the yield curve, and so on), bonds can be an important part of a well-balanced investment portfolio. If we enter deflation and the dollar retains its reserve status (where the world continues to appreciate dollars), bonds will be tremendous investments. This assumes the Fed retains control and investors maintain confidence.

But if we enter a serious inflation or the currency collapses, with or without a financial terror attack, bonds will be the worst investment. Even if we simply see a return to a normal interest-rate environment, bonds will be hurt.

You need professional help from advisors who understand all the risks of economic warfare.

CHAPTER EIGHT

Beyond the Dollar: Why Money in the Mattress Is a Bad Idea

A Chinese woman thought the best way to protect her substantial nest egg was to keep her four hundred thousand yuan in a plastic bag at home. Thieves didn't steal it and she didn't lose it. But termites got to it and ate a substantial amount—about sixty thousand yuan, a loss amounting to almost $10,000.[1]

A Queens woman hid her family's life savings in a refrigerator without telling her husband. He replaced the fridge and dumped it at a recycling center, losing thousands of dollars. Cash literally became trash.[2]

An Israeli woman hid $1 million in her mattress. Her dutiful daughter replaced the lumpy, worn-out mattress and left it on the curb. A scramble to find the most valuable mattress in the world ensued at the Tel Aviv dump.[3]

Christ teaches, "Lay not up for yourselves treasures upon earth, where moth and rust doth corrupt, and where thieves break through and steal: But lay up for yourselves treasures in heaven, where neither moth nor rust doth corrupt, and where thieves do not break through nor steal: For where your treasure is, there will your heart be also" (Matthew 6:19–21).

Destruction by insects and the risk of theft was as real in Jesus' time as it is today. There's a lot in the Bible about money, and in the parable of the talents Jesus warns against hoarding it out of fear. Don't bury it in the backyard, He says—put it to work, or at least draw interest:

> For the kingdom of heaven is as a man travelling into a far country, who called his own servants, and delivered unto them his goods.
>
> And unto one he gave five talents, to another two, and to another one; to every man according to his several ability; and straightway took his journey.
>
> Then he that had received the five talents went and traded with the same, and made them other five talents.
>
> And likewise he that had received two, he also gained other two.
>
> But he that had received one went and digged in the earth, and hid his lord's money.
>
> After a long time the lord of those servants cometh, and reckoneth with them.
>
> And so he that had received five talents came and brought other five talents, saying, Lord, thou deliveredst unto me five talents: behold, I have gained beside them five talents more.
>
> His lord said unto him, Well done, thou good and faithful servant: thou hast been faithful over a few things, I will make thee ruler over many things: enter thou into the joy of thy lord.

He also that had received two talents came and said, Lord, thou deliveredst unto me two talents: behold, I have gained two other talents beside them.

His lord said unto him, Well done, good and faithful servant; thou hast been faithful over a few things, I will make thee ruler over many things: enter thou into the joy of thy lord.

Then he which had received the one talent came and said, Lord, I knew thee that thou art an hard man, reaping where thou hast not sown, and gathering where thou hast not strewed:

And I was afraid, and went and hid thy talent in the earth: lo, there thou hast that is thine.

His lord answered and said unto him, Thou wicked and slothful servant, thou knewest that I reap where I sowed not, and gather where I have not strewed:

Thou oughtest therefore to have put my money to the exchangers, and then at my coming I should have received mine own with usury.

Take therefore the talent from him, and give it unto him which hath ten talents.

For unto every one that hath shall be given, and he shall have abundance: but from him that hath not shall be taken away even that which he hath.

And cast ye the unprofitable servant into outer darkness: there shall be weeping and gnashing of teeth. (Matthew 25:14–30)

Despite this two-thousand-year-old warning, people are people, and in tough times they become paralyzed and hold on to money. They certainly did it in the aftermath of the 2008 collapse. Everyone was buying stock before the crash. Now everyone seems to be hoarding cash, as the AP reports:

> Five years after U.S. investment bank Lehman Brothers col-
> lapsed, triggering a global financial crisis and shattering
> confidence worldwide, families in major countries around
> the world are still hunkered down, too spooked and distrust-
> ful to take chances with their money.
>
> An Associated Press analysis of households in the 10 big-
> gest economies shows that families continue to spend cau-
> tiously and have pulled hundreds of billions of dollars out of
> stocks, cut borrowing for the first time in decades and poured
> money into savings and bonds that offer puny interest pay-
> ments, often too low to keep up with inflation.[4]

The reality is that even if your life savings is safe from termites, if you keep it all in paper money, you are running a huge risk. The average life expectancy for a fiat currency is twenty-seven years, and our dollar has been off the gold standard since 1971.[5] DollarDaze's study of 775 fiat currencies found that no fiat currency has ever held value—12 percent were destroyed by hyperinflation, another 21 percent by war, 12 percent by independence, and 24 percent by monetary reformation. The rest are awaiting their deaths. The most successful fiat currency in history is the British pound sterling, which has lasted since 1694—but even that cur-rency is a shocking 0.5 percent of its original value.[6] No wonder Steph-anie Pomboy, the founder of MacroMavens, says that currencies unbacked by gold or other assets will collapse. Inflation, she says, isn't the solution:

> Some believe that, with another round of quantitative easing,
> we move forward, emerge from the morass, and the need for

further intervention will dissipate. But the Fed is really the only natural buyer of Treasuries anymore. It will have to continue to monetize Treasury issuance at the same time all the other major developed economies—from the Bank of Japan to the Bank of England to the European Central Bank—are doing the same. Pursue that to its natural conclusion, and you see the inevitable demise of fiat money. To look at our policies and not be concerned about the risks to our currency would be dangerously naive.[7]

Lord Monckton, a former advisor to Margaret Thatcher, has suggested that it is time to reset the United States dollar. He's not kidding. In fact, he has argued that a complete reset of the monetary system may be required:

> "Forget the dollar. It is finished. America needs a sound currency. The easy option would be to adopt the Canadian dollar, for hard-headed, common-sense Canada avoided the foofaraw of nonsensical credit-default swaps and dodgy derivatives that brought down the sillier banks...."

Monckton doesn't stop with suggestions of Canadian monetary integration, however. He suggests a complete "reset" of the American financial system.

> "There is a more dirigiste solution, which I prefer much less than the free-market solution.... It is possible simply to cancel all public and private debt and tell everyone to start again. One takes a deep breath, presses the RESET button and reboots the entire system," he said.

> "The Emperor Augustus did this in ancient Rome, and the result was 400 years of prosperity, notwithstanding the flashy and often spectacularly incompetent absolute tyrants

who succeeded him," he said. "Again, the more recent precedent is in postwar West Germany in 1948, when Mr. Erhardt,
then the finance minister, waited until the occupying Allied
commanders were away for a weekend's shooting and called
in the Reichsmark, replacing it with the Deutsche Mark.
Everyone was given 50 new Deutsche Marks and told to get
on with it."

Financial analysts are aghast at the idea, but Monckton dismisses
such concerns, again reaching into history: "'When Gen. Clay, the U.S.
commander of the occupying forces, got back after his weekend and
found out what had been done [in Germany], he called at the Finan-
zministerium and said, 'Herr Erhardt, my advisers tell me you're making
a terrible mistake.' Erhardt's famous reply: 'Don't worry, general: mine
tell me the same.' Again, the rest is history. Germany, even after enduring the staggering cost of rebuilding East Germany upon the happy
reunification of the nation, remains Europe's economic powerhouse.'"[8]

If Monckton were right, what would happen to the greenbacks being
hoarded now? This is a sobering thought and should give pause to anyone who believes that cash is the safest investment.

Even if you believe the dollar will survive as a viable currency and
retain its status as the most important reserve currency of the world (in
spite of economic warfare against it), history has proved that those who
hold paper will lose purchasing power even in the best of times. From
1913, when the Federal Reserve was created, to 1933, the dollar lost
almost 30 percent of its value. By 1944, it had lost another 10 percent of
its value. By 1971, the dollar was about 30 percent of its 1913 value, and
today it represents just 5 percent of its original value. According to the
Bureau of Labor Statistics' inflation calculator, it takes one hundred dollars to buy today what cost $4.24 in 1913. And that calculation is based
on the consumer price index, which many think understates inflation.

If you factor in the risks of a currency attack or collapse, it is easy to see that keeping all your wealth in paper is a bad idea.

What about Banks?

Banks are wonderful things. They serve important functions in our economy. But, while far better than a mattress, bank deposits are not the only place to store wealth.

There are many reasons not to stick your cash in a bank. First, banks may offer very low rates for savers, often below the rate of inflation. Catherine Rampell of the *New York Times* explains,

> The fact that interest yields are so low in so many parts of the world is no coincidence. Rates are determined not only by markets, but also by government policy. And right now many governments say they have good reason to keep their own borrowing costs as low as they possibly can.... Though bad for people trying to live off their savings, low interest rates happen to be quite good for anyone borrowing money, like governments themselves. Over time, interest rates below the inflation rate allow governments to refinance, erode or liquidate their debt, making it easier to live within their budgets without having to resort to more unpalatable spending cuts or tax increases.[9]

So you can thank the U.S. government for making sure that you make no money on your deposits.

Banks also charge a variety of fees for holding your money. IRA fees, for example, may be up to fifty dollars per year. On a $5,000 deposit, that fee would wipe out a 1-percent interest rate.[10] Banks commonly charge fifteen or twenty dollars per month to maintain checking accounts below a certain minimum balance (as high as $15,000). "Nothing in banking is free anymore," reports the Associated Press.[11]

One reason that banks can get away with charging such high fees is that they are flush with deposits. In fact, some banks now try to discourage deposits because they don't have good places to put all the cash. According to Reuters:

> "Banks were fighting each other for deposits in 2004, 2005, and 2006, but since then, deposits have become easy. I've had bankers tell me, 'I can't turn the deposit faucet off,'" said Scott Hildenbrand, a strategist at investment bank Sandler O'Neill who advises banks on their assets and liabilities.
>
> Some banks have tried to turn down the faucet. In August 2011, during a U.S. debt ceiling crisis, Bank of New York Mellon Corp announced a plan to charge some corporate and fund management clients a fee for adding too much to their deposits, although it never acted on that threat. It thought about making a similar move last year amid euro zone turmoil.[12]

It's not all good times in the banking business, however. More than five hundred banks have failed since October 2000, some big, some small. Many others were bought and merged away. Virtually all of those failures have occurred since the beginning of the Great Recession.

But your money is safe even if it's in a failed bank, right? Wrong. Federal Deposit Insurance Corporation guarantees have limits. During the financial crisis, the limit per account was raised to $250,000,[13] but it can be adjusted. The insured amount varies by type of account. Savings accounts, trust accounts, money-market deposit accounts, individual retirement accounts, and certificates of deposit are insured up to the $250,000 limit, but mutual funds, annuities, life insurance policies, and the like, are not. Limits have ranged from $2,500 to $250,000. Some non-interest-bearing checking accounts enjoyed unlimited coverage during the crisis, but this ended in 2012.

The FDIC's reserves are limited. At the end of 2011, its backstop fund was about $12 billion, and it predicted that it would need $12 billion to cover bank shutdowns through 2016. The FDIC said that it would take until 2018 for the fund to recover fully; the fund actually had a deficit of $20.9 billion at the end of 2009, when the banks began to collapse.[14] The deposit fund grew nicely in 2012 to almost $33 billion, as member bank assessments far exceeded bailouts.[15]

Sounds like they have it covered—as long as the dramatic slowdown of failures from recent history continues. From 2007 through 2012, the FDIC paid out almost $100 billion, according to the *Los Angeles Times*, while taking in less than $1 billion: "Since 2007, 471 U.S. banks have failed, nearly depleting the FDIC deposit-insurance fund with $92.5 billion in losses.... Overall, the FDIC collected $787 million in settlements by pressing civil claims related to bank failures from 2007 through 2012—a fraction of its total losses."[16] At the start of 2013, assets insured were something like $9 trillion. That's right—the total amount insured is measured in *trillions* of dollars, while the insurance fund is measured in tens of *billions*. Barring a major catastrophe, the FDIC should be able to continue to guarantee deposits up to $250,000. But in the case of a massive failure from an act of economic warfare, there would be a problem. There's no way to cover $9 trillion in deposits with less than $50 billion on hand. And with a $17 trillion federal debt, it's hard to see how even the government could bail out $9 trillion of deposits in the event of a systemic collapse.

Government default is not all that uncommon, unfortunately. Germany and France have both defaulted eight times since 1800, the United States has technically defaulted before, and Russia defaulted as recently as 1998.[17] Obviously, in the event of a default, government help beyond the FDIC limits is, shall we say, unlikely.

Looming Cyberattack

And let's not forget about cyberattacks. In February 2013, Bank of the West, a regional financial institution in California, came under a hack attack. Thieves were able to grab $900,000 from one of the bank's business customers.[18]

Now, even if your bank remains sound, hacking could deprive you of access to your funds temporarily or permanently. In 2009 alone, the Internet Crime Complaint Center reported that Americans lost over $550 million to internet thieves, double the 2008 amount. "Last year there were more online bank robberies than there were actual on-site bank robberies," Sean Sullivan, security advisor at F-Secure, said. "Banks have become very proactive in protecting accounts from hackers but it's still quite a large problem. We see all types of new attempts every day."[19] Dell SecureWorks estimates online thievery from small and midsized companies at over $1 billion per year.[20] What happens if those funds are stolen? It depends on whether you're an individual with a personal account, or a business account. Banks have to help you out if you have a personal account in some ways, and they have to provide "commercially reasonable" online security—but reimbursement does not apply to business accounts. Typical bank agreements include that language.[21]

There are those who think all the rich folks keep their cash in offshore banks. But while higher rates and diversification may seem attractive, there's always Cyprus, which simply confiscated wealth from depositors—60 percent from those who had over one hundred thousand euros.[22] London's *Financial Times* believes it could happen in the United Kingdom: "Could it happen here? You bet. The ghastly arithmetic underlying this week's Budget shows that, at best, Britain is travelling less fast in the wrong direction.... If bank deposits become a legitimate target, there's not much the ordinary citizen can do. Moth and rust doth corrupt the treasures you lay up for yourself but the state can simply take them away."[23]

Some believe that confiscation could happen here in tough times. Even a Federal Reserve governor seemed to indicate that in a financial catastrophe, the government would let private investors bear the bank losses rather than bailing them out. Jeremy Stein, a former economics professor at Harvard and a senior advisor to the secretary of the Treasury in the Obama administration said: "Perhaps more to the point for TBTF (Too Big Too Fail), if a SIFI (Systemically Important Financial Institution) does fail I have little doubt that private investors will in fact bear the losses—even if this leads to an outcome that is messier and more costly to society than we would ideally like. Dodd-Frank is very clear in saying that the Federal Reserve and other regulators cannot use their emergency authorities to bail out an individual failing institution. And as a member of the Board, I am committed to following both the letter and the spirit of the law."[24]

Confiscation of depositors' funds in a bank failure is essentially the same thing as enforcing deposit insurance limits. The legal mechanism to confiscate bank deposits in the United States is therefore in place.[25] Presumably, confiscation would occur only in the sort of calamitous bank failure to which Stein refers.[26] No one should be surprised by the possibility of confiscation. It happened in Poland recently,[27] and in Russia.[28] And the European Union is making contingency plans for confiscations as needed.[29] The problem is global. The key is to be prudently aware of the risks and know that they are universal.

What about Money-Market Funds?

Remember Representative Paul Kanjorski's sobering account in chapter four of the electronic run on the banks that almost sank our financial system? The target of that run—half a trillion dollars in two hours—was U.S. money-market accounts. So much for money markets being a safe haven during financial crises.

Money-market funds remain at risk. As Rex Nutting of MarketWatch writes, "Money-market funds, thought to be one of the safest investments, are actually some of the most dangerous.... The money-market funds are smaller than they were in 2008, but if anything, they are riskier. Current U.S. law prohibits the kind of federal guarantee that, in 2008, stopped the bank run before it could bring down the financial system. The next run on these shadowy bank-like institutions could be fatal." Why? Because money-market funds promise that people will have their capital returned, just like banks do—except there's no real guarantee of that promise. As Nutting points out, "Money-market funds are popular precisely because there's no cushion to back them up. Cushions cost money, cutting into the profits the funds make and the returns (meager as they are) that depositors receive.... If money-market funds were regulated like banks, then what advantage would they have? You might as well park your money in a commercial bank, with its boring FDIC insurance and access to the Federal Reserve's discount window in the event of a liquidity squeeze."[30] Current law prohibits the Fed and Treasury from bailing out the money-market funds the way they did in 2008. So next time, it's kaboom.

Now, money funds held at a brokerage house may be insured by the Securities Investor Protection Corporation (SIPC). But that insurance protects against a failure of your brokerage account and not of your holdings. If your money-market fund loses value, you have no insurance against that loss. These funds are designed to keep you from losing money—the net asset value is never supposed to drop below one dollar. Dropping below one dollar is called "breaking the buck." Money-market funds are invested in short-term securities that can, in a crisis, lose value. In a panic, investors could pull money out of money-market funds, forcing the funds to dump short-term securities, further depressing their price and setting off a downward spiral. The Securities and Exchange Commission notes, "While investor losses in money market funds have been rare, they are possible."[31] Eric Rosengren, president of the Federal Reserve Bank of Boston, said that runs on money-market mutual funds were still quite possible because of their lack of capital. There is about $3 trillion in money-market funds, and Rosengren calls the risk of runs a "significant unresolved issue."[32]

There are risks even to cash and "cash equivalents" like money-market funds. Whether you try to keep money in the mattress or at the bank, there can be problems.

So what should you do? Diversify where you keep your cash. If you have more than $250,000 in cash, open accounts at multiple banks. If you are worried about the FDIC, put some cash in safety deposit boxes. You won't gain interest, but you won't be at risk of confiscation either. (But watch out for counterfeit cash—something being pumped out by nation-states like Iran and North Korea with the help of the drug cartels.)[33]

Buy U.S. Treasuries rather than money-market funds. These can be insured at a broker by SIPC. If SIPC is a concern, keep them in a safety deposit. Stick to short-term maturities, or buy a Treasury-only fund, which will protect you unless there is a sudden onset of hyperinflation. In that case, all bets are off, as currencies can lose almost all their purchasing power overnight. Millions of dollars could become virtually worthless in such circumstances.[34] And, of course, there remains the risk of government default.

If you are concerned about the dollar, you can buy multi-currency money-market funds. Or open foreign bank accounts denominated in foreign dollars (although such an arrangement can have some implications for currency transfers).

If you are concerned about inflation, you need to move away from cash and into growth-oriented investments or hard assets. Again, a professional is necessary to help you navigate these shark-infested waters. And they are most definitely shark infested—and those sharks include America's enemies.

CHAPTER NINE

Guaranteed Investments

Ultimately, there are only two types of investments, and everything else is derived from them. You either own or loan. You can own businesses or things like real estate, gold, collectibles, or coins. Even holding cash is a form of loaning or owning. If you put the cash in a safety deposit box, a no-interest deposit account, or a mattress, you simply own paper certificates guaranteed by the government. If you put the cash in an interest-bearing bank account or money-market fund, you are loaning the money directly or indirectly.

Every other investment is ownership, a loan, a combination of the two, or a derivative of some kind. Guaranteed investments are no different. If the underlying investments fail in some way, the guarantee may become worthless. If you buy insurance, and your insurer goes out of business, it won't help you to invoke your insurance—there's nobody left to pay it. In other words, there are no absolute guarantees when investing. In a world where the economic future is uncertain, investors naturally look for safety. Thus investments that say they're guaranteed have an allure for those concerned about the vicissitudes of the economy. It's worthwhile to examine "guaranteed" investments, whether they're annuities or guaranteed investment contracts (GICs), in order to have a clear picture of the rewards as well as possible pitfalls.

Annuities date back to the Roman Empire. Citizens would make one lump-sum payment into what was called the "annua," then they would be paid a certain sum every year until they died or for a period that had been agreed upon.

In the Middle Ages, kings raised money for their wars with fixed annuities. In early America, annuities started as a retirement pool for church pastors in Pennsylvania. Benjamin Franklin left annuities in his will to the cities of Boston and Philadelphia. Amazingly, the Boston annuity was still paying out in the 1990s; it stopped only because the city chose to take the rest in a lump-sum payment.

The signal change in buying annuities occurred when Americans' attitude about supporting family members in their later years changed. Wary of the stock market after the crash of 1929, Americans invested more in annuities. Variable annuities appeared in 1952, and indexed annuities followed in the late 1980s and early 1990s.[1]

Annuities offer payments for a fixed term or for life from an insurance company to the investor, or even to his heirs. That is, you get your money back over time plus interest. Ongoing payments, of a fixed or variable amount, are guaranteed. Annuities are offered only by insurance companies. Once you buy one, you can't change the amount of the payments or withdraw more than the scheduled amount. The terms are etched in stone.

So why invest in an annuity? There are two main reasons. First, an annuity allows you to defer taxes, which can be especially useful if you have maxed out your contributions to an IRA, 401(k), or 403(b). Second, an annuity can give you a monthly income for the rest of your life, which is useful now that people are living longer.[2]

Deciding to Buy an Annuity

The first decision you have to make about an annuity is whether you want the payout to begin immediately or to be deferred. If you decide on an immediate annuity, you will begin to receive money as soon as you invest. You can receive payments for a "period certain"—that is, a period with a set beginning and end—or you can receive payments for the rest of your life or your spouse's life.[3]

A deferred annuity, on the other hand, does not begin payments until some later date, which could be as early as thirty days after you invest. The advantage of a deferred annuity is that taxes are deferred on your gains until you receive payments.

Once you've decided to purchase an immediate or deferred annuity, you'll have to decide whether you want a fixed annuity or a variable one. Fixed annuities have the advantage of letting the money invested grow while being tax deferred.

You can buy a fixed annuity with a lump-sum payment, or you can make a series of payments while you are still working. When you are considering purchasing a fixed annuity, it is important to remember that you can often negotiate the price of these products. Also, the amount of money that an annuity will pay out varies (sometimes greatly) between financial intermediaries selling these products, so it's best to shop around and avoid making quick decisions.

Variable annuities offer fluctuating payments based on the returns of the underlying investment. Like fixed annuities, variable annuities have two phases: the accumulation phase, in which the investor makes purchase payments to the insurance company, and the annuitization (or payout) phase, in which the investor collects payments. You can allocate your purchase payments to different kinds of investments, from the conservative to the aggressive. For example, you could allocate part of the payments to bond funds, part to an international stock fund, and part to a U.S. stock fund. You could put part of your payment into an investment that pays a fixed rate of interest, which is set by the insurance company and can fluctuate, but would likely have a guaranteed minimum.[4] Variable annuities are expected to outperform fixed annuities in the long run, but you will experience the ups and downs of the market along the way. If you are looking for a quick income payout or guaranteed result, you should avoid variable annuities.

You should also be aware of the charges variable annuities can incur. If you want to withdraw money early, you might incur a penalty known as a surrender charge—a stipulated percentage of the amount withdrawn, which usually decreases over time. Variable annuities with a surrender charge may offer a bonus for leaving your funds invested. If you want to be able to withdraw funds at a moment's notice, you should buy an annuity with no surrender charges, but you won't get the bonus. Mortality and expense risk charges are a percentage of the value of your annuity, usually about 1.25 percent per year. Administrative charges can be deducted as flat fees or a percentage of your account value, usually about 0.15 percent per year.[5]

What Kind of Annuity Is Right for You?

Once you have decided on immediate or deferred payout, fixed or variable payments, and the ability to withdraw with or without a penalty, you can consider which kind of annuity is for you. There are many types of annuities: term-certain annuities, life annuities, prescribed annuities, non-prescribed annuities, and insured annuities among them.

A term-certain annuity makes fixed payments over a guaranteed period. If you die during the guarantee period, the annuity continues making payments to your beneficiaries.

A life annuity guarantees regular payments for the rest of the annuitant's life; when the annuitant dies, the payments end unless the contract names a beneficiary. A straight life annuity makes payments until the annuitant dies and does not offer payments to beneficiaries after the annuitant's death. A straight life annuity, therefore, does not make sense for an investor who wants to leave something for his survivors unless it is combined with a separate life insurance policy. A life annuity with a guaranteed term will make a one-time payment of any unpaid benefits to a designated beneficiary upon the annuitant's death, but that payment is in a lump sum, so there can be tax implications.

If you have a serious health problem, you may want to look at a substandard health annuity, which is a life annuity whose price is determined by the health of the annuitant.

A joint life annuity, which can be reducing or non-reducing, is bought for two people and may or may not have a guarantee period. If one of the annuitants dies, the survivor will receive a smaller payment. If the annuity is reducing and has a guarantee period, the smaller payment would occur only after one annuitant dies and the guarantee period is over.

An insured annuity is guaranteed by a life insurance policy matching the amount of the annuity. If you die early, your beneficiaries obtain the full proceeds of the life insurance, tax free.[6]

Another possibility is the equity-indexed annuity (EIA), a complex fixed annuity with a call option on a stock index (almost always the S&P 500). EIAs, which can be useful for target-date income planning, have little downside risk. The upside potential, though greater than a conventional fixed annuity's, is limited.[7] A newer type of annuity—a bonus annuity—is sometimes attached to an EIA. The insurance company adds a "bonus" to your principal when you make your investment, but there are tradeoffs in the form of higher fees, caps on your returns, and limits on cashing out early.[8]

What about holding annuities in an IRA? One of the major advantages of an annuity is the deferral of taxes, but an IRA already has that covered. The Financial Industry Regulatory Authority states, "Investing in a variable annuity within a tax-deferred account, such as an individual retirement account (IRA) may not be a good idea. Since IRAs are already tax-advantaged, a variable annuity will provide no additional tax savings. It will, however, increase the expense of the IRA, while generating fees and commissions for the broker or salesperson."[9]

In general, because of the lack of liquidity, the surrender charges, and the limitations on the investor, many annuities are best for those who want to invest their money for more than fifteen years, those making considerably more money at the time of investment than they will when they retire, or those without beneficiaries.[10] You will not be taxed on the funds in your annuity until you receive payments, but those payments will be taxed at ordinary income rates, not at the lower rates for capital gains.[11]

A good insurance company should be able to weather ordinary economic troubles. The retirement investment advisor Shelby Smith writes, "First and foremost, insurance companies have an operating history of stability that is the envy of banks and brokerage firms. Their investments are limited to conservative, boring options that rarely carry inordinate market risks." States regulate insurance companies closely, and Smith says that no insurance policyholder has ever lost his invested principal. Nor has the holder of a fixed annuity ever lost money because of the vicissitudes of the market.[12] Then again, we aren't in normal economic times, so it is very important to be selective when committing your capital, even to annuities.

Because annuities can be complicated and because they offer so many options, you will need a trusted advisor to help you determine what is best for your situation.

Guaranteed Investment Contracts

Guaranteed investment contracts, like annuities, are bought from insurance companies. The period of time for the guarantee can range from thirty days to decades. Unlike annuities, with a guaranteed investment contract you receive your original investment when the contract ends. You get interest, as with an annuity, but you also get the return of your principal. The advantage of buying GICs is that your investment is similar to a money-market fund but also guaranteed by the insurance company, bank, or trust company that issues the contract. The downside is that the fees are higher than money-market funds, the fixed rates of the GICs sometimes don't keep up with inflation, and, like annuities, they are not guaranteed by the U.S. government the way that Treasury securities are.[13]

GICs usually offer a higher return than bank CDs, most often 0.1 percent to 1 percent higher at the time they are bought. But they are not protected by the FDIC as bank CDs are. GICs are most often bought by investors through 401(k) retirement plans.

Employees who invest in a company's 401(k) retirement plan can commonly choose from four options for investing their pensions: GICs, money-market mutual funds, equity mutual funds, or the common stock of the company. For the GIC option, the company's pension-plan manager allocates the funds to one or more insurance companies. The insurance companies then invest variously in residential mortgages; government, corporate, or high-yield bonds; and private placements.

GICs come in two types: participating and nonparticipating. Participating GICs allow investors to participate in the risks and rewards of fluctuating interest levels, providing a variable rate of return as interest rates rise or fall. Nonparticipating GICs have a fixed rate of return. Participating GICs are therefore a better investment when it looks as if interest rates will be rising, and nonparticipating GICs are better if interest rates are high and look as if they will descend.[14]

It is essential to understand that the guarantee of a GIC refers only to the promise of the issuer to pay. If the insurer fails, the investor could lose all of the investment, although some states may have funds to protect investors in GICs in such cases. If an insurance company does go belly-up, however, under most state laws the policyholders of the company will get paid before the holders of GICs. Fortunately, most big insurance companies do not go bankrupt, and the manager of a 401(k) program will likely diversify among various GICs from different insurers so the failure of one insurer would not wipe out the entire investment.[15]

Bank investment contracts (BICs), are similar to GICs but are issued by banks. In this case, the investor buys the underlying securities, which are put in a trust fund and are thus untouchable by the bank's creditors if the bank goes bankrupt. Unlike regular bank deposits, BICs may or may not be covered by FDIC insurance; it depends on how they are structured by the bank. Most banks do not cover BICs with FDIC insurance. Although BICs are insured by the bank, and GICs by the insurance company, GICs usually have a higher rate of return.[16]

Do Guaranteed Investments Protect You?

All the questions about the relative merits of the different kinds of annuities and GICs could be moot, of course, if there were a massive economic crisis in which only the strongest institutions survived. There is no FDIC coverage for insurance companies, though there are state insurance guaranty associations (GAs) that do support insurance companies if they go bankrupt. Like FDIC coverage, however, the protection provided by a GA is limited; it also varies by state. For the most part, you can demand your money from a bank at any time, but even if your insurance company survived an economic catastrophe, you would have to wait for the scheduled monthly payment to get your hands on your funds. Still, insurance companies are far less leveraged than banks, so they have less exposure in a crisis. From 1987 to 2009, only seventy-four multistate insurance companies failed. In 2010 alone, 157 banks failed, and ninety-two more went under in 2011.[17]

So how do you know how strong your insurance company is? Four independent agencies—A.M. Best, Fitch, Moody's, and Standard & Poor's—rate the strength of insurance companies. The agencies often disagree, so you should try to find a consensus among them before you make a judgment. The ratings change day to day, and the agencies use different scales, making comparisons more difficult.[18] The agencies tarnished their reputations in 2008 by giving investment-grade ratings to Lehman Brothers, AIG, and Washington Mutual until the financial sky fell on September 15. The agencies may have become more careful, but they do not deserve your blind trust.

There are some strong arguments against annuities. They lock up your money, they lack liquidity, and their investment profits are ultimately taxed as ordinary income rather than capital gains, which can negate the advantage of tax deferral. William Reichenstein, a professor of investment management at Baylor University, cautions that investments in conservative stocks and bonds or exchange-traded funds outperform annuities by as much as 2 percent a year over the long term.[19]

David Babbel of the Wharton School and two colleagues, however, conducted an extensive study of fixed-index annuity funds and quarrel with Reichenstein's conclusions. Annuity returns, they argue, can be competitive with alternative portfolios of stocks and bonds.[20]

Ultimately, the returns of a guaranteed investment depend on the performance of the underlying investment. Fixed annuities are based on debt (loaning money), so debt performance will determine how the annuity does. If there is serious deflation, guaranteed debt with fixed rates will do quite well. On the other hand, if inflation is high, debt will do poorly, and the purchasing power of your annuity returns will be harmed. In an inflationary environment, even index annuities will suffer because their returns are often capped. They will nevertheless do better than fixed annuities. If the dollar crashes, annuities will be poor investments because they are primarily dollar linked. Foreign currency annuities may offer a solution, but they lose tax-deferral benefits.

You must conduct a proper analysis of your personal situation and work with a reputable company and a trusted, well-informed advisor who will fully disclose all the pros and cons. You must understand that you are trading flexibility for safety in some but not all areas. The challenge is to understand the effects of economic warfare and financial terrorism and how they will affect your supposedly guaranteed investments. Insurance companies can become targets of bear raids, but the stability of insurance companies is ultimately the guarantee behind annuities and GICs.

Circumstances change rapidly in a crisis, so flexibility is the key to survival. Contracts can be changed in a crisis, and it's usually not to the investor's benefit. That is why you must have good advice from professionals fully aware of the economic-warfare risks.

Obviously, guaranteed investments can get very complicated. This book is not an all-purpose guide to investing. It's about what to do in the event of a serious economic crisis, particularly one resulting from financial terrorism or economic warfare. That's what the next section is about.

CHAPTER TEN

Hedge Funds and Other Out-of-the-Box Investments

M any investors are looking for something different. They are tired and afraid of traditional choices like stocks, bonds, and cash. Unfortunately, many naive investors ignore the proverbial warning about exchanging the devil they know for the devil they don't. Because some alternative investments are not subject to the same regulatory scrutiny as traditional investments, it is often difficult to get the information necessary for objective comparison. This chapter is intended to demystify the alternatives and help you understand how they might perform during economic difficulties.

Alternative investments, according to Blackrock, the world's largest investment management firm, are simply investments other than stocks or bonds, and they behave differently in a portfolio than traditional investments. The term encompasses different investment classes and includes hedge funds, long and short strategies, commodities, private equity, and real estate.[1]

Let's start with hedge funds. These are private investment partnerships, largely unregulated, that give the manager the greatest possible flexibility. Hedge funds can buy stocks; sell short; use derivatives; buy or sell bonds; and invest in real estate, collectibles, private equity, or just about anything else. The general partner is more often than not the fund manager, while the investors are the limited partners, usually represented by institutions and accredited investors. There is usually a limit of ninety-nine limited partners.[2] Hedge funds typically have a high minimum investment and require investors to leave their money in for at least a year.

Hedge funds started as investments for wealthy people. Alfred Winslow Jones, an Australian-born financial journalist, decided in 1949 to create a private investment partnership that he hoped would protect him from the ebbs and flows of the market. He borrowed shares of stock, then short sold them because he figured the market was going to drop. Because it was risky if the market rose, regulators ruled that only rich people could afford to take the chance. The idea was that with the gyrations of the market, the hedge funds would have modest but less risky gains.

Roger Ibbotson, a finance professor at the Yale School of Management, analyzed 8,400 hedge funds from 1995 to 2012 and found that they averaged a gain of 2.5 percent of alpha, which is very good. Alpha is a measure of a fund's risk-adjusted performance compared with its benchmark index. For example, if a fund has 1.0 alpha, that fund has done better than its benchmark index by 1 percent.[3] Ibbotson said, "They have done a good job, historically. Now, I think it's overcapacity. I doubt that the alphas are completely gone, but alphas are going to be harder to get in the future than they have been in the past."[4]

Although hedge funds are for the most part unregulated, a majority of the investors in a fund must be accredited, meaning they meet a minimum annual salary and have a net worth of at least $2 million.[5] Hedge-fund managers charge much higher fees than managers of mutual funds, who take an average of 1.44 percent,[6] and they also charge more than people who offer funds that track stock market indices. The fees for hedge-fund management are typically 2 percent of the original investment per year, plus 20 percent of the profits in addition to the costs of trading. For the most part, hedge-fund managers, not their clients, make a fortune.[7] From 1998 to 2010, the managers of hedge funds amassed $379 billion, while their investors earned $70 billion. The managers wound up with 84 percent of the investment profits; the investors kept 16 percent.[8]

Hedge funds get even more expensive when investors go through "funds of funds." The original idea was to pool investors' dollars and distribute them among a variety of hedge funds. The fund of funds would conduct manager due-diligence, selection, and monitoring. But this arrangement adds another layer of fees and makes it even harder for the investor to win.

Hedge funds have become an important part of the international financial market. They manage over $2 trillion, over 1 percent of all assets held in financial institutions.[9] As of March 2013, forty of the world's billionaires earned a huge chunk of their income managing hedge funds. The list of these supermanagers includes Carl Icahn, George Soros, Ray Dalio, James Simons, John Paulson, Steven Cohen, David Tepper, Leon Cooperman, and David Einhorn.[10]

Despite the glamour, most investors would do well to avoid hedge funds. The S&P 500 outperformed the average hedge fund every year but one from 2003 to 2012. The equity-bond index doubled in that period, while hedge funds only gained 20 percent. The sole exception was 2008, when both hedge funds and the stock market were big losers. That year hedge funds lost a little less.[11] Hedge funds only returned 3.5 percent in 2012, according to the HFRX Global Hedge Fund Index; the

S&P 500 stock index rose 16 percent. From 2007 to 2012, the hedge-fund index lost 13.6 percent, while the indices rose 8.6 percent. From January 1 to May 23, 2013, hedge funds rose only 5.4 percent, while the stock market rose 15.4 percent and mutual funds rose 14.8 percent.[12]

The Hedge-Fund Mentality

Early in the life of a hedge fund, its managers are hungry, motivated, and often humble enough to know what they don't know. This tends to be the best time to put money in, but also the hardest, as the funds tend to be very small. Stage two occurs once the fund has achieved some success, when those making the decisions have gained some confidence but aren't yet so well known that the fund is impossible to get into.

In stage three, the fund's success becomes well known, and there is no room for more investors. Finally, in stage four, the fund manager who has been wildly successful becomes overconfident, and the fund is too unwieldy to move quickly. As Jim Kyung-Soo Liew, assistant professor in finance at the Johns Hopkins Carey Business School, said, "The bigger a fund gets, the more difficult it gets to maintain strong performance. That's just because the number of opportunities is limited in terms of putting that much money to work."[13]

Then, of course, there are the numerous stories of hedge-fund managers who have acted in a criminal fashion. The most famous, Bernie Madoff, with $50 billion, could well have been the world's best hedge-fund manager if he weren't a complete fraud.[14] (It turns out that his firm wasn't even structured properly to be a hedge fund.)[15] Raj Rajaratnam, who founded the hugely successful Galleon Group hedge fund in 1997, was later sentenced to eleven years in prison for the largest hedge-fund insider-trading scheme in history.[16] Steve Cohen, the head of the $14 billion SAC Capital, saw his firm charged with a five-count criminal indictment that seemed to be ultimately targeting him.[17]

Some argue that the hedge-fund mentality encourages criminality. Lynn Stout of the UCLA School of Law explains that hedge funds, by their very nature, suppress "prosocial" behavior. Hedge-fund managers tell their traders to maximize portfolio returns. Traders are competitive and would rather boast of their achievements than sacrifice gains if there is an ethical conflict. And since traders don't see the victims of their crimes, they remain indifferent to the consequences of acting unethically.[18] There's so much money and so little control that the temptation to cut corners or do whatever necessary to attract clients or increase returns becomes extremely powerful.

Hedge-Fund Economic Warfare

That's another risk—it's rarely clear what the motives of the hedge-fund manager might be. In *Secret Weapon*, I showed how large pools of wealth can influence hedge-fund investments. Sometimes, big-fund managers have objectives other than making the most money for clients. The famous George Soros is a case in point: In 2003 he said that removing President George W. Bush from office was the "central focus of my life" and "a matter of life and death." He said he would sacrifice his entire fortune to defeat President Bush, "if someone guaranteed it."[19] There are other reasons to question Soros's motivations. He was convicted of insider trading in France, and the conviction was upheld after years of effort to discredit it. He has also more recently been investigated for possibly violating U.S. insider-trading laws.[20] Has Soros been investing for himself or for his clients?

As the Soros example shows, hedge funds may be dedicated to values different from yours. Some are focused on compliance with Islamic law, and their clients include enormous Middle Eastern sovereign wealth funds. Sheikh Yusuf Talal DeLorenzo has become a key player in developing Islamic financial products in the United States. In

2000 he joined the Guidance Financial Group, which now offers U.S. Muslims a competitively priced mortgage that complies with sharia law. The company had raised $1 billion in financing by 2007. Sharia, he said, has "essentially been in a coma for several centuries.... It desperately needs reviving."[21]

The anonymity of hedge-fund investors can be a problem. You might not know what your fellow investors believe, and the fund could be used to pursue values you don't share.

We should not be surprised if sovereign wealth funds use their assets to pursue objectives other than simply making money. As the former Treasury secretary Lawrence Summers said: "Suppose a country ran an active trading operation and found itself in an investment much like George Soros' short position in the British pound in 1992. Would we be comfortable with the concept that nation X found that the fixed exchange rate of nation Y was untenable and wanted to launch a speculative attack against it?"[22]

If you don't know your manager, you may be investing against your own interests. If you don't know who else is in the hedge fund, you may be unaware of powerful interests pushing a conflicting agenda. You could be funding your own enemies.

Should You Use a Hedge Fund?

This is not to say that hedge funds are always bad for investors. But they can be expensive ways to invest in alternatives. You need the right manager, with the right strategy, at the right time. A handful of hedge funds actually averaged returns of 50 percent per year over a recent three-year period.[23]

There has been a push to make hedge funds accessible to retail investors. Two major investment firms, Fidelity and Blackstone, have recently combined to offer hedge-fund alternatives with expense ratios lower than those of typical hedge funds and minimum investments as low as $50,000. They also removed some of the withdrawal restrictions.[24]

Some experts nevertheless believe that hedge funds are a bad idea for retail investors. Adrian J. Larson, the president and portfolio manager of Pathlight, found that in the ten years between 2003 and 2013, someone who invested $1 million dollars in the S&P 500 index gained $661,070 more than an investor in the HFRI Fund of Funds Composite Index.[25] Hedge funds, he concluded, represent "an investment style that is simply not worth the money."

In any case, investing in hedge funds requires professional help. These funds can be nothing more than glorified mutual funds—underperforming, overpriced mutual funds at that. A fund that sticks to stocks and bonds requires a truly exceptional manager to beat the market by enough to justify his keep. The hedge funds that stand out focus on alternative investments. To evaluate such funds, you have to understand the alternatives in which the fund is investing.

Alternative Investments

There are several basic categories of alternative investments. You can invest in financial assets like corporate stock, which is equity. You can lend money, which is debt. You can invest in real estate, commodities, or collectibles. Or, you can hold cash in various currencies. Every investment can be affected by the world around it. Economic warfare will have a substantial effect on all investments. Depending on the type of attack, the effect could be positive or negative.

Financial assets are also called "paper assets" because you buy a piece of paper that represents an agreement. *Investopedia*'s online dictionary defines a financial asset as one "that derives value because of a contractual claim. Stocks, bonds, bank deposits, and the like are all examples of financial assets. Unlike land and property—which are tangible, physical assets—financial assets do not necessarily have physical worth."[26] Alternative assets that fit in this category include private equity and alternative loans.

Private equity is ownership of corporate stock that is not traded on public stock exchanges. When you buy shares of stock on an exchange, the price is publicly quoted, and you buy through a broker. The investment is highly liquid—you can usually sell your investment any time you want. Shares of Facebook are public equity; they have been publicly traded since May 2012. In its initial public offering (IPO), Facebook raised $16 billion of new investment capital in a day.[27] Facebook had shareholders before its IPO, however. The lucky few who got in early made fortunes. They enjoyed returns of about 1,000 percent within four years.[28]

With gains like that, who wouldn't want to dive into private equity?

Private equity comes in all flavors and varieties. It can be a small personal investment in your cousin's bakery. Or it can be taking a very formal stake in a pre-IPO company like Facebook. There is always the potential for gain, but there is also the potential for complete loss. You can invest in private equity on your own or through a manager or private-equity fund. There are many private-equity firms that act like a combination of hedge funds, and there are venture capital firms focused on true start-ups. These firms charge relatively high fees to oversee a portfolio of private-equity holdings on behalf of their shareholders. The investment can be in an early-stage start-up or a later-stage investment to provide working capital or growth opportunity for a business that is already operating. It is best to seek professional guidance from someone who understands your personal situation and goals, thoroughly reviews the opportunity, and appreciates the economic situation and economic warfare risks.

The more exotic (and high-risk) options for private-equity investments include Broadway plays and feature films. The *New York Times* reported about such investments, "[F]or some amateurs, being part of the film festival circuit, let alone making it to a big Hollywood premiere, can be glamorous. For a serious investor, with more at stake, there are many ways to make money in films that have little to do with box-office success."[29] It takes more than a few million to take a stake in a major Hollywood project, but smaller independent filmmakers might accept as little as $10,000.

Other outlets for the glamour-seeking investor are racehorses[30] and NASCAR teams.[31]

Private equity is riskier than public equity. The disclosure requirements and regulations are less stringent. Companies listed on an exchange are established businesses. Public shares are more liquid. As a general rule, the risk of complete failure is much greater with private equity.

Only licensed broker dealers are allowed to sell equity, even private equity, for compensation.[32] A word of caution is in order. Although having an advisor is highly recommended for a private-equity investor, make sure that your advisor is sitting on the same side of the table as you. It is common to offer "finder's fees" for capital raising, which creates incentives for the advisor that can run contrary to your interests.

One way around this problem is for the advisor to negotiate the greatest possible incentive and then require that the company raising capital return that fee to the client directly. This eliminates the conflict of interest and simultaneously creates a better deal for the investor. Finder's fees can be 5 percent or more of the investment, so the client ends up with a 5-percent discount and trust in his advisor.[33] Be certain to ask if your investment includes finder's fees or other commissions.

There may be circumstances in which a finder's fee is appropriate. In those cases, the advisor must be a properly licensed broker dealer, and the commission on the sale of the private investment should be in lieu of advisory fees. Finally, the client must fully understand the implications of the finder's fee.

There are some real advantages to private equity:

1. The upside can be substantially larger. Imagine if you were one of Steve Jobs's early supporters and bought even a few thousand dollars' worth of Apple pre-IPO.
2. Private equity is not subject to the daily pricing whims of the markets. You don't have to worry about what others think of your investment as reflected in the daily tick of the market. On the other hand, your investments aren't so liquid that you can sell them on a moment's notice.
3. Your investment in private equity won't be directly affected if the stock exchange is hacked or prices are manipulated.
4. With private equity you can have a greater influence on management and company direction.

The benefits of private equity can make it a reasonable investment option if you have professional support in evaluation and monitoring, objectivity, and a long-term horizon.

Microinvesting is a recent innovation that allows investors to take small stakes in companies. It used to cost $50,000 or even much more to get in on a start-up, but microinvesting lets you invest as little as $250. The risk with microinvesting, according to MicroVentures CEO Bill Clark, is that "seeing a return could take five to seven years. And you could also lose all your money. It's high-risk."[34]

Warrants, Options, and Other Incentive "Kickers"

Sometimes companies issuing private equity will attach other instruments—usually "warrants"—to make the investment more interesting.

Options are usually given to employees of start-ups as a part of their compensation. They allow employees to take an ownership stake in the company if the shares become more valuable. An option is the right to buy shares at a predetermined price for a limited time period. A warrant, on the other hand, is usually given to investors. It is not compensation but rather a "sweetener" for those taking a stake early. An early-stage company might, for example, offer fifty warrants for every hundred shares of stock purchased. The warrants would allow the investor to buy additional shares at a predetermined price for a set period. The warrants themselves have value and can be sold separately in some cases.[35] Both warrants and options have tax implications.

Private Debt

Private debt is to the bond markets what private equity is to the stock markets. Many of the same rules apply.

Private debt can be informal, such as loaning money to a sibling to buy a car or open a coffee shop. Or it can be formal, such as participating in a private offering from a larger company. As with private equity, there can be finder's fees and warrants. Private debt can contain "conversion" privileges that allow the debt holder to convert the balance due into another form of security of asset. A mortgage is an example of a convertible debt.[36]

Both entrepreneurs and investors like convertible debt. It can be flexible, but there are three critical choices to make. First, what event will trigger the conversion? It is usually a financing event, such as a revenue or financing threshold. Second, what discount, if any, will there be upon conversion? If there is no discount or it is too low, investors might back away; if the discount is too high, investors in the next round might factor the discount in when they value the stock. Third, what happens to the investment if the conversion event never occurs?[37]

You might consider a species of private debt known as microloans, fixed-interest loans given to small-business owners in developing countries. Minimum investments can be as small as twenty dollars, but the yields can be 1 to 6 percent annually.[38] For lending to people who, because of their poverty, normally would not qualify for a loan, the microlending pioneer Muhammad Yunus, the Bangladeshi founder of Grameen Bank, won the 2006 Nobel Peace Prize. The "security" for microloans is the good name of the borrower's family.[39]

Hard-money loans, which usually return 10 to 12 percent to the lender, are secured against an asset. An investor, for example, might offer a mortgage to a real estate buyer who is short of cash or needs bridge financing.[40]

Tangible Investments ("Stuff")

In contrast to paper investments (financial assets), tangible investments are essentially investments in "stuff." The range is huge, from land to diamonds, from food and wine to comic books and stamps. Each has unique attributes and pricing. Each has unique costs and quirks. But all have one thing in common: you own stuff.

Sometimes buying stuff involves a paper investment. For example, when you invest in an oil well, you are really making a private equity investment in a venture. You can also buy mineral rights or production royalties.

In most cases, you will own a piece of paper that entitles you to an income stream or other payout. It is a "tangible" asset because the underlying investment is a thing rather than an idea or service. The value of the investment, if successful, will be based on the value of the stuff it represents.

Tangible investments include real estate, commodities, fine art, stamps, oil and gas properties, precious metals, guns and firearms, antique cars, and equipment that can be leased. We can break these tangible assets down into three categories: property, commodities, and collectibles.

Property

Property can be real estate (undeveloped or developed) or equipment. You might own a rental home or a stake in a shopping center.[41] Your investment can be direct or pooled with others. One way to invest in property is through a real estate investment trust (REIT), which is often publicly traded on an exchange. REITs invest in a great variety of commercial properties.[42]

REITs pay dividends and shield investors from some of the liabilities associated with direct property ownership. They are convenient and liquid and don't require much money to invest. You are not personally responsible for maintenance, and you can diversify your investments. At the same time, REITs, when traded on exchanges, are subject to the daily ups and downs of the market. If you own investment real estate directly, you manage it yourself, and you can get additional tax benefits.[43]

There are many considerations in real estate investing. The famous aphorism is that only three things matter: "location, location, location." But it's more complicated than that. Without going into detail about real estate investing, let's mention some of the plusses and minuses.

As an investor in real estate, you have leverage. You can take advantage of the appreciation and cash flow of the investment while using a small amount of money on a large investment. You have more security than if you were flipping houses, you reap tax benefits, and you control the investment, as opposed to a stock, where you are at the mercy of the company's directors.[44] There are choices ranging from single-family homes, with their attendant ease of financing; small multifamily properties, where two or four units protect you if one of the families moves out; and large multifamily properties, which can give you higher cash flow.

But there are risks to investing in real estate. Christopher J. Mayer, a professor of real estate, finance, and economics at Columbia Business School, warns, "There is a lot of idiosyncratic risk associated with rental income. That is the word that economists use for when a lot of things can go wrong, even if on average they don't go wrong very often."[45] Home values can decline, your money is concentrated in one place, your rental property might sit vacant, and the upkeep is your responsibility.

In all cases, having professional advice can help with property investing. It is especially important to have an awareness of global economic factors and how they may affect your property investments.

Commodities

I have already devoted a whole chapter to precious metals, which are a subset of commodities. But you might also invest in rare gems and diamonds, food, timber, or energy. You can purchase commodities directly, on the futures market, and through funds and ETFs. You can also invest in companies that produce the commodities. I will briefly describe each of the investments and then run through the mechanisms.

Diamonds: Investing in "ice" has become hot. Diamonds and other rare gems are universally appealing, contain a great deal of value in a small package, and can be easily stored and transported. They don't wear out or go bad,[46] and diamonds produced a higher rate of return than equities between 1999 and 2010: white diamonds yielded 6.4 percent, while stocks and bonds returned 0.1 percent and 3.3 percent, respectively.[47]

Business Insider gives eight rules to follow when investing in gems:

1. Either buy the gems themselves or invest in a company such as a mining company that is part of the gem industry.
2. Make certain that your average rate of return matches the rate of inflation.
3. Know that gemstones are not liquid. You can't look up the "going rate" for diamonds as you can for gold; there are many factors determining the value of a diamond.
4. Try to buy the stones below retail.
5. Get professional help.

6. Keep your eyes open for fraud.
7. Remember that selling the gem will be as difficult as buying it.
8. Remember that capital gains taxes apply.[48]

Food: One problem with diamonds and precious metals is that you can't eat them. The necessity of eating makes food an interesting alternative investment. And there are multiple ways to invest in food:

1. You can grow your own. Of course, this requires land, seeds, know-how, fertilizer, and luck for weather.
2. You can buy food someone else has grown. In this case you will need storage and maybe processing capabilities and distribution.
3. You can buy food someone else has already processed. Again, you still have to store and distribute.
4. You can buy contracts for food delivery and then sell the contracts prior to delivery. This is usually how the futures market operates.

At some point, for the food to have value, it will need to be delivered to a consumer. Food is mostly perishable, although the shelf life can vary greatly.

Many people buy food futures. Futures are *not* for the average investor, especially without professional help. I won't go into all the specifics, but there are plenty of dangers to watch out for. High-pressure brokers or inadequate capital can lead to trouble.[49] The futures market is so unpredictable that you could lose your entire investment, and possibly more than you even invested. Futures are not covered by the Securities Investor Protection Corporation (SIPC).[50]

A friend of mine recently devised a unique and beneficial way to invest in food. Richard Lackey—a great investor in his own right with experience as a trader and fund manager, and a bestselling author—established the Global Food Exchange, now the world leader in strategic food reserve development.[51] "Over the past decade," Lackey observes, "communications technology, transportation technology, power systems and food manufacturing technology alike have improved; and yet record numbers of people around the globe are dying because we are not able to get adequate quantities of food and clean water to victims following a natural disaster."

Lackey predicts that because of the massive quantities of food needed and the lack of funds by governments to maintain stored food, food prices will be higher ten years from now.[52] Already, funds are forming to pool investment capital for investing in food through the Global Food Exchange.[53] Investors may soon be able to buy and hold meals that can be stored for the long term and sent as needed for disaster relief. You can invest in these meals when food is plentiful and sell when it becomes scarce. This type of food storage also enhances national security.

Industrial metals, raw materials, and energy: Industrial metals are commodities used in construction and manufacturing, such as steel, copper, lead, aluminum, nickel, and tin.[54] The prices of these metals rise and fall because of two things: supply and demand. The best time for these metals is when the economy starts to grow after a lengthy slow period. The slow period will have reduced production, keeping supply low, and new growth will increase demand sharply. Because mining operations have a long lead time, demand grows much more rapidly than supply. Late in the growth cycle, the opposite is true. Supply will be coming on line as demand wanes. Metals are thus considered cyclical investments. As with most commodities, you can invest "long" or "short." Long investments profit from price gains, and "shorts" benefit from falling prices. If you don't understand shorts, you need to be educated and have professional support before you invest in commodities.

Exchange-traded funds (ETFs) are one way to invest in commodities. An ETF manager buys and sells the commodity on behalf of the shareholders. The fund is also responsible for storage and protection. This is a direct way to own copper, for example, and the price of the ETF will rise and fall with the price of copper.

You can also buy shares in mining companies, whose fortunes also tend to rise and fall with the price of what they are mining.

There is a lot of talk recently about the importance of rare earth minerals for things like hybrid cars and iPhones. China controls the market, and many developed countries no longer mine for elements such as neodymium, dysprosium, or cerium.[55]

There are ways to invest directly in minerals, but I caution against that. It would be a nightmare to store, keep track of, and later sell such an investment. The market is simply not mature enough. The only rational way to make such an investment would be buying shares in a company that produces them. An expert from *Forbes* agrees with that assessment.[56]

Investing in timber is another option. This commodity's fortunes are tied to those of the housing market.[57]

You can buy timber through ETFs and REITs as well as through the paper companies. Timber has outperformed the S&P 500 ever since 1910. In the quarter century after 1987, the NCREIF Timberland Index grew about 15 percent per year, while the S&P 500 averaged about 11 percent. In 2008, the S&P plummeted 38 percent; Timberland rose by 9.5 percent.[58] Timber can be a helpful diversification play that works in times of inflation, and even depression if the circumstances are right.

Energy, essential for life and economic growth, is an extremely important component of tangible investing. The United States is enjoying a well-timed energy boom. Our most nagging national security risk over the past forty years has been our dependence on foreign oil, which has tethered us to one of the most dangerous regions on earth. So, investing in energy is one way to hedge against economic attack.

You can buy the commodities directly through the futures markets or buy shares in energy producers. You can focus on so-called fossil fuels

such as natural gas, coal, and oil. You can buy shares in uranium producers. Or you can invest in alternatives such as wind, solar, and hydrogen.
These investments have to be made in companies that produce the
equipment or use the equipment to produce energy for sale.

You can also own shares in companies that transport energy, like the
railroads or pipeline companies. You can participate in ETFs, REITs, and
even master limited partnerships (MLPs), which are publicly traded.
The limited partner provides the capital to the MLP and receives peri-
odic income. The general partner runs the MLP's affairs and is paid
according to the partnership's performance. In an MLP the partnership
must derive roughly 90 percent of its cash flow from real estate, natural
resources, and commodities. The advantage of an MLP is that the partnership does not pay taxes from the profit, only when partners get paid.[59]

You can invest in energy company stocks, in mineral rights or producing wells, or even energy exploration. All of these investments carry
risks, of course, but the biggest risk is probably to ignore the potential
of energy in your portfolio.

Collectibles

The final category of tangible-asset investing is collectibles. These
can be toys, comic books, stamps, coins, autographs, baseball cards,
jewelry, classic cars, antiques, guns, and even fine wine. It takes intuition,
savvy, and general awareness to win with these investments. I remember
that in the mid-1970s my brother once begged my parents to let him
spend forty dollars on a comic book. They thought he was crazy but let
him do it anyway, and he bought something called *Amazing Fantasy 15*.
It turns out that comic in mint condition sold for over a million dollars
in 2011.[60] Now, my brother's copy wasn't close to mint condition, but it
was worth a lot more than the forty dollars he paid for it!

I once bought twenty bottles of Dom Perignon 1998 at Costco in
anticipation of high champagne demand for New Year's 2000. I paid seventy

dollars per bottle and eventually sold them all on consignment through a wine shop for a net $140 per bottle, a quick doubling of my money.

Not all investments in collectibles work out so well. In the late 1990s, my family had an ice cream and candy shop in Carmel, where we sold Beanie Babies. They retailed for around six dollars, but a strong after-market drove the prices of the "rare" ones to astronomical prices. People were paying one hundred, three hundred, and even five hundred dollars for a little purple bear called Princess. Some parents bought several, believing they would make enough profit to put their kids through college. Today you'll find people trying to sell them on eBay for hundreds and even thousands of dollars, though you can get Princess for five to fifty dollars, depending on the production run. Not bad if you paid five dollars in 1998, but a serious disappointment if you paid five hundred![61]

The best collectors are those who have a passion for the collection but a willingness to take advantage of price discrepancies. Suitable items for collecting include antique motorcycles, watches, and even autographs.[62] The *Financial Times* reported in 2013 that "the best-performing luxury investments—cars, coins, stamps and art—have matched or out-performed prime property investments, over one-, five- and 10-year periods, in the indices of five key world cities: London, Paris, New York, Hong Kong and São Paolo."[63]

Judith Miller of TV's *Antiques Roadshow*, the coauthor of *Miller's Collectibles Price Guide*, champions collectibles: "They have done much better than most other investments. Do you want a piece of paper over which you have no control or something really nice like a table that you can not only enjoy but eventually sell for a good price at market?" James Daley, the money editor at the British consumer-advocacy magazine *Which?*, is more cautious: "It might seem like an exciting idea but these investments are only suitable for a minority of investors. Not until you have a cash reserve and a relatively large portfolio of equities, bonds and property should you even consider them."

Tim Schofield, the director of the motorcar department at the British auction house Bonhams, is bullish about cars as investments. He said, "If you have got money earning nothing in the bank, view the stock market as a bit hit and miss, and have petrol in the veins, then why not buy an old car? It is a tangible asset that is kept in your garage and you cannot put a figure on the fun you get out of its use." Geoff Anandappa, investment portfolio manager at Stanley Gibbons, pushes stamps, noting that they "can be a good way of diversifying your portfolios because they do not correlate closely with any other asset classes."[64]

A word of caution about collectibles: you are not allowed to hold them in an IRA,[65] although you can buy them in British retirement accounts.[66]

Alternative Assets in Times of Economic Warfare

We have covered a variety of alternative investments ranging from hedge funds to stamps. But you're wondering, "How will these perform in an economic attack?" It depends on the investment and on the kind of attack.

In the case of a network heart attack or systems disruption, anything related to the market could be hurt. Hedge funds that rely on complex trading strategies could well be toast. Private equity and private debt, if focused on the right areas, could do quite well. Imagine investing in a startup company with the latest network-protection software. Or owning a piece of a survival gear company in the case of an EMP.

In a deflation, many types of private equity would suffer, but private debt, with the right issuer, could become more valuable. In an inflationary period, just the opposite is true. The right kind of private equity would do well, but private debt would be paid back with ever-diminishing dollars.

The best alternative investments in an inflationary attack or currency meltdown would probably be "stuff." Real assets tend to hold value during inflation. In fact, they can be ideal hedges. Food, energy, and basic materials all can do well in inflation but can be hurt badly by deflation.

Collectibles are questionable. They can do well in mild to medium inflation but can become nearly worthless in a hyperinflation. That's because collectors may be forced to sell to pay for food, energy, clothing, and shelter. In a currency collapse, the only collectibles that will retain their value are those with global appeal. If the Chinese aren't interested in a 1969 Nolan Ryan baseball card, it might be hard to get a decent price if the dollar collapses.

There are no simple solutions. Good investors have to be flexible. And it is extremely important to understand what the economic climate will be and to have professional, trained guidance to get you through it.

CHAPTER ELEVEN

A Sane Strategy
for an Insane World

A strategy built upon incomplete information may be doomed to failure. That is why it is so important to understand the geopolitical events swirling around us. For example, even if you build the perfect portfolio to maximize dollar returns, if the dollar fails, you are out of luck.

This chapter will cover some of the basics needed to develop a proper investment approach, accepting the reality of a very fluid situation. The key is to apply time-tested disciplines with situational awareness to protect and grow wealth. The times can be treacherous, but with proper understanding and the benefits of professional advice, it is possible not only to survive but to prosper. Furthermore, it is possible to invest in a way that enhances America's economic security.

There are a number of books that offer excellent advice about investment strategies, and in this chapter I will borrow from a few of them. Developing an investment strategy is the first half of our task. The other half is adapting that strategy for a treacherous world.

Dean Junkans, the chief investment officer at Wells Fargo Private Bank, is the author of *The Anatomy of Investing*, an outstanding primer for individual investors. I will borrow liberally from that work, confirming the adage that "imitation is the sincerest form of flattery." The other guides to investing that I rely on are *The Wealthy Barber* by David Chilton,[1] *The Intelligent Investor* by Benjamin Graham,[2] *The Templeton Touch* by William Proctor and Scott Phillips,[3] *Investment Policy* by Charles Ellis,[4] *On My Own Two Feet* by Manisha Thakor and Sharon Kedar,[5] *Global Investing the Templeton Way* by Norman Berryessa and Eric Kizner,[6] and a book I coauthored with Erik Davidson, *Investing in Separate Accounts*.[7]

The starting point for all investors is determining their goals. *The Anatomy of Investing* lists four broad categories of needs:

- Basic (meeting needs for food, clothing, shelter, medical, and other basic necessities)
- Lifestyle (which Dean Junkans defines as "maintaining a satisfactory or specific lifestyle throughout your life")
- Philanthropy (defined by Junkans as "supporting causes or charities that you are passionate about")
- Legacy (which Junkans defines as "making significant bequests during or after your lifetime")

Then we must consider how financial terrorism would affect each of these goals. An attack on the dollar as reserve currency would affect your ability to meet basic needs and would certainly change your lifestyle. But the damage would not stop there. If the dollar lost half its purchasing power, any hopes for philanthropy or legacy would be destroyed. Imagine what it must have been like in Zimbabwe when its dollar collapsed. Or Greece, where the turmoil caused by economic dislocations has shattered the dreams of investors. But those who accounted for the possibility of such destruction were protected.

You need, therefore, a fifth goal—economic security—that you pursue in connection with each of the other four.

In her highly regarded investment book for women, *On My Own Two Feet: A Modern Girl's Guide to Personal Finance*, Manisha Thakor, CFA, boils the goals of investing down to two: "The first reason you should invest is to combat the corrosive effects of inflation. Inflation is corrosive because it eats up the value of your money.... The second reason to invest is that if you do it right, you'll have the opportunity to actually grow your money faster than the rate of inflation."

Unless you are very wealthy to begin with, you need to invest if you want to be able to meet your own needs and the needs of those you care about. And if you address the threat of inflation, you will address much of the risk of economic warfare. So whether you think about meeting a list of needs or simply realize that you need to grow your money, investing is an essential course.

Most investors are concerned about more than just themselves. Junkans identifies five kinds of beneficiaries, and I have added one (number four) to his list:

1. Yourself
2. Spouse or partner
3. Children or other heirs
4. Neighbors and community
5. Society
6. Government

Junkans then identifies five concerns (what he calls "parameters") for your portfolio:

1. Return
2. Risk
3. Liquidity
4. Cash flow
5. Tax efficiency

According to Junkans, "Once you have determined your needs, goals, beneficiaries, and parameters, then it is time to determine how you can set up portfolios to meet those needs."

This is a desirable starting point, but that is all it is—a starting point. Early in my career, I was able to work with Bob Duggan, a self-taught investor from Santa Barbara, California. Bob shared with me that "Success equals Observation plus Action plus Responsibility." He abbreviates his formula S=O+A+R and says that to win in life, you have to learn to SOAR. Bob Duggan has gone on to become a billionaire and was recently added to the *Forbes* list of richest Americans.[8]

The Dean Junkans lists provide the framework for an investment policy statement. At the same time, they meet the criteria to SOAR.

The Secret of Success

To be successful you must observe your current circumstances. You have to know yourself and know where you are. For example, if you wanted to travel to New York but didn't know your starting location, you couldn't get there. If you thought you were starting in Miami but were actually in Seattle, following the directions to New York from Miami would really mess you up.

My grandfather was a great man. He served in the navy during World War II, ran a filling station after the war, and eventually became a rural mail carrier in Oklahoma. He was part Cherokee and deeply loved this country. Late in life he decided to take up flying with one of his friends. I remember his telling me how they would fly from Oklahoma to Kansas, but sometimes they got so lost that they had to land at the nearest airstrip. Too embarrassed to admit they were lost, they would look for a pay phone and consult the phonebook to find out where they were. The old joke is true—men hate to ask for directions. But before you get directions, you have to know where you are.

Observation is identifying your needs, your beneficiaries, and your circumstances. It is essential that you become aware of your personal risk tolerance (how well you might sleep at night if your investments are volatile) as well as the market environment (including what returns you can expect under what circumstances). You also have to know the time horizon of your needs (how long before you will need funds and for what) as well as the time horizon of possible investments (when they might provide returns and how liquid they might be when you need money). You also need to be aware of tax consequences and how those might change in the future.

The next step in Bob Duggan's success formula is to take action. You should begin by formulating an investment policy statement based on your observations. This is the point at which most people turn to professional assistance. Here's how to come up with an investment policy statement:[9]

1. Summarize your major financial goals, your feelings about risk, your expectations
2. Specify the purpose of certain investments and the rationale behind them

3. Outline general policies and procedures for managing the portfolio over the long term
4. Establish who calls the shots when picking investments

How do you know if you have a solid investment policy? Charles Ellis offers a five-part test:[10]

1. Is the policy carefully designed to meet your needs and objectives?
2. Is the policy written so clearly and explicitly that a competent stranger could manage the portfolio and conform to your intentions?
3. Would you have been able to sustain your commitment to your investment policies over the past fifty or sixty years—particularly over the past ten years—when conventional wisdom would have opposed them?
4. Would your investment manager have been able to remain faithful to the policy over the same periods, despite intense daily pressure?
5. Would the policy, if implemented, have achieved your objectives?

I would amend Ellis's third and fourth questions to ask how your investment policy would have performed under the various threats of economic warfare we face. Those are more difficult questions to answer, but they are necessary. That's why it is so important to have an advisor who understands the risks we will face in the years ahead and who is not wedded to the methods of the past.

Of course, it does no good to create a plan if you are unwilling to implement it. This also will require some assistance from pros who understand the risks involved. But you have to start, and the sooner the better. This is the "action" part of Duggan's formula. Once you know where you are and where you'd like to go, you have to head in the right direction.

Now you're ready to select investments if you want to build a portfolio on your own, or to select managers if you want professional help. Your investments need to meet the criteria of your investment plan and to be flexible enough to withstand a wide variety of threats. No portfolio will be perfect. But you can do your best with the best available information. We've covered all the key options—stocks, bonds, precious metals, "guaranteed investments"—and a host of alternatives including hedge funds, energy, and even collectibles. Taking action means matching those choices with your needs in light of the global risks we are all now facing.

Responsibility

The final component of Duggan's success formula—and it's critical—is to take responsibility. Even if you have an advisor, you bear responsibility for your investments. Your portfolio will require course corrections, which will send you back to observation and then action. Charles Ellis put it this way: "Clients—not their portfolio managers—have the most important job in successful investment management. Clients' central responsibilities are to decide on their long-term investment objectives and, with the expert advice of professional managers, determine a well-reasoned and realistic set of investment policies that can achieve the specified objectives of the client."[11]

So who is responsible for what? If you follow the Ellis pathway, you are responsible for outlining your objectives and determining the policies. If you choose to hire a professional, you can gain assistance in setting the policies, but ultimately the buck stops with you. Once the policies are set, you will be responsible for making it all happen or having a pro do it for you.

But what happens in a severe crisis? What do you do when there is massive deflation or hyperinflation or a currency collapse? To answer that question, we can turn to another of my mentors, Sir John Templeton.

John Templeton began his investment career in 1937. The world economy was in its eighth year of depression. Franklin Roosevelt was beginning his second term in office, threatening to "pack" the Supreme Court with justices who would uphold the New Deal. Japan invaded China. The Soviet Union began the "Great Purge," which killed more than seven hundred thousand people in a year. Spain was embroiled in a murderous civil war. Neville Chamberlain became the prime minister of the United Kingdom. And Adolf Hitler continued to tighten his grip on the German state.[12] It was hardly an auspicious time for a young man starting out, and the worst was yet to come. Yet each of the seven decades of Templeton's career would be remarkably successful.

My introduction to Templeton came in 1983 when I read a book called *The Templeton Touch* by William Proctor. I was attracted to the book by its cover, which featured a chart of the Templeton Growth Fund. A $10,000 investment in 1955 (when the fund launched) grew to $364,495 by the end of 1982. Over the last sixteen years of that run, the Dow was down 20 percent.

I wanted to learn more. In fact, this book sparked my desire to become a professional investor. Two years later I started writing an investment newsletter with a model portfolio. That's how I began working with Bob Duggan. Two years later my father, Kerry Freeman (a respected stockbroker and my original investing mentor), helped me get in touch with John Templeton. I interviewed him via fax for the August 1987 newsletter. The market had just attained a new all-time high, with the Dow Jones Industrial Average spiking to over 2,700, a huge gain from its low of 770 five years earlier. In our interview the great Templeton shared that a bear market could take stock prices down as much as 40 percent in a couple of months—an exceptionally bold statement. And he was absolutely right.

I met Templeton in person in December 1987, just before he was knighted by the queen of England. Our meeting came on the heels of the worst market crash since the Great Depression. The Dow was down about 35 percent from its August peak. Everyone was pessimistic. Thirty-three of the world's most respected economists had just opined that the global economy was entering its worst period since the 1930s.[13]

John Templeton understood the challenges, yet he was focused not on the problems but on the solutions and opportunities. Even after fifty years as arguably the most successful investor in the world, this great man was preparing to protect and grow his clients' portfolios. He had the energy and the optimism of a man who has seen it all. He invested in the Great Depression. He invested during a world war. He invested during the boom years of the 1950s and the go-go 1960s. He invested throughout the Cold War. He invested during the malaise of the 1970s—the oil embargo, stagflation, and the recession. He invested during the Reagan recovery. And that was just in the United States! Since Templeton's operations were global, he had also seen the hyperinflation in Latin America, witnessed currencies collapse, and seen revolutions, depressions, and just about everything else. He often looked for a crisis rather than stability, aware that crisis brought opportunity. He was among the first Americans to invest in Japan, Korea, Africa, and Eastern Europe after World War II.

When I met Templeton, it was obvious that the crisis of a market crash in America hadn't fazed him. And when I went to work for him a couple of years later, he taught me to remain unfazed as well.

There are important strategic lessons that I learned from Templeton. Indeed, they were drilled into me. They are more than homespun wisdom. They are true strategy, proved over a lifetime of investing in good times, bad times, and outright crises. The following are ten Templeton Maxims[14] followed by my comments on how to apply them:

Number One: Invest for Real Returns

Maxim: The true objective for any long-term investor is maximum total real return after taxes. This is significant because the goal is REAL RETURNS, which account for the loss of purchasing power due to currency devaluation or inflation.

Game Plan Application: One of the first things you must do is to realize that inflation could climb to much higher than where it has been in the recent past. So the strategy that worked over the past thirty years (when price growth slowed dramatically) may not be appropriate going forward. If you don't prepare for a potential change, you may get caught in the wrong strategy. Investors who expected the 1960s and 1970s to be similar to the 1940s and 1950s were shocked to discover that inflation in America could reach double digits (peaking near 15 percent in early 1980) and that the prime interest rate (charged to the best borrowers) could reach over 20 percent.[15] Those unprepared for such dramatic changes suffered greatly.

Likewise, a proper strategy must account for changes in tax rates. The top income-tax rate started out a hundred years ago at 7 percent, jumped to 67 percent by 1917, peaked at 94 percent in 1945, and hit a low of 28 percent in 1988. When Templeton began investing in 1937, the top rate was 79 percent.[16] So any strategy you develop must be able to generate real returns after the effects of inflation and taxes, since the rate of either can change dramatically.

Number Two: Keep an Open Mind

Maxim: Never adopt permanently any type of asset or any selection method. Try to stay flexible, open minded, and skeptical. Long-term top results are achieved only by changing from popular to unpopular types of securities and varying your methods of selection.

Game Plan Application: We don't know what challenges will come our way. It could be deflation, it could be inflation. The currency could come under attack, but another currency might rise. The only way to be prepared for the risks is to be open minded enough to watch for them, even if they go against your preconceptions, and to be flexible enough to adjust.

Number Three: Never Follow the Crowd

Maxim: If you buy the same investments as other people, you will have the same results as other people. It is impossible to produce a superior performance unless you do something different from the majority. To buy when others are despondently selling and to sell when others are greedily buying requires fortitude but pays the greatest potential reward.

Game Plan Application: Economic warfare and financial terrorism will create panic. This can mean opportunity. In March 2009 everyone was panicked out of the stock market. Wise investors were able to buy when the Dow Jones Industrial Average bottomed out in 2009. Four years later it was over 15,000. Some investments increased more than tenfold.

Number Four: Everything Changes

Maxim: Bear markets have always been temporary, and so have bull markets. Share prices usually turn upward from one to twelve months before the bottom of the business cycle, and vice versa. If a particular industry or type of security becomes popular with investors, the popularity will always prove temporary and, when lost, may not return for many years.

Game Plan Application: We've already explained that the period from the 1930s through the 1950s began with depression and later saw modest growth and low inflation. The 1960s and 1970s had higher growth but ended with stagflation. The 1980s and 1990s were a time of higher growth and low inflation. No trend lasts forever. Things change, and you have to be ready to adapt. In a global economic war, we may see trends that seem permanent, but they could shift quickly. Imagine if another nation were to attack our market, causing it to fall sharply, and then our government took a series of steps to shore it up, causing it to rise dramatically. That's the kind of story I tell in *Secret Weapon*: the Dow fell from 14,100 to 6,500 but was over 15,000 by early 2013.

Number Five: Avoid the Popular

Maxim: When any method for selecting investments becomes popular, switch to unpopular methods. Too many investors can spoil any selection method or any market-timing formula.

Game Plan Application: Even with a seemingly sound strategy, the crowd can mess things up. An example is the rise of gold from $800 per ounce to over $1,900 per ounce within a couple of years. Even though there were still good reasons to own gold, the price fell sharply. Yes, the Federal Reserve's money printing ought to have supported gold. But so many people owned gold that there were few new buyers. The rise was too rapid, and gold had to cool off a bit. No matter how right your thesis, too much popularity will lead to at least a short-term pullback.

Number Six: Learn from Your Mistakes

Maxim: "This time is different" are among the most costly words in market history.

Game Plan Application: Some people will cite this maxim and argue that because the U.S. economy has always come through its difficulties before, it should always be the "go-to" location for your investments. A true follower of Templeton, however, will look at a much longer historical period. You might notice, for example, that every empire in history has eventually fallen from preeminence. You might also notice that no paper currency has ever been permanently on top. Don't put all your eggs in the American basket.

Number Seven: Buy during Times of Pessimism

Maxim: Bull markets are born in pessimism, grow on skepticism, mature on optimism, and die of euphoria. The time of maximum pessimism is the best time to buy, and the time of maximum optimism is the best time to sell.

Game Plan Application: There is every reason to expect panic and euphoria in coming years. Even with the risks of financial terrorism and economic warfare, there will be plenty of opportunities to buy and sell.

Number Eight: Hunt for Value and Bargains

Maxim: Too many investors focus on outlook and trend. More profit is made by focusing on value. In the stock market, the only way to get a bargain is to buy what most investors are selling.

Game Plan Application: When you focus on outlook and trend, you too often miss the "black swan" events that can wreak havoc on your investments. Terrorism, by definition, breeds fear, which causes panic. It is most successful when unexpected. "The trend is your friend" is a market adage that holds true until the trend changes.

Number Nine: Search Worldwide

Maxim: To avoid having all your eggs in one basket at the wrong time, diversify. If you search worldwide, you will find more and better bargains than by studying only one nation. You will also gain the advantage of diversification.

Game Plan Application: Possibly the best all-around approach to the risks we have identified is to be broadly diversified. You can't put all your faith in a single type of asset, industry, country, or currency. While diversification won't prevent some dramatic short-term losses, it will stabilize your portfolio over time.

Number Ten: No One Knows Everything

Maxim: An investor who has all the answers doesn't even understand the questions.

Game Plan Application: Arrogance is the greatest enemy of investment success. You may be right for a season, but seasons always change. Having humility allows you to follow the other nine maxims and enjoy long-term success.

Amazingly, these ten simple maxims can lead you through virtually any economic crisis.

There is a lot to know and a lot to monitor on a regular basis. That's why I encourage you to seek out professionals who not only understand how to invest but are also prepared to adapt to a complex environment. We have had it pretty easy in America for all of our lifetimes. Yes, we have gone through difficulties, but America has enjoyed economic dominance since World War II. That prosperity has not prepared us for what can take place over the next few decades. As we were wholly unprepared for 9/11 and the effects of physical terrorism on our shores, so we are mostly unprepared for the coming reality of financial terrorism.

I recommend that your strategy incorporate two critical elements. First, make a sensible disaster plan for your family. I'm not saying you have to plan for forty years of living in an underground bunker. But I am saying you should anticipate serious dislocations for at least a short time. This is above and beyond the "basic" set of needs that Dean Junkans advocates in *The Anatomy of Investing*.

Here are supplies you should consider for a two-week power outage. If the situation were worse, you would of course need more:

- Two weeks' supply of water—one gallon per day per person
- Non-cooked food: crackers, peanut butter, fresh fruit, canned juice, trail mix, dry cereal, pretzels, nuts, dried fruits, tuna[17]
- Other foods (quantities are per person): two bottles of juice, two canned goods, peanut butter, jelly, honey, mustard, ketchup, barbeque sauce, spices, cooking oil, flour, powdered milk, powdered potatoes
- Portable propane heater
- Sanitation: heavy-duty garbage bags and kitty litter (place a bag either in your drained toilet or in a bucket)
- Lighting: garden stake solar lights, candles, kerosene lamps, flashlights, hand-cranked camping lantern, matches
- Tools and supplies: lighter or waterproof matches, batteries, manual can opener, pliers, screwdriver, wrench, hammer, duct tape
- First-aid kit: bandages, antibiotic ointments and sprays, pain relief capsules, cold medicine, cough syrup, anti-nausea pills, allergy medication, and anti-diarrheal medications[18]

Second, make a diligent search for a trained investment professional who understands how to develop a proper strategy according to sound investment philosophies like those of John Templeton, Dean Junkans, Erik Davidson, David Chilton, Bob Duggan, Manisha Thakor, or Charles Ellis.

Unfortunately, few investment pros have gone beyond traditional financial training to study the kind of risks we now face. That's why my colleagues and I established the National Security Investment

Consultant Institute.[19] The NSIC started at the Keating Center at Oklahoma Wesleyan University. The center's namesake, Frank Keating, served in the Reagan administration's Treasury and Justice Departments. He later became the governor of Oklahoma and now heads the American Bankers Association. The NSIC Institute trains investment professionals to recognize economic warfare threats and prepare strategies to combat the problem. Clients interested in protecting their investments as well as finding ways to promote America's national security interests through their investments will gravitate toward advisors who have earned the NSIC credential.

Over time, as more advisors receive NSIC training, the collective client assets available to invest in America's security will grow large enough to make a difference. Imagine if a pool of capital in the tens or hundreds of billions were unleashed to promote American energy independence, for example? Without government funding, these advisors and clients could help our country on an enormous scale.

———————————

There is an absolute correlation between our economic strength and our ability to defend our nation. It's time to recognize that our enemies' threat doctrine is targeted against our economy, and to respond. Enemies of the United States have targeted our financial markets and economic infrastructure, and a new generation of leaders will be required to protect them.

CHAPTER TWELVE

There Is Hope

The amazing thing about the current global economic war is that the United States of America is still ideally positioned to win. If we act properly, it's not too late to usher in a period of global peace and prosperity. It's not too late, even though we have accumulated the largest budget deficits and national debt in history. Even though we have over-shackled our people with crippling rules and regulations. Even though we have nearly abandoned all the things that made America great in the first place. It's still not too late. But it is close.

There are dozens of reasons to believe that the American experiment will end in failure. We have plenty of internal problems—out-of-control spending, paralyzing political agendas, a government that operates more like a confidence game, an apathetic population, and a system that rewards failure and punishes success. In many ways, we are our own worst enemies.

Externally, we have enemies who want to see America go away. Some of them are parasites on our prosperity and intend to bleed us dry over the long term. Others hate us ideologically. Some simply resent our success. Whatever their motivation, they are intent on our destruction.

In your heart you know this country faces enormous perils.

So how can I say there is hope? Because America continues to have unique and powerful advantages. Despite what the doomsayers say, the worst doesn't always happen. This is something you have to remember. While the case for collapse seems compelling, history is replete with examples where certain doom failed to materialize.[1]

The good news is that the doomsday doesn't have to happen now, even though we are in a global economic war. Our natural advantages can carry us through to victory. Unfortunately, we have let our advantages make us arrogant, and our arrogance has made us vulnerable. There are eight steps we must take to restore our greatness. The first is to admit we have a problem.

Step One:
Recognize the Global War Under Way

I've been to Washington, D.C., dozens of times over the past five years, meeting with current and former senior officials in the Pentagon, CIA, FBI, Defense Intelligence Agency, Senate Intelligence Committee, House Intelligence Committee, House Armed Services Committee, Defense Advanced Research Projects Agency, Securities and Exchange Commission, and Federal Reserve. I have met with multiple congressmen and senators and members of their staffs. Very few of those leaders understand the challenges we are facing in this global economic war.

Officials in defense and intelligence have little training in economics. Even those who appreciate our economic problems don't understand that our enemies could use economic weapons to damage us. Juan Zarate, former assistant secretary of the Treasury for terrorist financing and financial crimes, explained the problem in his book *Treasury's War: The Unleashing of a New Era of Financial Warfare*: "The United States faces direct challenges to its economic predominance and financial influence, and is unprepared to defend itself from the looming external threats and internal vulnerabilities.... The United States needs to redesign how it thinks about, treats, and addresses national economic security to prepare for the coming financial wars.... The financial wars are coming. It is time to redesign a national economic security model to prepare for them. If we fail to do so, the United States risks being left vulnerable and left behind as other competitors race toward the future."[2]

The old paradigm, which was on display in virtually every meeting I had in Washington, views national security and economics as separate disciplines. I met with the top people on the economics team at one of the capital's leading think tanks, and then I met with the national security people down the hall. The economists didn't doubt that our financial systems might be vulnerable, but they questioned why anyone would want to attack them. They were confident that the market would financially punish those who tried to manipulate our system. The defense experts fully understood that our enemies would be willing to suffer harm to achieve their objectives, but they didn't grasp the seriousness of the financial risk. Each discipline keeps to itself and doesn't cross-pollinate the other.

The first step to restoring our security is simple. We have to recognize that we have a problem. There is a global economic war (or financial war, as Zarate calls it), and it threatens our national existence. Admiral Mike Mullen, a former chairman of the Joints Chiefs of Staff, hinted at the scope of our financial peril when he declared that our debt was "the most significant threat to our national security."[3] But the danger goes beyond our debt, as I have explained in this book. There is a broad array of economic vulnerabilities. We must acknowledge our vulnerabilities and respond to them. The good news is that we can do so if we will wake up to the challenge. Zarate holds out this hope: "More than any other state and culture, America—enabled and accelerated by globalization and new technologies—still enjoys a comparative advantage in leveraging power and influence in ways that are commensurate with our enduring strategic security heritage and our prosperity."[4]

He's right. We're in a position to win the global economic war. But we have to decide that we are in it to win it.

Step Two:
Take Reasonable Precautions

The United States should take a few reasonable precautions to protect its financial system and infrastructure. These measures are not costly, but they will provoke opposition from some powerful interests that benefit from the status quo, so they will require political will.

First, we should prohibit naked short selling and naked credit-default swaps. These transactions are ways of manipulating shares that you don't actually own and haven't even borrowed, and they played important roles in the collapse of 2008. While Wall Street would likely balk at their prohibition, the risks they pose to our financial system are too great to leave unaddressed. Germany eliminated such transactions in 2010.[5] The many warnings of calamity that would follow such a ban[6] were not fulfilled,[7] and the European Union followed suit in 2011.[8] There is no reason for the United States to continue to tolerate what have been called "financial weapons of mass destruction."[9]

Under the leadership of Representative Ken Ivory, Utah passed legislation developed by the state's accountants and businesses that is a model for other states and the federal government.[10] Intended to ensure Utah's "financial earthquake preparedness," the legislation establishes a Fiscal Risk Management Commission to address a variety of economic threats.[11] Representative Matt Krause of Texas introduced similar legislation in the Texas legislature, but it died in committee in the 2013 session.[12]

Another initiative at the state level that merits attention is the Texas Bullion Depository, proposed by Representative Giovanni Capriglione with support from Governor Rick Perry[13] and the approval of Jim Rickards, the author of *Currency Wars*.[14] If the measure had passed, the state would have sold the billion dollars' worth of physical gold that it held in New York and bought an equivalent amount to be stored in Texas. The depository would be open to anyone seeking physical protection for his gold, making Texas an economic leader in the event of dollar catastrophe. There were even discussions about providing depositors with the equivalent of an ATM card, enabling them to exchange gold for goods, with electronic record keeping down to small fractions of an ounce. With a Texas gold card, you could buy a pack of gum or cup of coffee with gold and never have to hold paper currency. Gold would be added to the seller's account or converted into dollars for exchange. As long as the dollar held up, there would be no need to move to such a system. But in the case of a dollar failure, wouldn't it be good to have a contingency plan ready to go?

Second, we should also look into ways to strengthen the cybergrid. The military has developed a Cyber Command, and that is a start.[15] But we have little in the way of private-sector defense.[16] It doesn't have to be this way. If we recognize that a war is already under way, we can mobilize national priorities to protect one of our most vital assets. We must go on the offensive to win.[17]

Third, we should reinstitute the civil defense measures that were maintained during the Cold War. There was a time when every school-child in America had an action plan in case of an attack.[18] Such lessons have long been forgotten. If a cyberattack were to take down the electric grid, is anyone prepared to respond? The National Geographic Channel's *American Blackout* depicted what could happen in a prolonged power failure, and it wasn't pretty.[19] Yet some simple civil defense preparations could mitigate the worst effects.

Finally, there is promising legislation aimed at preventing disaster from an electromagnetic pulse—either natural, from solar flares, or from a deliberate missile attack—that should be adopted. Representative Andrea Boland pushed through some groundbreaking legislation in Maine that can serve as a model for other states.[20] Representative Trent Franks has sponsored critical legislation at the federal level.[21] A natural EMP disaster is only a matter of time,[22] but its impact can be mitigated with prior planning. The cost of preparation for the electric grid would amount to a few extra cents each month on everyone's electric bill.[23] In fact, the total combined cost of the measures I have outlined here would be only a fraction of the $700 billion spent on the bailout of the financial system after Lehman Brothers failed.

The key is to take sensible steps in response to the reality that we face a global economic war. Now is the time to prepare—before disaster strikes.

Step Three:
Get Money Moving without
Money Printing

Since 2009 the Federal Reserve has conducted three rounds of "quantitative easing." It has pumped trillions of dollars into the system, and yet the economy remains stagnant. Just before the 2008 crash, the

Federal Reserve's balance sheet was around $800 billion. Five years later it was in the range of $3.6 trillion.[24] The unemployment rate has barely dipped, and that minimal decrease is attributable to workers' getting discouraged and giving up the search for a job.[25]

So why isn't all this new money from the Fed making the economy strong? The answer from economists is that the "velocity of money" is too low. In plain English, that means that individuals and businesses have been hoarding cash. Consumers have been reluctant to spend, and companies have been slow to expand.

So where has all the money gone? Corporations now hold a record amount of cash, and they have kept almost $2 trillion of that overseas.[26] A mere eighty-three companies hold almost $1.5 trillion among them. The reason that American companies hold so much cash in offshore accounts is our tax code. The United States has the highest official corporate tax rate in the world.[27] Even accounting for various deductions and manipulations that allow companies to pay less than the stated rate, we are ranked ninety-fourth out of one hundred nations in tax competitiveness.[28]

Great American companies that have plenty of cash to spend and grow are unwilling to bring that cash back home. Instead of building a plant here, they will build or buy one abroad.[29] The *New York Times* reports: "Kathleen M. Kahle, a finance professor at the University of Arizona, said, 'As risk increases, executives get nervous and they want to hold cash for a rainy day.... I have little doubt that the United States corporate tax code is causing companies like Apple to hold cash overseas.'"[30]

Corporate leaders have made it clear that if the U.S. tax system didn't penalize them, they would invest and spend at home. Cisco's John Chambers has pleaded for tax reform so he can spend and invest at home. But if the current system remains intact, he will be creating jobs overseas. Of Cisco's $446 billion, 80 percent is stored in foreign countries because of our 35-percent tax rate.[31]

There are a lot of proposals to encourage the return of that cash. Any effective strategy would rely on the free market rather than top-down government mandates. As an example, the government could grant a "tax holiday" if corporations used the cash for domestic acquisitions, paying dividends for shareholders, or investing in something that creates jobs. The goal would be to let the corporations define the specifics.

Contrast that with government-controlled "stimulus" projects that are so subject to politics that virtually nothing gets achieved. The American Recovery and Reinvestment Act will wind up costing taxpayers over $800 billion. Yet according to the nonpartisan Congressional Budget Office, the act created somewhere between 200,000 and 1.5 million jobs. Each job, in other words, cost somewhere between $540,000 and $4.1 million.[32]

At least half of the $2 trillion sitting idle overseas might come home with the right opportunity. And the return of that cash would contribute far more to economic growth than government borrowing and spending. The new jobs created would generate tax revenues and reduce government welfare expenses. The investment of that enormous mountain of cash would strengthen the American economic position substantially, helping us win the global economic war.

Step Four:
Achieve Energy Independence

One of the areas in which we could let American companies invest that overseas cash is energy. The same government that wants to tax corporations' overseas cash at 35 percent set aside $80 billion of the $800 billion stimulus for green energy.[33] While not all of that money was spent, at least thirty-four of the recipients of this federal subsidy have already gone bankrupt, taking billions of taxpayer dollars with them.

Were these projects chosen solely because of their economic merit? Not according to the Hoover Institution's Peter Schweizer. In *Throw Them All Out*, he writes that 71 percent of the Obama Energy Department's grants and loans were given to "individuals who were bundlers, members of Obama's National Finance Committee, or large donors to the Democratic Party...."[34] *Politico* reported in late 2011, "The Energy Department's inspector general has launched more than 100 criminal investigations related to 2009 economic stimulus spending."[35] Everyone knows about Solyndra's bankruptcy (costing taxpayers a half billion) and should understand that the government isn't the ideal venture capitalist.[36]

There is an understandable interest in developing new forms of energy with the hope that they will create jobs and strengthen our economy. But when you contrast the government failures with private-enterprise successes, you begin to see why we should promote the free-market approach to energy development. Apple is building a massive new solar power farm.[37] We can be certain that Apple thinks the project makes economic sense. What would happen if Apple were able to use its $100 billion in cash hoarded overseas on domestic investments without a tax penalty?[38]

Which is the better idea—tax Apple, take its cash, and hand it out as political favors, hoping that something useful gets developed, or let Apple keep its cash to invest profitably, benefitting shareholders and later generating taxes at home?

Germany has made important progress in alternative energy by leaving control with individuals and communities. In 2011, renewables contributed 20 percent of Germany's electricity; 65 percent of these renewables are owned by individuals or communities.[39]

Alternative energy is only one step toward American energy independence. What if we allowed some of that corporate cash to accelerate fossil fuel development as well? Every day the United States sends about $1 billion overseas just to keep up with its hefty energy appetite. If that money were spent on domestic energy instead, we would generate as much as $1 trillion per year in new economic activity, raising GDP by perhaps 2.5 percent—which would double the growth rate from recent levels—and creating as many as three million new domestic jobs.[40]

Thanks to technological advances like hydraulic fracking and horizontal drilling, we are already reducing our dependence on foreign energy. In fact, Citigroup analysts estimate that we could eliminate every foreign energy source except Canada in as little as five years. Doing so, they calculate, would strengthen the dollar as much as 5.4 percent.[41] The United States is now projected to surpass Saudi Arabia in oil production by 2017.[42]

What if American corporations were allowed to repatriate foreign cash if they invested to promote energy independence? What if government allowed the pipelines we need and opened federal lands and offshore opportunities to development? Wow! Sadly, none of that is happening. As Daniel Kish, a senior vice president of policy at the Institute for Energy Research, said, "Where the feds are in charge, production is sucking wind. Where they aren't, we're breaking records."[43] The Daily Caller reported the Obama administration's shameful record: "While production booms on non-federal lands and boosts U.S. exports, production on federal lands is lagging. In fact, all of the increased oil production from 2009 to 2012 took place on non-federal lands.... [O]il production on federal lands was down 31% from 2011 levels, while production on state and private lands increased by 15%."[44]

Some argue that fracking is not worth the risks, but experts disagree.[45] Even Daniel Yergin, who was an advisor for Barack Obama on shale gas, dismisses the danger of contamination of drinking water, expressing concern only about "manag[ing] the waste water that is produced with drilling" and "maintaining air quality because you have a lot of diesel engines pumping away."[46]

Lifting the ban on offshore drilling could result in a million new American jobs, according to some estimates, and reduce our reliance on foreign oil.[47] Our energy future is bright—if we don't foolishly spoil it. Stephanie Catarino Wissman, the executive director of the Associated Petroleum Industries of Pennsylvania, makes the case for a smarter energy policy: "With the right policies in place, America could meet 100% of its liquid fuel needs through safe, reliable North American sources by 2024.... Hydraulic fracturing provided $62 billion in additional government revenue in 2012 and will provide more than $111 billion in 2020. 1.7 million jobs are currently supported by unconventional oil and natural gas activity, and that number grows to some 2.5 million jobs in 2015, 3 million jobs in 2020, and 3.5 million jobs in 2035."[48]

There is troubling evidence that those who decry fracking are funded by interests such as the United Arab Emirates and Vladimir Putin— economic enemies of the United States. The late Hugo Chavez of oil-exporting Venezuela, Putin, and various oil sheiks all opposed fracking.[49] Prince Alwaleed bin Talal of Saudi Arabia frets that his country's economy will be hurt by foreign fracking. "The world's reliance on OPEC oil, especially the production of Saudi Arabia, is in a clear and continuous decline," he writes, adding that "rising North American shale gas production is an inevitable threat."[50] Russia, which sits on $13 trillion of natural gas deposits, attacks shale gas as "unsafe," "uneconomical," and "irrelevant."[51]

Developing our domestic energy resources is essential to our fight in the global economic war. James Woolsey, a former director of the CIA, warns, "By and large, it is oil money that is funding the madrasas that teach little boys that becoming suicide bombers is a good, reasonable life choice for them. Next time you go to a filling station, you will know where that money is coming from. So, to put it mildly, we are paying for both sides of this war on terrorism."[52]

We must and we can do more to achieve energy independence. We can unleash entrepreneurs like Tesla's Elon Musk. Not only has he created a sensation with his electric luxury car, but also he's made a lot of investors very wealthy.[53] He has plans for a high-speed train known as the Hyperloop, which would use solar power and yet cost a fraction of what other proposed systems would cost.[54] There are doubters, to be sure, but given Musk's track record, doesn't it make sense to encourage his entrepreneurship?

We can encourage promising developments in transportation like automobiles that run on compressed natural gas or methanol. It will require investment but is certainly doable. That's the vision of Clean Energy Fuels and T. Boone Pickens.[55] The major barrier to getting America off foreign oil and on to domestic natural gas, says Pickens, is the need for investment capital. To him, it's a no-brainer and a matter of time.

We can achieve energy independence and are in fact tantalizingly close to doing so. We can achieve it by unleashing American ingenuity and expanding domestic production. In an era of economic warfare, energy independence is a matter of life and death.

Step Five: Reduce Regulation

A couple of years after President Ronald Reagan left office, I had the privilege of presenting him with the Adam Smith Award for Individual Excellence in Free Enterprise. Reagan's modest response was: "Really, all I did was get the government the hell out of the way so good people like you could grow the economy."

Since the end of Reagan's presidency, however, the regulatory burden has grown uncontrollably. Back in 1974, Reagan, then the governor of

California, complained about forty-five thousand pages of new federal regulations.[56] Today there are about 175,000 pages of new regulations.[57]

Accumulated regulation has been enormously costly. America's nominal GDP in 2011 was $15.1 trillion. One study calculates that if regulation had remained at the same level as in 1949, GDP in 2011 would have been about $53.9 trillion. That's a difference of $129,300 per person."[58] The Competitive Enterprise Institute finds that compliance with federal regulations costs about $1.8 trillion—roughly 11 percent of 2013 GDP—per year.[59] To put it starkly, federal regulation has made the average American 75 percent poorer.[60]

Now, we know that some regulation is necessary. But much of the regulation we live with is the "nanny state" at work. We have built an unaccountable regulatory regime that employs quite a few people but chokes economic growth. It is a slow form of economic suicide. The implementation of Obamacare's regulations—which are estimated to impose 127 million hours of paperwork per year[61]—is going to make the situation even worse.

The Heritage Foundation offers some suggestions, including a freeze on new regulations until the national unemployment rate drops under 6 percent, a ban on "midnight" regulations (issued after an election by an outgoing administration), and making the regulatory process far more transparent.[62] The problem is serious, but it can be tackled.

Step Six: A Workable Tax Code

Reform of the tax code should go hand in hand with a reduction of regulation. Nearly everyone agrees that the current tax system is a convoluted mess. It does not maximize revenues, and it hampers economic growth.[63]

So how do we fix it? There are four basic options:

1. Simplify the system by stripping it of numerous breaks, leaving only those which help grow the economy or make the tax code fairer.[64]
2. Implement a flat tax, which would give people more incentive to work and invest their earnings back into the economy.
3. The so-called fair tax would eliminate the payroll tax and impose a national sales tax on purchases of new goods and services, excluding necessities. The fair-tax rate after necessities would be 23 percent, which equals the lowest current income-tax bracket (15 percent) plus the employee's share of payroll taxes (7.65 percent).[65]
4. A combination of the flat tax and the fair tax might ameliorate the problems with each. The flat tax does not eliminate the payroll tax, while the fair tax, depending on one's state sales tax, could leave someone with a tax burden of close to 40 percent of his income. One proposal is to combine a flat income tax of about 16 percent (eliminating altogether the tax liability of the poorest) with a national sales tax or VAT of roughly 10 percent.[66]

Each idea has merit, and each has its proponents. Regardless of what we do, we have to fix the tax code. Such a fix would dramatically enhance our ability to fight in the global economic war.

Step Seven:
Teach What America Is All About

Immigration is a serious problem. Some argue that because our native population is declining, we need more immigrants to fuel growth and allow America to compete in the global market.[67] Others argue that uncontrolled immigration will destroy the fabric of society. Richard Lamm, as governor of Colorado, "saw how employers were using illegal immigration for cheap labor and in some cases firing Americans so they could hire illegals who they could pay less and work harder. I saw the incredible flow of illegal aliens who crowded out American workers in construction, packing plants, the service industry, etc, many of whom were paid 'off-books' so we got no state income taxes from them."[68]

Others worry that our lax immigration policies will allow terrorists to infiltrate our nation. C. Stewart Verdery Jr., a former assistant secretary of homeland security, said in 2006, "[O]thers seeking to cross our borders illegally do present a threat—including potential terrorists and criminals. The current flow of illegal immigrants and people overstaying their visas has made it extremely difficult for our border and interior enforcement agencies to be able to focus on the terrorists, organized criminals, and violent felons who use the cloak of anonymity that the current chaotic situation offers."[69] Deputy Secretary of Homeland Security Admiral James Loy told the Senate Select Committee on Intelligence, "Several al-Qaeda leaders believe operatives can pay their way into the country through Mexico and also believe illegal entry is more advantageous than legal entry for operational security reasons. At home, we must prepare ourselves for any attack, from IEDs (improvised explosive devices) to Weapons of Mass Destruction . . . from soft targets like malls to national icons."[70] Congressman Louie Gohmert said in 2013, "We know Al Qaeda has camps on the Mexican border. We have people that are trained to act Hispanic when they are radical Islamists."[71]

Immigrants built our nation, and immigration is an essential part of the American story. What's different, however, is that immigrants are no longer taught the uniqueness and greatness of America. It used to be that we were a cultural melting pot. Now political correctness teaches us to maintain and celebrate our differences rather than coming together.

Our educational institutions seem intent on developing disdain for America by highlighting failure rather than celebrating success. Professor Haunani-Kay Trask of the University of Hawaii told students, "We need to think very, very clearly about who the enemy is. The enemy is the United States of America and everyone who supports it."[72] Princeton's Richard Falk said the Boston Marathon bombings were a result of "all kinds of resistance" generated by "the American global domination project." Darry Sragow of the University of Southern California told his students that Republicans are "angry old white people" who are "stupid, racist losers." Rod Swanson, a UCLA economics professor, tells students, "The United States of America, backed by facts, is the greediest and most selfish country in the world." Penn State's professor Matt Jordan says supporters of voter ID laws are like the Ku Klux Klan, and the Georgetown law professor Louis Michael Seidman says America's problems are derived from the Constitution, which he called "archaic" and "idiosyncratic" with "downright evil provisions."[73]

Our own government is in on the act—often leading the way. The air force teaches that the Founders of the United States were extremists: "In U.S. history, there are many examples of extremist ideologies and movements. The colonists who sought to free themselves from British rule and the Confederate states who sought to secede from the Northern states are just two examples."[74]

This is a nation that has lost its moral compass and so has lost its way. The corrosion of Americans' self-understanding has seriously weakened us. But there is a solution. We can begin celebrating the Founders and their principles. We have to return to old-fashioned patriotism. And, we have to make such teaching a part of any immigration solution. Peggy Noonan described the challenge in 2006:

What is the legend, the myth? That God made this a special place. That [immigrants are] joining something special. That the streets are paved with more than gold—they're paved with the greatest thoughts man ever had, the greatest decisions he ever made, about how to live....

We fought a war to free slaves. We sent millions of white men to battle and destroyed a portion of our nation to free millions of black men. What kind of nation does this? ... Soviet communism stalked the world and we were the ones who steeled ourselves and taxed ourselves to stop it. Again: What kind of nation does this?

Only a very great one. Maybe the greatest of all....

Do we, today, act as if this is such a special place? No, not always, not even often. American exceptionalism is so yesterday....

When you don't love something you lose it. If we do not teach new Americans to love their country, ... then we will begin to lose it.[75]

Step Eight:
Return to Our Spiritual Roots

Of the eight steps, this one is the most important. American was founded on the Judeo-Christian principles of Western civilization. As George Washington affirmed, "It is the duty of all nations to acknowledge the providence of Almighty God, to obey His will, to be grateful for His benefits, and humbly to implore His protection and favor." He also said, "Of all the dispositions and habits which lead to political prosperity, religion and morality are indispensable supports."[76]

President Reagan warned us not to forget our national dependence on divine Providence: "If we ever forget that we are One Nation Under God, then we will be one nation gone under."[77]

I agree with President Reagan. Remembering our spiritual heritage is the most important step we can take in defending America, because our problem isn't really economic or even political. Our real problem is spiritual. "Blessed is the nation whose God is the Lord," writes the psalmist (Psalms 33:12). The Bible promises blessings to the obedient: "The Lord shall open unto thee his good treasure, the heaven to give the rain unto thy land in his season, and to bless all the work of thine hand: and thou shalt lend to many nations, and thou shalt not borrow. And the Lord shall make thee the head, and not the tail; and thou shalt be above only, and thou shalt not be beneath; if that thou hearken unto the commandments of the Lord thy God, which I command thee this day, to observe and to do them" (Deuteronomy 28:12–13).

To the disobedient, in contrast, God promises a curse: "thou shalt not prosper in thy ways: and thou shalt be only oppressed and spoiled evermore, and no man shall save thee" (Deuteronomy 28:29). "The fruit of thy land and all thy labors, shall a nation which thou knowest not eat up" (Deuteronomy 28:33). "The stranger that is within thee shall get up above thee very high; and thou shalt come down very low. He shall lend to thee, and thou shalt not lend to him: he shall be the head, and thou shalt be the tail" (Deuteronomy 28:43–44). By these verses, America today sounds more like a nation under a curse than a nation under blessing.

The Bible also warns that "the borrower is servant to the lender" (Proverbs 22:7). The decline of American influence has been rapid and has coincided with the rise in our federal debt. The Canadian newspaper publisher and biographer Conrad Black has observed, "Not since the disintegration of the Soviet Union in 1991, and prior to that the fall of

France in 1940, has there been so swift an erosion of the world influence of a Great Power as we are witnessing with the United States."[78]

Now, if the problem is spiritual, the solution will be spiritual as well. America needs wise economic and security policies, but those policies alone will not restore our greatness. America needs a spiritual revival: "If my people, which are called by my name, shall humble themselves, and pray, and seek my face, and turn from their wicked ways; then will I hear from heaven, and will forgive their sin, and will heal their land" (2 Chronicles 7:14).

Conclusion

After in-depth research on behalf of the Pentagon, it became obvious to me that America suffered a financial terror attack in 2008. I explained what happened in *Secret Weapon*. As I continued my research, I uncovered a long history of economic warfare, which others, including Jim Rickards and Juan Zarate, have discovered as well. I have spent countless hours giving briefings to a host of agencies in our nation's capital. Make no mistake; we are in a global economic war.

The bad news is that we are fighting blindly. Too few in our nation's leadership have grasped what we are facing. Call it ignorance or arrogance. Either way, we are not prepared to defend the dollar in world trade, protect trade secrets from corporate espionage, or safeguard our financial systems from cyber attack. There are even more serious risks, like the EMP that could send us back to a pre-industrial age. Our $17 trillion debt creates a whole host of vulnerabilities. Yet we go on as if American supremacy will endure forever.

The implications are serious, and you need to be aware and prepare. This requires a thorough understanding of your investment options and how they might perform under different scenarios. Unfortunately, there aren't any simple answers. What works for one problem may not work for another. Things can and will change. As a result, you will likely want to identify and work with a professional investment advisor who has been trained on these national security issues. That's why my colleagues and I formed the National Security Investment Consultant Institute to train and credential investment advisors.

Despite all this, you should have hope. There are eight steps that America can take to maintain its position as the best and strongest economy in the world. There are also seven spiritual truths, which I share in the appendix, that you can apply in your life for greater prosperity and success.

This is your game plan. It is a practical understanding of economic warfare and how you can defend against it.

Preparing Your Family

I n chapter twelve, I outlined eight steps to restore American greatness. Whether or not we take those steps as a nation, you have to take care of yourself and your family. I have given you a game plan for your investments. Now I'll share seven basic truths that will help in good times and bad. For the most part, these are lessons I learned from John Templeton, the greatest mentor I ever had. They're based on the Bible, and I have seen their truth confirmed time after time in my own life and in others'.

1. Order Your Priorities

Much of our nation's vulnerability is the result of misplaced priorities, even on the personal level. Jesus' instructions about our priorities couldn't be clearer: "But seek ye first the kingdom of God, and his righteousness; and all these things shall be added unto you" (Matthew 6:33).

Many of the most successful people I know put their priorities in that order—God first, then family, then business. But too many of us put business first. When that happens, life loses meaning.

2. Know Where Your Treasure Is

Jesus said, "Where your treasure is, there your heart will be also" (Matthew 6:21). Most people get this backward: they let their treasure follow their heart. But that's not what Jesus says. He says your heart follows your treasure. It was a dramatic revelation when Pastor Robert Morris of Gateway pointed out this truth to me. You can actually direct your heart by moving your treasure.

When you consider this verse from Matthew in its full context, it becomes obvious that storing earthly riches keeps your heart set on earthly things, which will surely disappoint. But heavenly riches are permanent. "Lay not up for yourselves treasures upon earth, where moth and rust doth corrupt, and where thieves break through and steal: But lay up for yourselves treasures in heaven, where neither moth nor rust doth corrupt, and where thieves do not break through nor steal: For where your treasure is, there will your heart be also" (Matthew 6:19–21).

3. Count Your Blessings

John Templeton devoted a good deal of time to what he called "discovering the laws of life." He even wrote a book with that title, and I treasure the autographed copy he gave me in 1995. "Counting your blessings," he wrote, "can transform melancholy into cheerfulness; laughter and joy are expressions of praise and thanksgiving for life's glories.

When looking at the glass that symbolizes our life, we can view it as half full or half empty. The choice is ours." Templeton also wrote: "Thanksgiving is a creative force that, if lived on a continuous basis and not just for one day each year, will create more good in your life and more to be thankful for. Perhaps we could call this the life of thanksliving. Thanksliving is an attitude of perpetual gratitude that will draw good to you. It is based on the premise that 'thanksgiving leads to having more to give thanks for.'"[1]

I can tell you that the most successful investor I ever met, John Templeton, believed this with all his heart and practiced it daily. And he became a billionaire following his laws of life.

4. Giving Is Living

As his coining of the word "thanksliving" suggests, John Templeton was struck by the relationship between *giving* and *living*. The words ultimately denote the same reality, he believed. "Life's greatest investment," he declared, "is the tithe"[2]—that is, the biblically enjoined return to the Lord of a tenth of your income. As Templeton wrote:

> Tithing often brings prosperity and honor because it's an important aspect of the law of giving and receiving, which is an integral part of the law of cause and effect. As you give forth, so shall you receive.
>
> A lot of people right now are seeking economic healing. Many of them are probably thinking, But I can barely make ends meet with the money I'm currently making. How can I give 10%, 5%, or even 1% to charity? Well, this is a case where conserving your resources in order to give a portion away actually has a paradoxical effect. Many people who are living

paycheck to paycheck are so focused on their own financial situation that they rarely have time to think of the needs of others. But … spiritual and material abundance can result only by focusing on the needs of others. By conserving your money and spending it more efficiently, perhaps through a budget, you will not only find money that you were previously wasting on trivialities, but your tithing will actually bring about economic healing.…

Tithing establishes a consistent method of giving and for stewarding the bounty in one's life.… I can say that, almost without exception, the family that tithes for more than 10 years becomes both prosperous and happy. This is the one investment suitable for all people.[3]

The prophet Malachi wrote, "Bring ye all the tithes into the storehouse, that there may be meat in mine house, and prove me now herewith, saith the Lord of hosts, if I will not open you the windows of heaven, and pour you out a blessing, that there shall not be room enough to receive it" (Malachi 3:10).

The important thing is to recognize that everything you have belongs to God, Who asks that we give a tenth of it back. Sometimes we give beyond that as well. If one of the greatest investors of all time says that tithing is the best investment, we ought to take it seriously.

5. Depend on Your Trust Fund

Most people think of a trust fund as a store of money set aside for their use. But I think of Proverbs 3:5–6: "Trust in the Lord with all thine heart; and lean not unto thine own understanding. In all thy ways acknowledge him, and he shall direct thy paths."

In this complicated and crazy world, no one can figure out everything. At some point, you have to trust God and move forward. That's why this proverb is so powerful. It gives you confidence that if you put your trust in God and start taking steps, He will direct your path.

6. Never Give In

There will no doubt be many challenges in the days and years ahead. We can take comfort from the wisdom of one who went before us and in terribly dark days persevered. Winston Churchill had watched his beloved nation lose its grip on the greatest empire in history, and then its very existence was threatened by Hitler's Germany. In October 1941 he returned to the ancient Harrow School to speak to the students. Standing before them, he simply said, "Never give in, never give in, never, never, never...."[4]

7. Only One Thing Is Necessary

The final truth to share comes from the tenth chapter of the Gospel of Luke:

> Now it came to pass, as they went, that he entered into a certain village: and a certain woman named Martha received him into her house.
>
> And she had a sister called Mary, which also sat at Jesus' feet, and heard his word.
>
> But Martha was cumbered about much serving, and came to him, and said, Lord, dost thou not care that my sister hath left me to serve alone? Bid her therefore that she help me.
>
> And Jesus answered and said unto her, Martha, Martha, thou art careful and troubled about many things:

But one thing is needful: and Mary hath chosen that good part, which shall not be taken away from her.

Martha was so busy worrying about the things of this life that she missed out on the best things—in this case, spending time with her Lord. Mary didn't miss it.

I know that this book has given you a great deal to worry about and a whole lot to do. Don't get so caught up in such worries that you miss out on living: "Take therefore no thought for the morrow: for the morrow shall take thought for the things of itself. Sufficient unto the day is the evil thereof" (Matthew 6:34).

Acknowledgments

The past five years has been an evolving mission. At first, my goal was simply to make certain our government was awake and aware of the threat of financial terrorism. As an investment manager, I watched firsthand as our financial system's vulnerabilities were exploited by those who meant to do us harm. I wanted reassurance that our federal government was busy at work protecting our interests in this area. Sadly they were not, presumably because they were simply uninformed. So the mission morphed into one of warning and education for our nation's leadership. My basic premise was that once our government became informed, it would be prepared to act and all would be well. That focus lasted for at least two years. Unfortunately, it became clear that more than ignorance was at work. Politics, worsened by information operations efforts, greed, and outright confusion over a complex topic made it impossible for our government to recognize, let alone properly respond to, this threat. That's why I wrote *Secret Weapon*. The American people deserved to know what was really happening, why, and what should be done about it.

As I traveled across the country sharing the reality of the economic war we are in, the mission morphed again. Good people, from all backgrounds and political persuasions, intuitively understood that something was wrong. Our message resonated with them and provided answers they had been seeking. But they needed more. They asked for a game plan for responding individually and collectively. That was the genesis of this book. I must therefore thank the hundreds of groups that let me speak to them and the thousands of people willing to listen. Many of them joined my prayer teams, provided research and contacts, or volunteered to help spread the word.

Ultimately, I believe that spreading the word is a spiritual requirement. Several people I've met along the way have likened my quest to that of a watchman as described in Ezekiel 33:6. I've felt that, recognizing the powerful leading of the Holy Spirit. The greatest acknowledgment, therefore, must be given to God, Maker of Heaven and Earth (Genesis 1:1), to His only begotten Son, whom He sent in love to save the world (John 3:16), and to the Holy Spirit of promise, sent by the Son (Acts 2:38-39).

Because the number of people to thank is extensive, I am just listing names without title or personal comment. I have grouped them into categories. Some fit into more than one group, so their names may be repeated. They are listed alphabetically by first name for the most part. The list has grown quite a bit since the release of *Secret Weapon* and continues to grow almost daily.

The Team, Volunteers, and Others Who Played a Part

Even though I was the primary author of the report to the Department of Defense, *Secret Weapon*, and the book you are now reading, there is a significant team and numerous volunteers who make it possible. Thank you to Allen Clark, Ann Canfield, Ben Shapiro, Bert Smith, Brad Worley, Brannon Preston, Bruce Cook, Caren Wheaton, Carol Taber, Christine Brim, Christy Brooks, Danny Herrera, David Hemenway, David Krauza, David Preston, Deana Morgan, Ducky Hemenway, EJ Kimball, Everett Piper, Frank Gaffney, Ginni Thomas, Giovanni Capriglione, Jack Langer, Jayne Carter, John Actis, John Guandolo, John Lenczowski, Jonathan Low, Karen Lake, Kathy Smith, Keith Green, Ken Ivory, Kevin Hiles, Kimberly Tipton, Laurie Bolton, Luke Macias, Marci Piper, Marilyn Britton, Matt Krause, Michael Colonetta, Michael Del Rosso, Mike Carter, Mitchell Morgan, Pat Calhoun, Patrick Maloy, Paul Bigham, Paul Janiczek, Peggy Dau, Rachel Ehrenfeld, Roger Robinson, Ron Brooks, Russell Lake, Scott Bradford, Shelli Baker Manuel, Stephen Coughlin, Steve Zidek, Steven Tipton, Tammy Worley, Ted Yadlowski, Trayce Bradford, Tom Dodd, and many others, some of whom must remain unnamed.

Those Who Provided Support, Encouragement, or Prayer

There is an even broader group who supported in a variety of ways including prayer. At the top of this list are my wife and our children, family, and extended family (including Miss Joy). Some of these have passed on to the Lord since the quest began but remain loved and appreciated.

My heartfelt thanks go to Aaron Wronko, Adam and Tara Ross, Aileen and Tom Milton, Al Proo, Al and Tracie Denson, Al Micallef, Alan and Michelle Schnacke, Aldon and Cheryl Rutherford, Alex Cortes, Alice Linahan, Alida Jacob, Alan Weigleitner, Allan and Dolores Wood, Allen and Leslee Unruh, Allen and Linda Clark, Ambree and Will Stone, Amos Ross, Amy Duncan, Amy Dunn, Amy Pearce, Andra Dunn, Andrew Stewart, Andy and Jenny Hickl, Andy and Jennifer Strachan, Angie and John Anderson, Ann and Bill Quest, Ann and Cliff

Bruder, Annette McPhetridge, Arch Bonnema, Archer and Elizabeth Martin, Avi Lipkin, Barbara Adamson, Barry Armstrong, Ben and Melanie Lasoi, Bernie and Lee Reese, Bert and Kathy Smith, Beth Palmer, Beth Williams, Bill Federer, Bill Floyd, Bill Garaway, Bill Mauerman, Bill and Anne Ashton, Bill and Caren Wheaton, Bill and Carolyn Doughty, Bill and Patty Stoner, Blake and Margaret Keating, Bill and Jane Mason, Bill Koenig, Bill NeSmith, Bill Zedler, Billy Joe and Sharon Daughtery, Bob Hall, Bob Reccord, Bob and Char Reehm, Bob and Rita Fisher, Brad Thor, Brad and Patty Harber, Brad and Tammy Worley, Brandon and Dana Pollard, Brannon and Noelle Preston, Brandon Freeman, Brenda Peterson, Brent and Carrie Blake, Brent Beraducci, Brent Phillips, Brian Wrenn, Brian Birdwell, Bridget and Rick Losa, Brooks Douglas, Bruce Hallett, Bruce and Laura Bellamy, Bruce and Tracy Levinson, Bruce Dunham, Bryce Freeman, Buddy and Hazel Atkinson, Buddy Pilgrim, Byron and Sally Todd, Carl and Sue Richards, Carlos and Marilyn Morales, Camille Johnson, Carolyn Hunt, Carolyn Wakefield, Carter Schuld, Casey and Amy Cook, Casey and Angela Jones, Cathy Adams, Chad Hennings, Charles and Jana Fay Bacarisse, Charles and Paulet Garrett, Charles Robinson, Charlie Levitt, Cheri Duncan Hubert, Chris and Amy Davis, Chris and Kathy Howard, Chris McKinzie, Christopher Williams, Chuck and Elaine Hewitt, Chuck and Vicky Watson, Chuck Molyneaux, Cindi Sherrod, Cindy Barnett, Cindy Youell, Clynt Taylor, Colin Hanna, Cory Huddleston, Craig Goldman, Crystal Gause, Dale and Vi Gibson, Dan Sullivan, Dane and Twyla Bartel, Darin and Christy Sloan, Darrell and Janelle Woolsey, Dave and Michael Cook, Dave Rambie, David and Cheryl Barton, David and Rochelle Bader, David and Shauna Rothman, David and Shelli Manuel, David Hamon, David Keyston, David Lambertsen, David Lane, David Morris, David Preston, David Rambie, David Simpson, Dawn Horton, Dean Forman, Dean and Kim Gillitzer, Dean and Michelle DeCavitte, Deb Gatzke, Denise Gerrich, Dennis and Beth Dribin, Derrick and Tammy Leupen,

Diane Truitt, Diana Denman, Don Munson, Don Walker, Don and Barbara Thornton, Don and Tiffany Willet, Don and Vivian Blakeman, Dorrie Obrien, Doug and Cynthia Nurss, Doug and Suzanne Wright, Doug and Sylvia Carter, Doug Wakefield, Drew and Linda Springer, Drew Springer, Ed Belan, Ed Smith, Ed Martin, Ed Wolff, Elise and Jeff Pistor, Edwin and Ursula Meese, Elizabeth Tolhurst, Ellen Grigsby, Elliott Griffin, Eric Bleiken, Evan Loomis, Eric Jackson, Erik and Lori Davidson, Erin Anderson, Everett and Marci Piper, Foster and Lynn Friess, Fran Sherwood, Frank Bragg, Frank Gaffney, Fredrick Wolcott, Gabe and Karen Joseph, Gail Gause, Gale Sears, Gary Moore, Gateway Church Pastoral Staff, Gene and Barbara Graves, Gerald Broadhurst, George Mauerman, George Rodriguez, Georgia Stapleton, Ginni Thomas, Ginny and Jason Noble, Giovanni Capriglione, Gordon and Nita Chen, Graham Morgan, Greg and Connie Williams, Gunnar Johnson, Hiram Sasser, Hunt Neurohr, Jack and Rose Fredricks, James and Cecelia Leininger, James and Lynda Dickey, Jamie Waller, Jason and Abi Landry, Jane Hogan, Jane Orient, Janet Sullivan, Janice and Charlie Drake, Jason Jones, Jay and Shonda Wagner, Jensine Bard, Jerry and Martina Ledzinski, Jeff and Amy Fredrick, Jeff and Carolyn Wakefield, Jeff and Kim Hassell, Jeff and Melanie Burns, Jeff Myers, Jenna Milleson, Jennifer Wortham, Jeremy Boyd, Jerry Boykin, Jerry Nichols, Jerry Tuma, Jessica and Marco Juarez, Jessica Spawn, Jim Czirr, Jim and Gene Edwards, Jim and Jeanne White, Jim and Laurie Bolton, Jim and Tisha Ghormley, Jim and Patti Jo Peevy, Jim Griffith, Jim Johnson, Jim Martin, Jim Whitehead, Joan Neuhaus Schaan, Joanne Herring, Joe and Kimberly Colonetta, Joe Ferguson, Joe Galindo, Joe Musser, Joe Kerry, Joe and Peggy Smith, John Anderson, John Antal, John and CJ Early, John and Kelley Kasperbauer, Jana Inge, John and Lynn Pohanka, John Hemenway, John Sandoz, John Spurling, John Stemberger, John Templeton Jr., John Westberg, Jon Lorenzon, Jonathan Stickland, Johnson and Feyi Obamahinti, Jonathan and Jennifer Weiss, Jonathan Low, Jonathan

Rotenberg, Jonathan Saenz, Jose and Kathleen Lopez, Josh Duggar, Joshua and Casey Tolhurst, Julie and Jeff Luke, Julie McCarty, K Carl Smith, KT Freeman, Kaaren Teuber, Karen Clark, Karen England, Kassie Dulin, Katherine Gorsuch, Kay and Paco Jordan, Kay Godwin, Keith and Michelle Swyers, Ken Davidson, Kent and Christie Glesener, Keet Lewis, Keith and Jeanna Green, Kellie Black, Kelly and Scott Luttenberg, Keith Kelly, Kelly and Karen Shackelford, Kelly Nichols, Ken and Joanna Wiesinger, Ken and Sandy Campbell, Kerrie and Phillip Oles, Kerry and Donna Freeman, Kevin and Liz Horn, Kevin and Lolita Minor, Kevin Blacquiere, Kirk and Nancy Freeman, Kirk Launius, Kris Humber, Kristi Davis, Kyden and Melanie Reeh, Kyla Reeves, Larry & Joan Ezell, Larry and Staci Wallace, Laura Bentz, Laura Lake, Lawrence and Joanne Kersten, Leah and Robert Morris, Leigh Wambsganns, Leighton and Lynette King, Les Pierce, Leslie Brosi, Leslie Kent, Liberty Institute Prayer Team, Linda Redd, Linwood Bragan, Lisa Byrd, Lisa Piraneo, Luke Macias, MM Freeman, Madge and Forest Williams, Marc and Libba Hanna, Marcus and Lexa Brecheen, Marie Howard, Marla and Chad Swandt, Mark and Jennifer Connell, Mark and Rebecca Ritchie, Mark and Robyn Tolhurst, Mark Fisher, Mark Swafford, Mark Yearout, Mary Jane Dodds, Mary K. Boston, Mary Lou Daxland, Maryann Christensen, Mason Area, Matt Krause, Matthew Taylor, Michael Farris, Michael and Peggy Lee, Michael Del Rosso, Michelle Scholtz, Michelle Smith, Mike and Julie Katzorke, Mike and Jayne Carter, Mike and Laura Oakley, Mike and Lisa Moore, Mike and Marika Olcott, Mike Farris, Mike Lewis, Mike McGuire, Mike Studer, Miriam (Joy) Mager, Mimi Buser, Mitchell and Deana Morgan, Nathan and DeeDee Ng, Nic and Janine Stevens, Nicholas Papanicolaou, Nick Ryan, Ollie and Marlaina Wick, Pam Nance, Pat and Deborah Calhoun, Pat Tippett, Patrick and Amy Maloy, Nina Speairs, Patrick Smith, Patricia Lee, Paul and Eleanor Mullen, Paul and Grace Hallen, Paul and Nancy Pressler, Paul and Paula Martin, Paul and Sharla Vinyard, Paulett Standefer, Peggy and Jim Dau, Peggy Eubanks,

Penny Eargle, Peter and Maggie Ashton, Peter Lee, Phil Wiltfong, Phillip Midkiff, Phillip Parton, Phillip Jauregui, Prasad and Beulah Rao, Preston Noell, Randall Christy, Randall Swanson, Randy and Lydia Long, Randy and Becky Isbell, Randy Simmons, Raphael Cruz, Ray and Jacquie Brooks, Ray and Nancy Ashton, Ray and Sharon Loveless, Ray Myers, Rebecca Berry, Rebecca and Andrew Hagelin, Rene Poe, Rex and Janie Lake, Rhonda Lacy, Richard and Jacquie Patterson, Richard Bott, Richard and Deborah Garreau, Richard and Gina Headrick, Richard and Robin Bernstein, Richard Lackey, Richard Viguerie, Rick Cott, Rob Smith, Robert England, Robert LaCosta, Robert Lowry, Robert Shreve, Robin and Cindy Carriger, Robyn Hancock, Rod and Sherri Martin, Roger and Moe Westfall, Rolla and Lisa Goodyear, Ron and Christy Brooks, Ron Fister, Roxanne Phillips, Roy Stuart, Russ and Laura Finlay, Russ Ramsland, Russell and Karen Lake, Russell Clements, Ryan Mauldin, Salina Duffy, Samantha Ryall, Samuel Luttenberg, Sarah and David Area, Scott and Gaylynn McBrayer, Scott and Megan Richards, Scott Sanford, Scott Turner, Shane Luttenberg, Shay Beard, Shawn and Anita Maloney, Sharon Ford, Sharron and Ted Angle, Simon Bull, Somers White, Spencer Luttenberg, Stephanie Klick, Stephen and Erin Luttenberg, Steve and Wendy Riach, Steve Dulin, Steve Gritton, Steve Kirkpatrick, Steve Monson, Steve Weinberg, Steve and Tracy Gallemore, Steven and Emily Dilla, Steven and Kim Tipton, Sue Freeman, Sue and Lanny Peden, Sue Richardson, Summer Luttenberg, Suzanne Blackstone, Tarek Saab, Ted Baehr, Terry Campbell, Tiffany Neurohr, Tim and Amy LeFever, Tim and Tuyet Cahill, Tim and Virginia Shepherd, Tim and Amy LeFever, Tisha Casida, Tod and Tammy Williams, Todd and Heidi Barnett, Todd and Maria Horchner, Todd and Penna Dexter, Todd and Salina Lorch, Tom Barrett, Tom Dodd, Tom Harrison, Tomi and Daryl Jarrell, Tony and Kathy Gayanich, Torsten Mann, Trayce and Scott Bradford, Tracy Hancock, Travis and Vanessa Howard, Troy and Erica Andrews, Troy Newman, Tricia Erickson, Vicki and Dan Nohrden,

Virginia Prodan, Wade Parkhill, Wanda and Bev Brown, Wendell Brock, Will and Kelly Angus, Will and Sandra Mills, Will King, Zach and Jen Neese, Zeldon Nelson, Zodie Christakos, and all others who have prayed and helped so much.

Groups That Invited Me to Speak

In two years, I've been honored to speak to more than one hundred groups of all types ranging from twenty people in a book club to five hundred in a large assembly hall. I'll mention here a few specific groups because of their uniqueness as well as broad categories wherein the various groups are too numerous to individually mention. The first category includes political groups made up of Tea Parties, 9/12 groups, Patriot groups, Eagle Forums, Freedom Forums, Republican Assemblies and Societies, as well as various progressive organizations. It is amazing how our message and concerns have resonated across partisan lines. The more right-leaning groups are very concerned about national defense and protecting our economy. The left-leaning groups are concerned about systemic manipulation and national security as well. It has been interesting connecting with Tea Parties from Florida to California and also groups supporting progressive causes.

Another category of organization that has shown keen interest in our work has been the national security groups. Included in these are the American Legion, Center for Security Policy, Doctors for Disaster Preparedness, Corazon De Leones, Irregular Warfare Symposiums, Oak Initiative, Reserve Officers Associations, West Point Society, and Military Order of World Wars. There are also a variety of government, defense, and intelligence organizations that have had me as a speaker or contributor, formally and informally. These include the DIA, the FBI, MITRE, DARPA, and IARPA, among others.

I've been privileged to speak at a variety of institutions of higher learning including Georgetown, Oklahoma Wesleyan University, Austin

Peay State University, the Naval War College, George Wythe College, Mercyhurst University, and the Naval Postgraduate School. I've addressed finance clubs, TIGER 21, real estate forums, and investment clubs. I've also been privileged to be the featured speaker at prestigious charities such as the Salesmanship Club of Dallas and United Way of Palm Beach. I've been featured at think tanks like the Heritage Foundation, Christian and Jewish religious groups, Wingmen, and retirement clubs.

Media Willing to Report

While financial terrorism, economic warfare, and Secret Weapons are intriguing concepts, it took courageous media to look beyond the popular narrative for the truth. I appreciate all who have studied, are studying, or have reported on the story, including Al Gainey, Alex Frean, AM Tampa Bay, American Family Radio, American Freedom Radio, American Legion Magazine, America's Morning News, America's Radio News, America's Workforce Radio, Andrea Tantaros, Ann Ubelis, Anthony Martin, Bartlesville Examiner, Ben Shapiro, Big John and Amy, Bill Gertz, Bill Koenig, Bill Lunden, the Blaze, Blu-News, Bob Dutko, Book TV, Brad Davis, Brad Watson, Brian Thomas, Breitbart, Bryan Biggs, Call to Rights Radio, Canada Free Press, CBS Philly, Cherokee Tribune, Chris Graham, Chris Versace, the Closing Bell, the Counter Terrorist, Craig Johnson, CSC Talk Radio, C-SPAN, Daily Caller, the Daily Mail, Daily Paul, Dan Cofall, David Arnett, David Hahn, David Morris, Don Smith, Dos Mundos, Doug Urbanski, the Dove Morning Show, the Epoch Times, Equity Strategies, Ernie and Molly, the Examiner, Family Security Matters, For the Record, Floyd Brown, Frank Beckman, Frank Gaffney, G. Gordon Liddy, Gabe Wisdom, Gayle Ruzicka, Ginni Thomas, Glenn Beck, Grant Stinchfield, Hugh Vail, Ideas Matter, John Griffing, Joseph and Elizabeth Farah, JR Nyquist, Jake Shannon, Janet Mefford, Jeff Stoffer, Jensine Bard, Jerry Corsi, Jewish

Voice, Joe Thomas, Joe Weasel, Joey Bourgoin, John Lee Walker Show, John Ostapkovich, Jonathan Bernis, Karen Clark, KDPQ, Ken Chandler, KFAQ Radio, KFUO, KMED Radio, KTCN, KZIM, the Lamplighter report, Lanigan and Malone Show, the Lifestyle Show, Lighthouse Journal, Maria Bartiromo, Mark Larson, Mark Mitchell, Matt Drudge, Matt Purple, Megyn Kelly, Michael Reagan, Michael Savage, Midland Reporter-Telegram, Mike Porenta, Money Riches and Wealth, MoneyNews, NewsMax TV, Nick Jones, Nick Reed, Pat Campbell, Pat Snyder, Paul Sperry, Penna Dexter, Point of View, Politickles, Peter Schiff, Poppoff Radio, Prepper Podcast, Ralph Smith, Ray Dunaway, Rich Bott, Richard Miniter, Robert England, Robyn Walensky, Ron Elz, Ron Insana, Roy Green, Ryan Cost, the Schilling Show, Secure Freedom Radio, 60 Minutes, Steve Deace, Southern Sense Radio, the Source, Steve Malzberg, Stu Taylor, Stuart Epperson, TBN, Tim Burg, Tracey and Friends, Tru News Radio, Tulsa Today, Tulsa World, 20/20 Radio, Virginia Grace, Warren Cole Smith, Washington Free Beacon, Wired Magazine, World Magazine, WKRC, and WND.

Those Who Helped Me with the Book

The professionals at Regnery have been terrific, as have other successful authors who have provided wise insights. I especially want to thank Ben Shapiro and Tom Spence for sharing their experienced wisdom in crafting this book. Others who have helped make this book a reality include Gene Brissie, Harry Crocker, Marji Ross, Maria Ruhl, Katharine Mancuso, Jason Sunde, Henry Pereira, and Randy Tunnell.

Some of Those Who Were Willing to Listen

I went through my travel schedule and emails over the past three years to get an idea of how many briefings I had given all across the country. There were hundreds of people involved, some of whom I briefed as many as six times each. I can't list all the names, as some must be withheld for security reasons. Thank you to all who took serious time to listen, including Adam Kaufman, Adam Miller, Al Micallef, Al Santoli, Alan Jackson, Alec Bierbauer, Alida Jacob, Andrew Davenport, Andrew May, Andy Marshall, Andy Wehrle, Andy Polk, Ann Canfield, Andrew Stewart, Anthony Arend, Avi Lipkin, Barrett Moore, Barry Smitherman, Bert Dohman, Bill Bergman, Bill Floyd, Bill Pascoe, Bill Posey, Bill Tucker, Bill Walton, Bob Reccord, Bob McEwen, Boone Pickens, Brady Cassis, Brett Heimov, Brian Kennedy, Brian Halstead, Bryan Hughes, Carol Taber, Chris Barkley, Charles Worrell, Christian Beckner, Christine Brim, Clarine Nardi-Riddle, Cliff May, Connie Hair, Craig Shirley, Dagne Florine, Dan Brandt, Dana Crane, Dane Bartel, David Bobb, David Britz, David Hamon, David Jackson, David Kotz, David Lane, David Patch, David Reist, David Yerushalmi, Diana Banister, Don Hodel, Don Nickles, Eamon Blanchard, Ed Koch, Ed McCallum, Ed Royce, Ed Soyster, Edwin Meese, EJ Kimball, Eric Bleiken, Ernest Istook, Everett Piper, Erik Davidson, EW Jackson, Foster Friess, Frank Bragg, Frank Keating, Frank Gaffney, Frank Wolf, Fred Grandy, Gary Fletcher, George and Becky Norton Dunlop, George Cecala, George Strake, Ginni Thomas, Gordon Chang, Hank Cooper, Harold Lanier, Herman Cain, Howard Kaloogian, HT Narea, James Hoge, James McGarrah, Jason Lee, Jay Rosser, Jay Schnitzer, Jeff Nyquist, Jeff Staubach, Jeff Taylor, Jeffrey Starr, Jenny Beth Martin, Jeffrey Roach, Jerry Boykin, Jerry Jones, Jim Gilmore, Jim Woolsey, Joan Neuhaus Schaan, Joe Ficalora, Joe Lieberman, Joe Schmitz, John Craig, John Guandolo, John Lenczowski, John Mauldin, John Miri, John Russo, John Ryan, John Sandoz, John Shadegg, John Sloan, Johnny A. Moncayo, Jon Kyl, Joseph and Sheryl Kaufman, K Carl Smith, Kara Schoeffling, Keith Poole, Kelly Ayotte, Kelly Hancock, Kelly Shackelford, Ken Ivory, Ken Jensen, Ken Timmerman, Kenny Marchant, Kevin Gates, Kevin Gentry, Kevin Hassett, Konni Burton, Lamar Smith, Larry Arnn, Lisa Pollard, Louie Gohmert, Luke Miller,

Mac Thornberry, Madeleine Pickens, Marc Colby, Marcus Brubaker, Mark Hafner, Mark Skinner, Matthew Elias, Matthew Marchant, Michael Burgess, Michael Conaway, Michael Del Rosso, Michael Flynn, Michael Grimm, Michael Hoehn, Michael Leary, Michael Mukasey, Michele Bachmann, Mike Lee, Mike Moen, Mike Moore, Mike Moncrief, Mike Pillsbury, Mike Rogers, Nancy Duncan, Neal Freeman, Newt Gingrich, Patrick Byrne, Patrick Maloy, Paul Blocher, Paul Broun, Paul McRory, Paulette Standefer, Peter King, Peter Wallison, Rachel Ehrenfeld, Rsand Paul, Rich Higgins, Richard Stoyeck, Richard Viguerie, Rick Bremseth, Rinelda Bliss, Rob Schwazwalder, Robert Boland, Robert Maguire, Robert Morgenthau, Roger Robinson, Roger Staubach, Ron Burgess, Roscoe Bartlett, Ruben Gonzalez, Russ Ramsland, Ryan Morfin, Sebastian Gorka, Serge Kabud, Sharron Angle, Shaun Brady, Simone Ledeen, Stephen Coughlin, Steve Feiss, Steve Stockman, Steve Weinberg, Stuart Burns, Stuart Epperson, Ted Cruz, Terry Wichert, Thomas Connolly, Thomas Culligan, Tim Cahill, Tim Morrison, Tim Slemp, Todd Wagnor, Tom O'Connell, Tom Pauken, Tom Sass, Tony Perkins, Van Taylor, Walid Phares, William Wright, and Zach Woodworth.

To all of these and the many others who have blessed us so much I share my heartfelt thanks.

Notes

INTRODUCTION

1. Qiao Liang and Wang Xiangsui, *Unrestricted Warfare: China's Master Plan to Destroy America* (Panama City, Panama: Pan American Publishing Company, 2002), 122. Originally published by People's Liberation Press, 1999.
2. James Dison, "A Nation Challenged: The New Tape; In Its Express Delivery and Its Details, Bin Laden's Latest Tape Differs from Past Ones," *New York Times*, December 28, 2001, http://www.nytimes.com/2001/12/28/world/nation-challenged-new-tape-its-express-delivery-its-details-bin-laden-s-latest.html.
3. George Soros, "One Way to Stop Bear Raids: Credit Default Swaps Need Much Stricter Regulation," *Wall Street Journal*, March 24, 2009, http://online.wsj.com/news/articles/SB123785310594719693.
4. Ibid.
5. Soros, "Does the Euro Have a Future?" *New York Review of Books*, October 12, 2011, http://www.nybooks.com/articles/archives/2011/oct/13/does-euro-have-future/.
6. Liang and Xiangsui, *Unrestrictred Warfare*, 36.
7. Alistair Barr, "Soros among Firms That Made Money in 2008, 2009: Caxton, Paulson, Brevan Howard, King Street, Bridgewater Also Up Both Years," MarketWatch, *Wall Street Journal*, January 13, 2010, http://www.marketwatch.com/story/soros-among-firms-that-made-money-in-08-and-09-2010-01-13.

8.   Bill Gertz, "Financial Terrorism Suspected in 2008 Economic Crash: Pentagon Study Sees Element," *Washington Times*, February 28, 2011, http://www.washingtontimes. com/news/2011/feb/28/financial-terrorism-suspected-in-08-economic-crash/?page=all.

9.   Gertz, "Inside the Ring: New WMD threats," *Washington Times*, October 10, 2012, http:// www.washingtontimes.com/news/2012/oct/10/inside-the-ring-new-wmd-threats/?page=all; and "Pentagon Cover-Up: 'For the Record' Reveals the Buried Details on Economic Terror Tactics Used by China, Russia, and Al Qaeda against America," The Blaze, September 18, 2013, http://www.theblaze.com/stories/2013/09/18/pentagon-cover-up-for-the-record-reveals-the-buried-details-on-economic-terror-tactics-used-by-china-russia-al-qaeda-against-america/.

10.   Juan Zarate, *Treasury's War: The Unleashing of a New Era of Financial Warfare* (New York: PublicAffairs, 2013), 420–21.

11.   "Jim Rickards: Pentagon's Financial War Game Playing Out," Financial Sense, September 20, 2013, http://www.financialsense.com/contributors/jim-rickards/world-playing-out-pentagon-financial-war-game.

12.   "Billion Dollar Soros Bet Right on the Money," Yahoo! Finance, May 8, 2013, http://au. finance.yahoo.com/news/billion-dollar-soros-bet-right-on-the-money—010432812.html.

CHAPTER ONE

1.   Ruth Sherlock, "Al-Qaeda Chief Calls for Attacks on U.S. in 9/11 Speech to Followers," *Telegraph*, September 13, 2013, http://www.telegraph.co.uk/news/worldnews/al-qaeda/10306755/Al-Qaeda-chief-calls-for-attacks-on-US-in-911-speech-to-followers.html.

2.   "Bin Laden: Goal Is to Bankrupt U.S.," CNN.com, November 1, 2004, http://www.cnn. com/2004/WORLD/meast/11/01/binladen.tape/.

3.   Susan Crabtree, "FLASHBACK: Obama: Al Qaeda Is on 'a Path to Defeat'; Calls for Resetting Terror Policy," *Washington Times*, May 23, 2013, http://www.washingtontimes. com/news/2013/may/23/obama-al-qaeda-is-on-a-path-to-defeat/?page=all.

4.   Yassin Musharbash, "The Future of Terrorism: What al-Qaida Really Wants," Spiegel Online, *Der Spiegel*, August 12, 2005, http://www.spiegel.de/international/the-future-of-terrorism-what-al-qaida-really-wants-a-369448.html.

5.   Ibid.

6.   Robert C. Martinage, *The Global War on Terrorism: An Assessment* (Washington, D.C.: Center for Strategic and Budgetary Assessments, 2008), 41.

7.   Musharbash, "The Future of Terrorism."

8.   Garry Blight, Sheila Pulham, and Paul Torpey, "Arab Spring: An Interactive Timeline of Middle East Protests," *Guardian*, January 5, 2012, http://www.theguardian.com/world/interactive/2011/mar/22/middle-east-protest-interactive-timeline.

9.   Tim Lister, "New al Qaeda Message Reinforces Focus on Arab Spring," CNN.com, September 13, 2011, http://security.blogs.cnn.com/2011/09/13/new-al-qaeda-message-reinforces-focus-on-arab-spring/.

10.   Keith Wagstaff, "Freedom Fighters or al Qaeda? What You Need to Know about the Syrian Rebels," *Week*, September 5, 2013, http://theweek.com/article/index/249178/freedom-fighters-or-al-qaeda-what-you-need-to-know-about-the-syrian-rebels.

11.   Maureen Farrell, "High Speed Trading Fueled Twitter Flash Crash," CNN Money, CNN. com, April 24, 2013, http://money.cnn.com/2013/04/24/investing/twitter-flash-crash/index.html?iid=EL.

12. Michael Kling, "CNNMoney: A Dozen Mini Flash Crashes Hit Stock Market Daily," Moneynews.com, March 21, 2013, http://www.moneynews.com/InvestingAnalysis/flash-crash-stocks-mini-SEC/2013/03/21/id/495652?s=al#ixzz2fZGzbdZK.

13. Kevin D. Freeman, *Secret Weapon: How Economic Terrorism Brought Down the U.S. Stock Market and Why It Can Happen Again* (Washington, D.C.: Regnery Publishing, 2012), 1.

14. Ibid., 220.

15. Freeman, "Progress in Washington," GlobalEconomicWarfare.com, May 13, 2011, http://globaleconomicwarfare.com/2011/05/progress-in-washington/.

16. Jamie Weinstein, "Meet Andrew Marshall, the Unknown but Immensely Influential Figure behind American National Security Strategy," Daily Caller, July 11, 2011, http://dailycaller.com/2011/07/11/meet-andrew-marshall-the-unknown-but-immensely-influential-figure-behind-american-national-security-strategy/.

17. Marcus Weisgerber and John T. Bennett, "Pentagon Determining Fate of Revered Net Assessment Office," DefenseNews.com, October 15, 2013, http://www.defensenews.com/article/20131015/DEFREG02/310150031/.

18. "Pentagon Cover-Up: 'For the Record' Reveals the Buried Details on Economic Tactics Used by China, Russia, and al Qaeda against America," The Blaze, September 18, 2013, http://www.theblaze.com/stories/2013/09/18/pentagon-cover-up-for-the-record-reveals-the-buried-details-on-economic-terror-tactics-used-by-china-russia-al-qaeda-against-america/.

19. National Intelligence Council, *Global Trends 2030: Alternative Worlds* (Washington, D.C.: Government Printing Office, 2012), 68.

20. Gertz, "Inside the Ring," *Washington Times*, November 10, 2010, http://www.washingtontimes.com/news/2010/nov/10/inside-the-ring-716343977/?page=all.

21. Lauren Tara LaCapra, "Wall Street Goes to War with Hackers in Quantum Dawn 2 Simulation," Reuters, June 13, 2013, http://blogs.reuters.com/unstructuredfinance/2013/06/13/wall-street-goes-to-war-with-hackers-in-cyber-dawn-2-simulation/.

22. Ryan Tracy, "Cyber Attack Test Finds Flaws in Equity Market: Results Find Industry, Government Can Do More to Harden System," *Wall Street Journal*, October 21, 2013, http://online.wsj.com/news/articles/SB10001424052702303672404579147713406361036.

23. Juan Zarate, *Treasury's War: The Unleashing of a New Era of Financial Warfare* (New York: PublicAffairs, 2013), 420–21.

24. National Commission on Terrorist Attacks, *The 9/11 Commission Report: Final Report of the National Commission on Terrorist Attacks upon the United States* (New York: W. W. Norton, 2011), 153.

25. Philip J. Cooper and Claudia Maria Vargas, *Sustainable Development in Crisis Conditions: Challenges of War, Terrorism, and Civil Disorder* (Lanham, MD: Rowman and Littlefield, 2008), 65.

26. Jan Sejna, *We Will Bury You* (London: Sidgwick and Jackson, 1985), 107–9.

27. Charles Duelfer and James Rickards, "Econo-Threats," *New York Times*, November 21, 2008, http://www.nytimes.com/2008/12/21/opinion/21iht-eduelfer.1.18844161.html?_r=0.

28. John Ware, "Panorama: Faith, Hate, and Charity," press release, December 30, 2006, http://www.bbc.co.uk/pressoffice/pressreleases/stories/2006/07_july/30/panorama.shtml.

29. "Casey," "The 39 Principles of Jihad," WorldAnalysis.net, http://worldanalysis.net/smf/index.php?topic=188.0;wap2.

30. Josh Pollack, "Statement by al-Qai'da Leader Usama Bin Ladin Carried within the 'First War of the Century' Program; Place, Date Not Given—Recorded: FBIS Translated Text," Mideast Web News Service, http://groups.yahoo.com/neo/groups/MewNews/conversations/topics/4339.

31. Interview with Mahathir bin Mohamad, *Commanding Heights*, PBS, July 2, 2001, transcript, http://www.pbs.org/wgbh/commandingheights/shared/minitext/int_mahathirbinmohamad.htm.

32. Liu Chang, "Commentary: U.S. Fiscal Failure Warrants a De-Americanized World," Xinhua News, October 13, 2013, http://news.xinhuanet.com/english/indepth/2013-10/13/c_132794246.htm.

33. Freeman, "Money, Money, Money," GlobalEconomicWarfare.com, March 7, 2013, http://globaleconomicwarfare.com/2013/03/money-money-money/.

34. Vedant Misra, Marco Lagi, and Yaneer Bar-Yam, "Evidence of Market Manipulation in the Financial Crisis," New England Complex Systems Institute, December 13, 2011, updated January 4, 2012, http://necsi.edu/research/economics/bearraid.html.

35. Ibid.

36. "U.S. Homeland Chief: Cyber 9/11 Could Happen 'Imminently,'" Reuters, January 25, 2013, http://www.reuters.com/article/2013/01/24/us-usa-cyber-threat-idUSBRE90N1A320130124.

37. Alister Bull and Jim Finkle, "Fed Says Internal Site Breached by Hackers, No Critical Function Affected," Reuters, February 6, 2013, http://www.reuters.com/article/2013/02/06/net-us-usa-fed-hackers-idUSBRE91501920130206.

38. Tyler Durden, "Big Oops: Deutsche Borse Says 'Flash Crash Can't Happen Here' a Week before German Flash Crash," Zero Hedge, April 18, 2013, http://www.zerohedge.com/news/2013-04-18/big-ööps-deutsche-börse-says-flash-crash-cant-happen-here-week-german-flash-crash.

39. Mark Clayton, "Terrorist Tweets: How Al Qaeda's Social Media Move Could Cause Problems," Christian Science Monitor, February 7, 2013, http://www.csmonitor.com/USA/2013/0207/Terrorist-tweets-how-Al-Qaeda-s-social-media-move-could-cause-problems.

40. Simone Foxman, "Recent Cyberattacks Could Be Part of a Chinese Military Strategy Started Nearly 20 Years Ago," QZ.com, March 14, 2013, http://qz.com/62434/recent-cyberattacks-could-be-part-of-a-chinese-military-strategy-started-nearly-20-years-ago/.

41. Bill Gertz, "D.C. to Beijing: Stand Down on Cyber," Washington Free Beacon, March 11, 2013, http://freebeacon.com/d-c-to-beijing-stand-down-on-cyber/.

42. Freeman, "Why Did We Wait So Long?," GlobalEconomicWarfare.com, March 30, 2013 http://globaleconomicwarfare.com/2013/03/why-did-we-wait-so-long/.

43. Liberty Chick, "Islamic Hackers Vow Assault on U.S. Banks Until 'Innocence of Muslims' Removed," Breitbart.com, December 13, 2012, http://www.breitbart.com/Big-Peace/2012/12/13/Islamic-Hackers-Vow-Continued-Assault-on-US-Banks-Until-Innocence-of-Muslims-Removed.

44. Nicole Perlroth and Quentin Hardy, "Bank Hacking Was the Work of Iranians, Officials Say," *New York Times*, January 8, 2013, http://www.nytimes.com/2013/01/09/technology/online-banking-attacks-were-work-of-iran-us-officials-say.html.

45. Freeman, "Is the Cold War Really Finished?," GlobalEconomicWarfare.com, April 21, 2013, http://globaleconomicwarfare.com/2013/04/is-the-cold-war-really-finished/.

46. Freeman, "It Started in London……," GlobalEconomicWarfare.com, February 25, 2013, http://globaleconomicwarfare.com/2013/02/it-started-in-london/.

47. "Liberated Iraq Calls on Arab States to Use Oil as 'Weapon' against U.S.," FoxNews.com, November 16, 2012, http://www.foxnews.com/world/2012/11/16/liberated-iraq-calls-on-arab-states-to-use-oil-as-weapon-against-us/.

48. Jordan Hams, "The EMP Threat: Just a Scare?," *Foundry*, Heritage Foundation, March 22, 2013, http://blog.heritage.org/2013/03/22/the-emp-threat-just-a-scare/.

49. Gertz, "Inside the Ring."

50. Gertz, "Chinese Military Engaged in Political Warfare against the United States," Washington Free Beacon, October 22, 2013, http://freebeacon.com/chinese-military-engaged-in-political-warfare-against-the-united-states/.

CHAPTER TWO

1.   John Carney, "Jim Cramer Was Right—They Knew Nothing!," CNBC.com, January 18, 2013, http://www.cnbc.com/id/100392107.

2.   Tom Brennan, "Stop Trading! Financial Terrorism?," CNBC.com, September 18, 2008, http://www.cnbc.com/id/26778065/Stop_Trading_Financial_Terrorism.

3.   Randall W. Forsyth, "The Other Lance Armstrongs," *Barron's*, Barrons.com, January 19, 2013, http://online.barrons.com/article/SB50001424052748703596604578235580880655900.html?mod=djembwr_h#articleTabs_article%3D1.

4.   Jason Raznick, "Even in Death, Did Osama Bin Laden Win?" *Forbes*, Forbes.com, May 3, 2011, http://www.forbes.com/sites/benzingainsights/2011/05/03/even-in-death-did-osama-bin-laden-win/.

5.   Kevin D. Freeman, "Economic Warfare: Risks and Responses: Analysis of Twenty-First Century Risks in Light of the Recent Market Collapse," June 2009, contracted report prepared for the Pentagon by Cross Consulting and Services, LLC; archived copy available at http://ia600405.us.archive.org/16/items/EconomicWarfare-RisksAndResponsesByKevinD.Freeman/Economic-Warfare-Risks-and-Responses-by-Kevin-D-Freeman.pdf.

6.   "Geithner Tells China Its Dollar Assets Are Safe," Reuters, June 1, 2009, http://www.reuters.com/article/2009/06/01/usa-china-idUSPEK14475620090601.

7.   Greg McDonald, "Art Laffer: 'Whole Economy Is Shrinking,'" Newsmax, January 31, 2013, http://www.newsmax.com/Newsfront/shrinking-output-contraction/2013/01/31/id/488250?s=al.

8.   Freeman, "Stock Prices Up, Economy Down, Fed Printing Money While Social Unrest Builds," GlobalEconomicWarfare.com, February 1, 2013, http://globaleconomicwarfare.com/2013/02/stock-prices-up-economy-down-fed-printing-money-while-social-unrest-builds/.

9.   Tyler Durden, "Guest Post: Preparing for Inflationary Times," Zero Hedge, March 31, 2013, http://www.zerohedge.com/news/2013-03-31/guest-post-preparing-inflationary-times.

10. Michael Snyder, "Quantitative Easing Worked for the Weimar Republic for a Little While Too," *Economic Collapse Blog*, September 22, 2013, http://theeconomiccollapseblog.com/archives/quantitative-easing-worked-for-the-weimar-republic-for-a-little-while-too.

11. "How Much Is Eine Million Mark Dated 1923 Worth?," WikiAnswers, http://wiki.answers.com/Q/How_much_is_eine_million_mark_dated_1923_worth.

12. Doug Hagmann, "Intelligence Insider: Obama Administration Agenda to 'Kill U.S. Dollar,'" CanadaFreePress.com, April 1, 2013, http://www.canadafreepress.com/index.php/article/54163.

13. Reuters, "Like Rate Cuts, Unconventional Easing Weakens Dollar: Fed Study," CNBC.com, April 1, 2013 http://www.cnbc.com/id/100606680.

14. Terence Jeffrey, "Government Spending per Household Exceeds Median Household Income," PoorRichardsNews.com, http://poorrichardsnews.com/post/47734771083/unsustainable-government-spending-per-household.

15.   "The Debt to the Penny and Who Holds It," U.S. Treasury, September 27, 2013, http://www.treasurydirect.gov/NP/debt/current.

16.   Gene Epstein, "Next Stop, Greece," *Barron's*, Barrons.com, February 18, 2013, http://online.barrons.com/article/SB50001424052748704852604578298123148082456.html?mod=djembwr_h#articleTabs_article%3D1.

17.   Michael Pento, "Debt Ceiling Myths," *Forbes*, Forbes.com, July 21, 2011, http://www.forbes.com/sites/michaelpento/2011/07/21/debt-ceiling-myths/.

18.   "A National Debt of $14 Trillion? Try $211 Trillion," NPR.org, August 6, 2011, http://www.npr.org/2011/08/06/139027615/a-national-debt-of-14-trillion-try-211-trillion.

19.   Alex VanNess, "China and U.S. Debt," American Thinker, March 22, 2013, http://www.americanthinker.com/2013/03/china_and_us_debt.html.

20.   Bill Gertz, "Inside the Ring: New WMD Threats," October 10, 2012, *Washington Times*, http://www.washingtontimes.com/news/2012/oct/10/inside-the-ring-new-wmd-threats/?page=all.

21.   Ibid.

22.   VanNess, "China and U.S. Debt."

23.   Dan Weil, "Ex-Fed Gov. Mishkin, Other Experts: Fed Easing Could Lead to 'Surge in Inflation,'" Moneynews.com, March 8, 2013, http://www.moneynews.com/Economy/Mishkin-Fed-inflation-rates/2013/03/08/id/493842?s=al&promo_code=12B93-1.

24.   Jim Meyers and John Bachman, "Jeb Bush: Entitlement System Will Collapse If We Don't Act Now," Newsmax.com, March 31, 2013, http://www.newsmax.com/Headline/jeb-bush-economic-growth/2013/03/31/id/497076?s=al&promo_code=12FBC-1.

25.   Gene Epstein, "Sorry, Deniers, U.S. Debt Crisis Isn't Going Away," *Barron's*, Barrons.com, May 18, 2013, http://online.barrons.com/article/SB5000142405274870455150457848105 2623543848.html?mod=djembwr_h#articleTabs_article%3D1.

26.   Jeff Cox, "Is the Dollar Dying? Why U.S. Currency Is in Danger," CNBC.com, February 14, 2013, http://www.cnbc.com/id/100461159.

27.   Glenn J. Kalinoski, "Dick Bove: U.S. Dollar Will Be 'Overthrown' as World's Reserve Currency," Moneynews.com, February 15, 2013, http://www.moneynews.com/FinanceNews/Bove-dollar-currency-reserve-China/2013/02/15/id/490589?s=al&promo_code=1278E-1.

28.   Cox, "Is the Dollar Dying? Why U.S. Currency Is in Danger."

29.   Scott Rose and Olga Tanas, "Putin Turns Black Gold to Bullion as Russia Outbuys World," Bloomberg.com, February 10, 2013, http://www.bloomberg.com/news/2013-02-10/putin-turns-black-gold-into-bullion-as-russia-out-buys-world.html.

30.   Andrew Osborn, "As If Things Weren't Bad Enough, Russian Professor Predicts End of U.S.," *Wall Street Journal*, December 29, 2008, http://online.wsj.com/article/SB123051100709638419.html.

31.   Kevin D. Freeman, "Putin Prepares for a Currency War That He Thinks (Hopes?) Will Collapse America," GlobalEconomicWarfare.com, February 11, 2013, http://globaleconomicwarfare.com/2013/02/putin-prepares-for-a-currency-war-that-he-thinks-hopes-will-collapse-america/.

32.   Tyler Durden, "Thanks, World Reserve Currency, but No Thanks: Australia and China to Enable Direct Currency Convertibility," Zero Hedge, March 31, 2013, http://www.zerohedge.com/news/2013-03-31/thanks-world-reserve-currency-no-thanks-australia-and-china-enable-direct-currency-c.

33. Ryan Villarreal, "So Long, Yankees! China and Brazil Ditch U.S. Dollar in Deal before BRICS Summit," *International Business Times*, March 26, 2013, http://www.ibtimes.com/so-long-yankees-china-brazil-ditch-us-dollar-trade-deal-brics-summit-1153415#.

34. Mike Cohen and Ilya Arkhipov, "BRICS Nations Plan New Bank to Bypass World Bank, IMF," Bloomberg.com, March 26, 2013, http://www.bloomberg.com/news/2013-03-25/brics-nations-plan-new-bank-to-bypass-world-bank-imf.html.

35. Denise Roland, "Bank of England Closes In on China Currency Deal," *Telegraph* (UK), February 22, 2013, http://www.telegraph.co.uk/finance/currency/9888141/Bank-of-England-closes-in-on-China-currency-deal.html.

36. Joe Parkinson and Emre Peker, "Turkey Swaps Gold for Iranian Gas," *Wall Street Journal*, November 23, 2012, http://online.wsj.com/article/SB10001424127887324352004578136973602198776.html.

37. Chris Blasi, "India to Pay Gold Instead of Dollars for Iranian Oil," Goldseek.com, January 24, 2012, http://news.goldseek.com/GoldSeek/1327417200.php.

38. Gao Changxin, "Asian Economies Turn to Yuan," *China Daily*, October 24, 2012, http://usa.chinadaily.com.cn/business/2012-10/24/content_15840920.htm.

39. Mike Larson, "International Investors Dump $40.8 Billion in Treasuries, the Most Ever," Money and Markets, August 15, 2013, http://www.moneyandmarkets.com/international-investors-dump-40-8-billion-in-treasuries-the-most-ever-53693.

40. Dhara Ranasinghe, "Are Treasurys Falling Out of Favor with China?," CNBC.com, May 20, 2013, http://www.cnbc.com/id/100752563.

41. "U.S. Embassy Cable—09Beijing1134," http://cables.mrkva.eu/cable.php?id=204405.

42. Deepanshu Bagchee, "Yuan Likely to Be Fully Convertible in 5 Years: PBOC Advisor," CNBC.com, September 14, 2011, http://www.cnbc.com/id/44512934.

43. Gordon Chang, "China's Currency Will Be Fully Convertible in Months," *Forbes*, Forbes.com, September 15, 2013, http://www.forbes.com/sites/gordonchang/2013/09/15/chinas-currency-will-be-fully-convertible-in-months/.

44. Marina Maksimova, "China Reportedly Planning to Back the Yuan with Gold," Russia Beyond the Headlines, July 17, 2013, http://rbth.asia/business/2013/07/17/china_reportedly_planning_to_back_the_yuan_with_gold_47997.html.

45. "How China Deals with the U.S. Strategy to Contain China," ChinaScope translation of *Qiushi* article, December 10, 2010, http://chinascope.org/main/content/view/3291/92. Original article in Chinese available through ChinaScope at http://chinascope.org/main/PDF/R20101213A_GoogleCache.pdf.

46. Freeman, "Putin Prepares for a Currency War That He Thinks (Hopes?) Will Collapse America."

47. "Year of the Yuan: China's Explosive Currency Goes Global," Russia Today, May 1, 2013, http://rt.com/business/yuan-china-currency-global-561/.

48. "Putin Wants Russia and China to Join Forces against the West," Pravda, May 6, 2012, http://english.pravda.ru/russia/politics/05-06-2012/121315-putin_china-0/#.

49. Murtaza Hussain, "Why China Might Be a Better Superpower," Al Jazeera, June 25, 2013, http://www.aljazeera.com/indepth/opinion/2013/06/201362584334716870.html.

50. Jerry Robinson, "The Rise of the Petrodollar System: 'Dollars for Oil,'" Financial Sense, February 23, 2012, http://www.financialsense.com/contributors/jerry-robinson/the-rise-of-the-petrodollar-system-dollars-for-oil.

51. "China Exceeds U.S. to Become Saudi Arabia's Top Oil Customer," *Global Times*, February 23, 2010, http://www.globaltimes.cn/business/china-economy/2010-02/507404.html.

52.   Kaleem Kawaja, "Are Petrodollar-Rich Muslims Responsible for Muslim-on-Muslim Oppression?," Ummah, April 9, 2013, http://www.ummah.com/forum/showthread. php?374003-Are-petrodollar-rich-Muslims-responsible-for-Muslim-on-Muslim-oppression.

53.   Howard LaFranchi, "How Arab Spring Turned into Protests and 'Death to America!,'" Christian Science Monitor, September 17, 2012, http://www.csmonitor.com/USA/Foreign-Policy/2012/0917/How-Arab-Spring-turned-into-protests-and-Death-to-America!

54.   John Rubino, "China, Russia, and the End of the Petrodollar," DollarCollapse.com, October 9, 2012, http://dollarcollapse.com/dollar-5/china-russia-and-the-end-of-the-petrodollar/.

55.   "China's Yuan Set to Become Global Reserve Currency with Gold Backing?," Zero Hedge, July 25, 2013, http://www.zerohedge.com/contributed/2013-07-25/china's-yuan-set-become-global-reserve-currency-gold-backing.

56.   Alan Wheatley, "China's Yuan Could Challenge Dollar Role in a Decade," Reuters, August 30, 2011, http://www.reuters.com/article/2011/08/30/us-economy-global-eclipse-idUSTRE77T2GX20110830.

57.   Ambrose Evans-Pritchard, "Beijing Hints at Bond Attack on Japan," Telegraph (UK), September 18, 2012, http://www.telegraph.co.uk/finance/china-business/9551727/Beijing-hints-at-bond-attack-on-Japan.html.

58.   Chris Mack, "Is This Time Different for the Dollar?," Resource Investor, January 24, 2011, http://www.resourceinvestor.com/2011/01/24/is-this-time-different-for-the-dollar.

59.   "Pimco's Gross Calls US Economy 'Supernova' on Path to Extinction," Moneynews.com, February 1, 2013, http://www.moneynews.com/StreetTalk/pimco-gross-economy-extinction/2013/02/01/id/488443?s=al.

60.   Brad Plumer, "Could Two Platinum Coins Solve the Debt-Ceiling Crisis?," Washington Post, December 7, 2012, http://www.washingtonpost.com/blogs/wonkblog/wp/2012/12/07/could-two-platinum-coins-solve-the-debt-ceiling-crisis/.

61.   James A. Kostohryz, "The Trillion Dollar Coin Idea: Beyond Stupid," Seeking Alpha, December 10, 2012, http://seekingalpha.com/article/1054491-the-trillion-dollar-coin-idea-beyond-stupid.

62.   James Rickards, Currency Wars: The Making of the Next Global Crisis (New York: Penguin/ Portfolio, 2011).

63.   Jeff Cox, "U.S. to Win Currency War, Then 'Implode': Schiff," CNBC.com, February 12, 2013, http://www.cnbc.com/id/100453993.

64.   Peter Schiff, "The Biggest Currency Printers Will Be the Biggest Losers," BusinessInsider. com, February 3, 2013, http://www.businessinsider.com/the-biggest-loser-2013-2.

65.   "China Ready to Go to War to Safeguard National Interests," Times of India, February 12, 2011, http://articles.timesofindia.indiatimes.com/2011-02-12/china/28545343_1_china-countries-communist-party.

66.   Ernest Hancock, "The End Is Nigh! No, Really. It Is!," FreedomsPhoenix.com, April 17, 2012, http://www.freedomsphoenix.com/Article/109991-2012-04-17-the-end-is-nigh-no-really-it-is.htm?From=News.

67.   Julie Crawshaw and Forrest Jones, "WSJ: Fed Buying 61 Percent of U.S. Debt," Moneynews. com, March 28, 2012, http://www.moneynews.com/Headline/fed-debt-Treasury/2012/03/28/id/434106?s=al&promo_code=E92C-1.

68.   Ben Shapiro, "Fed Announces Possible End to Quantitative Easing, Stocks Crash," Breitbart.com, June 19, 2013, http://www.breitbart.com/Big-Government/2013/06/19/Fed-chair-pump-stock-crash.

69. Freeman, "Lessons From Egypt," GlobalEconomicWarfare.com, February 11, 2011, http://globaleconomicwarfare.com/2011/02/lessons-from-egypt/.

70. Marco Lagi, Yavni Bar-Yam, Karla Z. Bertrand, and Yaneer Bar-Yam, "The Food Crises: A Quantitative Model of Food Prices Including Speculators and Ethanol Conversion," New England Complex Systems Institute, September 21, 2011, http://necsi.edu/research/social/foodprices.html.

71. Lagi, Bertrand, Bar-Yam, "The Food Crises and Political Instability in North Africa and the Middle East," New England Complex Systems Institute, August 10, 2011, http://necsi.edu/research/social/foodcrises.html.

72. Nafeez Mosaddeq Ahmed, "Why Food Riots Are Likely to Become the New Normal," *Guardian*, March 6, 2013, http://www.theguardian.com/environment/blog/2013/mar/06/food-riots-new-normal.

73. "Where Does All That Food Come From?," Discovery Channel, December 13, 2012, http://news.discovery.com/history/us-history/american-thanksgiving-dinner-121120.htm.

74. Luís Aguiar-Conraria and Yi Wen, "Understanding the Large Negative Impact of Oil Shocks," Federal Reserve Bank of St. Louis, Working Paper Series, January 12, 2006, http://research.stlouisfed.org/wp/2005/2005-042.pdf.

75. "Liberated Iraq Calls on Arab States to Use Oil as 'Weapon' against U.S.," FoxNews.com, November 16, 2012, http://www.foxnews.com/world/2012/11/16/liberated-iraq-calls-on-arab-states-to-use-oil-as-weapon-against-us/.

76. Robert Lenzner, "Speculation in Crude Oil Adds $23.39 to the Price per Barrel," *Forbes*, Forbes.com, February 27, 2012, http://www.forbes.com/sites/robertlenzner/2012/02/27/speculation-in-crude-oil-adds-23-39-to-the-price-per-barrel/.

77. "Beijing Diversifies Away from U.S. Dollar," *Wall Street Journal*, March 2, 2012, http://online.wsj.com/article/SB10001424052970203753704577254794068655760.html.

78. "No Risk to Dollar If China Expands Yuan's Role," Reuters, March 8, 2012.

79. Freeman, "Don't Worry, Tim Geithner Says the Dollar Will Be Fine," GlobalEconomicWarfare.com, March 12, 2012, http://globaleconomicwarfare.com/2012/03/dont-worry-tim-geithner-says-the-dollar-will-be-fine/.

80. Juan C. Zarate, *Treasury's War: The Unleashing of a New Era of Financial Warfare* (New York: PublicAffairs, 2013), 401–2.

81. Philip Aldrick, "Hu Calls on China to Develop Domestic Economy," *Telegraph*, November 8, 2012, http://www.telegraph.co.uk/journalists/philip-aldrick/9663920/Hu-calls-on-China-to-develop-domestic-economy.html.

82. "Asian Growth Needs Stronger Currencies: IMF," TerraDaily, October 6, 2010, http://www.terradaily.com/reports/Asian_growth_needs_stronger_currencies_IMF_999.html.

83. Freeman, "The Chinese Take a Long Term View; Evaluating Their 5YP," GlobalEconomicWarfare.com, February 21, 2011, http://globaleconomicwarfare.com/2011/02/the-chinese-take-a-long-term-view-evaluating-their-5yp/.

84. Freeman, "Unrestricted Warfare," GlobalEconomicWarfare.com, January 14, 2011, http://globaleconomicwarfare.com/2011/01/unrestricted-warfare/.

85. "Spiegel Interview with George Soros," Spiegel Online, *Der Spiegel*, August 15, 2011, http://www.spiegel.de/international/europe/spiegel-interview-with-george-soros-you-need-this-dirty-word-euro-bonds-a-780189.html.

CHAPTER THREE

1. Daniel Doherty, "Oh My: More People Collecting Food Stamps in the United States Than Living in Spain," Townhall.com, April 27, 2013, http://townhall.com/tipsheet/danieldoherty/2013/04/27/oh-my-more-people-collecting-food-stamps-in-the-united-states-than-living-in-spain-n1580000.

2. Wynton Hall, "Exclusive: Food Stamp Recipients Outnumber Populations of 24 States Combined," Breitbart.com, November 23, 2012, http://www.breitbart.com/Big-Government/2012/11/23/Exclusive-Food-Stamp-Recipients-Outnumber-Populations-Of-24-States-Combined.

3. "New Record: 15 Percent of Americans on Food Stamps," RT.com, March 11, 2013, http://rt.com/usa/food-stamps-record-americans-119/.

4. Siemond Chan, "Food Stamp Issue Derails Farm Bill as Recipients at Record High," Yahoo! Finance, June 27, 2013, http://finance.yahoo.com/blogs/the-exchange/food-stamp-issue-derails-farm-bill-recipients-record-150015885.html.

5. Neil Munro, "Native-Born Americans Gained No Jobs since 2000, Says Report," Daily Caller, July 3, 2013, http://dailycaller.com/2013/07/03/native-born-americans-gained-no-jobs-since-2000-says-report/#ixzz2Y1PGu7Q4.

6. "BLS Spotlight on Statistics: The Recession of 2007–2009," Bureau of Labor Statistics, February 2012, http://www.bls.gov/spotlight/2012/recession/.

7. Peter Ferrara, "Economically, Could Obama Be America's Worst President?," *Forbes*, Forbes.com, June 2, 2013, http://www.forbes.com/sites/peterferrara/2013/06/02/economically-could-obama-be-americas-worst-president/.

8. Markos Kaminis, "True Unemployment Is 17.6%, Not 7.6%," Seeking Alpha, June 7, 2013, http://seekingalpha.com/article/1488832-true-unemployment-is-17-6-not-7-6?source=google_news.

9. Paul Wiseman and Jesse Washington, "U.S. Labor Force Participation Rate Lowest since 1979," Huffington Post, April 6, 2013, http://www.huffingtonpost.com/2013/04/06/labor-force-participation-rate_n_3028135.html.

10. Nick Beams, "After Strong Growth, World Economy at a 'Turning Point,'" World Socialist Web Site, April 24, 2007, http://www.wsws.org/en/articles/2007/04/grow-a24.html.

11. David Feith, "Timothy Thomas: Why China Is Reading Your Email," *Wall Street Journal*, March 29, 2013, http://online.wsj.com/article/SB10001424127887323419104578376042379430724.html.

12. Ibid.

13. "China Ready to Go to War to Safeguard National Interests," *Times of India*, February 12, 2011, http://articles.timesofindia.indiatimes.com/2011-02-12/china/28545343_1_china-countries-communist-party.

14. Wayne M. Morrison and Marc Labonte, *China's Holdings of U.S. Securities: Implications for the U.S. Economy*, Congressional Research Service, August 19, 2013, 17, http://www.fas.org/sgp/crs/row/RL34314.pdf.

15. Rosa Prince, "George Soros Predicts Class War and Riots," *Telegraph* (UK), January 24, 2012, http://www.telegraph.co.uk/finance/financialcrisis/9036889/George-Soros-predicts-class-war-and-riots.html.

16. "George Soros Predicts Riots, Police State and Class War for America," RT.com, January 24, 2012, http://rt.com/usa/george-soros-class-war-619/.

17. John C. Williams, "The Risk of Deflation," Federal Reserve Bank of San Francisco, March 27, 2009, http://www.frbsf.org/economic-research/publications/economic-letter/2009/march/risk-deflation/.

18. Ibid.
19. A. Gary Shilling, "Why Global Economies Face an Age of Deflation," Bloomberg.com, March, 20, 2013, http://www.bloomberg.com/news/2013-03-20/why-global-economies-face-an-age-of-deflation.htm.
20. Rick Newman, "4 Reasons to Fear Deflation," *U.S. News & World Report*, July 20, 2010, http://money.usnews.com/money/blogs/flowchart/2010/07/20/4-reasons-to-fear-deflation.
21. Mark Gongloff, "Markets Sell Off Sharply after Bernanke Talks of Quantitative Easing Slowdown," Huffington Post, June 20, 2013, http://www.huffingtonpost.com/2013/06/19/bernanke-markets_n_3467940.html.
22. Charles Riley, "Bank of Japan Takes Fight to Deflation," CNN Money, CNN.com, April 5, 2013, http://money.cnn.com/2013/04/04/news/economy/bank-of-japan-decision/index.html.
23. Rodrigo Campos, "U.S. Stocks—Summers' Withdrawal Signals Dovish Fed, Wall St Rises," Reuters, September 16, 2013, http://www.reuters.com/article/2013/09/16/markets-usa-stocks-idUSL2N0HC17G20130916.
24. Alex Crippen, "Warren Buffett: Failure to Raise Debt Limit Would Be 'Most Asinine Act' Ever by Congress," CNBC.com, April 30, 2011, http://www.cnbc.com/id/42836791.
25. Martin Fridson, "Is S&P's U.S. Debt Warning Politically Motivated?," *Forbes*, Forbes.com, May 5, 2011, http://www.forbes.com/sites/investor/2011/05/05/is-sps-u-s-debt-warning-politically-motivated/.
26. "Obama Begins Push for New National Retirement System," National Seniors Council, originally posted October 13, 2010, http://www.nationalseniorscouncil.org/index.php?option=com_content&view=article&id=89:obama-begins-push-for-new-national-retirement-system&catid=34:social-security&Itemid=62.
27. Jerome Corsi, "Now Obama Wants Your 401(k)," WND, November 25, 2012, http://www.wnd.com/2012/11/now-obama-wants-your-401k/.
28. Dagmara Leszkowicz and Chris Borowski, "Poland Reduces Public Debt through Pension Funds Overhaul," Reuters, September 4, 2013, http://www.reuters.com/article/2013/09/04/poland-pensions-idUSL6N0H02UV20130904.
29. Ambrose Evans-Pritchard, "German 'Wise Men' Push for Wealth Seizure to Fund EMU Bail-Outs," *Daily Telegraph* (UK), April 14, 2013, http://www.telegraph.co.uk/finance/financialcrisis/9993691/German-Wise-Men-push-for-wealth-seizure-to-fund-EMU-bail-outs.html?utm_source=GraphicMail&utm_medium=email&utm_term=NewsletterLink&utm_campaign=2013+King+Report+Master&utm_content=.
30. Amy Feldman, "President Obama Thinks Your IRA Is Too Big," *Barron's*, Barrons.com, June 22, 2013, http://online.barrons.com/article/SB50001424052748704311204578555881264127620.html#articleTabs_article%3D0.
31. Richard Evans, "'There Will Be More Wealth Confiscation, without a Doubt,'" *Daily Telegraph* (UK), April 30, 2013, http://www.telegraph.co.uk/finance/personalfinance/investing/10027101/There-will-be-more-wealth-confiscation-without-a-doubt-Saxo-Banks-Lars-Christensen.html.
32. "Government Took Gold in 1930, Now They're Taking Bank Accounts," World Order News, April 5, 2013, http://www.worldordernews.com/government-took-gold-in-1930-now-theyre-taking-bank-accounts/.
33. "Hiking Taxes to Balance the Budget Would Require Doubling Tax Rates," Federal Budget in Pictures, Heritage Foundation, accessed September 2013, http://www.heritage.org/federalbudget/entitlements-double-tax-rates.

34. Lawrence Goodman, "Demand for U.S. Debt Is Not Limitless," *Wall Street Journal*, March 27, 2012, http://online.wsj.com/article/SB10001424052702304450004577279754275393064.html.

35. "IMF Members' Quotas and Voting Power, and IMF Board of Governors," International Monetary Fund, July 14, 2013, updated November 6, 2013, http://www.imf.org/external/np/sec/memdir/members.aspx.

36. "Top Ten Reasons to Oppose the IMF," Global Exchange, http://www.globalexchange.org/resources/wbimf/oppose

37. Matt Krantz and Elizabeth Weise, "China Continues to Target U.S. Companies," *USA Today*, May 29, 2013, http://www.usatoday.com/story/money/business/2013/05/29/china-shuanghui-smithfield/2369565/.

38. Kenneth Rapoza, "The Foreign Companies That Are Buying Up America," *Forbes*, Forbes.com, June 27, 2013, http://www.forbes.com/sites/kenrapoza/2013/06/27/the-foreign-companies-that-are-buying-up-america/.

39. Michelle Caruso-Cabrera, "Forget the Headlines: Chinese Buying Big in U.S.," CNBC.com, May 22, 2013, http://www.cnbc.com/id/100751502.

40. Michael Snyder, "The Federal Reserve Is Paying Banks NOT to Lend $1.8 Trillion to the American People," *The Economic Collapse Blog*, July 1, 2013, http://theeconomiccollapseblog.com/archives/the-federal-reserve-is-paying-banks-not-to-lend-1-8-trillion-dollars-to-the-american-people.

41. Martin Hutchinson, "Why There's No Real Inflation (Yet)," Money Morning, January 30, 2013, http://moneymorning.com/2013/01/30/why-theres-no-real-inflation-yet/.

42. "The Worst Hyperinflation Situations of All Time," CNBC.com, http://www.cnbc.com/id/41532451/page/9.

43. Matthew O'Brien, "Hyperinflation Hype: Why the U.S. Can Never Be Weimar," *Atlantic*, March 21, 2012, http://www.theatlantic.com/business/archive/2012/03/the-hyperinflation-hype-why-the-us-can-never-be-weimar/254715/.

44. Tyler Durden, "Guest Post: Preparing for Inflationary Times," Zero Hedge, March 31, 2013, http://www.zerohedge.com/news/2013-03-31/guest-post-preparing-inflationary-times.

45. Marc Slavo, "Just in Time: When the Trucks Stop, America Will Stop (With Immediate and Catastrophic Consequences)," SHTFplan.com, April 2, 2012, http://www.shtfplan.com/emergency-preparedness/just-in-time-when-the-trucks-stop-america-will-stop-with-immediate-and-catastrophic-consequences_04022012.

46. John S. Foster Jr., Earl Gjelde, William R. Graham et al., *Report of the Commission to Assess the Threat to the United States from Electromagnetic Pulse (EMP) Attack*, vol. 1: *Executive Report* (Washington, D.C.: Government Printing Office, 2004), 134–137, http://www.empcommission.org/docs/empc_exec_rpt.pdf.

47. Ibid.

CHAPTER FOUR

1. Frank Gaffney Jr., "E.M.P. Vulnerability Invites Catastrophe," Center for Security Policy, July 29, 2013, http://www.centerforsecuritypolicy. org/2013/07/29/e-m-p-vulnerability-invites-catastrophe/.

2. Christopher Klein, "A Perfect Solar Superstorm: The 1859 Carrington Event," History.com, March 14, 2012, http://www.history.com/news/a-perfect-solar-superstorm-the-1859-carrington-event.

3. Ellie Zolfagharifard, "A Near Miss for Earth: Solar Flare That Could Have Knocked Out Power, Cars and Phones Came So Close Two Weeks Ago," *Daily Mail* (UK), August 1, 2013, http://www.dailymail.co.uk/sciencetech/article-2382527/A-near-miss-Earth-Devastating-electromagnetic-pulses-knocked-power-cars-phones-occured-weeks-ago.html#ixzz2ggtgD0ws.

4. F. Michael Maloof, "Now Lloyd's of London Warns of EMP: Industry Giant Says 'Extended Outage' Could Be Measured in Years," WND, July 28, 2013, http://www.wnd.com/2013/07/now-lloyds-of-london-warns-of-emp/.

5. Zolfagharifard, "A Near Miss for Earth."

6. Ibid.

7. Office of Electricity Delivery and Energy Reliability, *Large Power Transformers and the U.S. Electric Grid*, U.S. Department of Energy, June 2012, http://energy.gov/sites/prod/files/Large%20Power%20Transformer%20Study%20-%20June%202012_0.pdf.

8. Eyder Peralta, "Kim Jong Il's Legacy? 'North Korea Is Dark,'" NPR, December 19, 2011, http://www.npr.org/blogs/thetwo-way/2011/12/19/143960966/kim-jong-ils-legacy-north-korea-is-dark.

9. Henry F. Cooper, "Former CIA Director Warns about the Existential EMP Threat," High Frontier, August 2, 2013, http://highfrontier.org/august-2-2013-former-cia-director-warns-about-the-existential-emp-threat/#sthash.WeuJhhzi.sMfshATu.dpbs.

10. "Preventing Armageddon Would Cost Only $100 Million ... but Congress Is Too Thick to Approve the Fix," Washington's Blog, November 22, 2012, http://www.washingtonsblog.com/2012/11/preventing-armageddon-would-cost-only-100-million-but-congress-is-too-thick-to-approve-the-fix.html.

11. F. Michael Maloof, "Congress Told: U.S. Life 'Unsustainable' after EMP," WND, September 12, 2012, http://www.wnd.com/2012/09/congress-told-u-s-life-unsustainable-after-emp/.

12. Michael Snyder, "A Massive Electromagnetic Pulse Could Collapse the Economy in a Single Moment," Infowars.com, January 1, 2013, http://www.infowars.com/a-massive-electromagnetic-pulse-could-collapse-the-economy-in-a-single-moment/.

13. Henry F. Cooper, "Former CIA Director Warns about the Existential EMP Threat," High Frontier, August 2, 2013, http://highfrontier.org/august-2-2013-former-cia-director-warns-about-the-existential-emp-threat/#sthash.WeuJhhzi.sMfshATu.dpbs.

14. See the EMP Coalition's website at http://stopemp.org.

15. Andrea Boland, "What Maine Did to Secure Its Electric Grid from Electromagnetic Pulse and Geomagnetic Disturbance," OurEnergyPolicy.org, August 8, 2013, http://www.ourenergypolicy.org/what-maine-did-to-secure-its-electric-grid-from-electromagnetic-pulse-and-geomagnetic-disturbance/.

16. Farhad Manjoo, "Apocalypse Then: A Two-Part Series on the Lessons of Y2K," Slate, November 11, 2009, http://www.slate.com/articles/technology/technology/features/2009/apocalypse_then/was_y2k_a_waste.html.

17. Qiao Liang and Wang Xiangsui, *Unrestricted Warfare: China's Master Plan to Destroy America* (Beijing: PLA Literature and Arts Publishing House, 1999). FBIS translated selections available at http://www.c4i.org/unrestricted.pdf.

18. "Doug Kass: Cyberattack Will Shut Down NYSE," Moneynews.com, November 23, 2010, http://www.moneynews.com/StreetTalk/Doug-Kass-Cyberattack-Shut/2010/11/23/id/377907?s=al&promo_code=B2B1-1.

19. Brian Wingfield, "Former Intelligence Chief Says a Cyber Attack Is Inevitable," *Forbes*, Forbes.com, November 23, 2010, http://www.forbes.com/sites/brianwingfield/2010/11/23/former-intelligence-chief-says-a-cyber-attack-is-inevitable/print/.

20. AFP, "Destructive Cyber Attack Inevitable: NSA Chief," Spacewar.com, February 17, 2011, http://www.spacewar.com/reports/Destructive_cyber_attack_inevitable_NSA_chief_999.html.

21. Devlin Barrett, "Hackers Penetrate Nasdaq's Computers," *Wall Street Journal*, February 5, 2011, http://online.wsj.com/article/SB10001424052748704709304576124502351634690.html.

22. Michael Riley, "U.S. Spy Agency Is Said to Investigate Nasdaq Hacker Attack," Bloomberg.com, March 30, 2011, http://www.bloomberg.com/news/2011-03-30/u-s-spy-agency-said-to-focus-its-decrypting-skills-on-nasdaq-cyber-attack.html.

23. Associated Press, "FBI Director: Cyber-Threats Will Become Top Worry," Newsmax, March 1, 2012, http://www.newsmax.com/Newsfront/FBIDirector-Cybersecurity/2012/03/01/id/431171?s=al&promo_code=E4F7-1.

24. Elisabeth Bumiller and Thom Shanker, "Panetta Warns of Dire Threat of Cyberattack on U.S.," *New York Times*, October 11, 2012, http://www.nytimes.com/2012/10/12/world/panetta-warns-of-dire-threat-of-cyberattack.html?pagewanted=all&_r=1&.

25. Jack Cloherty, "Cyber Terrorism: Al Qaeda Video Calls for 'Electronic Jihad,'" ABCNews.com, May 22, 2012, http://abcnews.go.com/Politics/cyber-terrorism-al-qaeda-video-calls-electronic-jihad/story?id=16407875#.UcyosmCCI6F.

26. Ken Jensen, "Cybersecurity: Still at the 'Closing the Barn Door after the Horse Has Bolted' Stage," *Weekly Standard*, May 6, 2013, http://www.weeklystandard.com/print/blogs/cybersecurity-still-closing-barn-door-after-horse-has-bolted-stage_722528.html?nopager=1%5D.

27. Shaun Waterman, "U.S. Banks Warned of Cyberattack on Accounts," *Washington Times*, December 14, 2012, http://www.washingtontimes.com/news/2012/dec/14/us-banks-warned-of-cyber-attack-on-accounts/.

28. David E. Sanger, "Mutually Assured Destruction: Old Concept in a New Venue," TwinCities.com, June 2, 2012, http://www.twincities.com/ci_20770936/mutually-assured-destruction-old-concept-new-venue.

29. Mark Buchanan, "Flash-Crash Story Looks More like a Fairy Tale," Bloomberg.com, May 7, 2012, http://www.bloomberg.com/news/2012-05-07/flash-crash-story-looks-more-like-a-fairy-tale.html.

30. Matthew Philips, "How the Robots Lost: High-Frequency Trading's Rise and Fall," Businessweek.com, June 6, 2013, http://www.businessweek.com/articles/2013-06-06/how-the-robots-lost-high-frequency-tradings-rise-and-fall#p1.

31. Barry Ritholtz, "What Happens during 1 Second of HFT?," *The Big Picture* (blog), May 7, 2013, http://www.ritholtz.com/blog/2013/05/what-happens-during-1-second-of-hft/.

32. David Zeiler, "High-Frequency Trading Could Cause Another Flash Crash," Money Morning, February 1, 2012, http://moneymorning.com/2012/02/01/high-frequency-trading-could-cause-another-flash-crash/.

33. "Expert: HFT Has Gamed the System—There's No Room for Traders Anymore," Financial Sense, April 17, 2013, http://www.financialsense.com/contributors/fs-staff/dave-lauer/hft-has-gamed-the-system.

34. Kara Scannell, "U.S. Brokerage Settles Manipulation Charges," *Financial Times*, September 25, 2012, http://www.ft.com/intl/cms/s/0/fb30556c-074a-11e2-b148-00144feabdc0.html#axzz2XiqVVp4g.

35. Maureen Farrell, "Mini Flash Crashes: A Dozen a Day," CNN Money, CNN.com, March 20, 2013, http://money.cnn.com/2013/03/20/investing/mini-flash-crash/index.html.

36. Jim McTague, "How Foreigners Could Disrupt U.S. Markets," *Barron's*, available through the University of Delaware Library, September 11, 2010, http://green.lib.udel.edu/webarchives/kaufman.senate.gov/press/in_the_news/news/-id=0a760c05-5056-9502-5df6-cc9220d44e1d.htm.

37. John Bates, "Sniffing Out Socialbots: The Combustive Potential of Social Media–Based Algorithms," Huffington Post, December 2, 2011, http://www.huffingtonpost.com/john-bates/financial-trading-algorithms_b_1125334.html?view=screen.

38. Heidi Moore, "AP Twitter Hack Causes Panic on Wall Street and Sends Dow Plunging," *Guardian* (UK), April 23, 2013, http://www.guardian.co.uk/business/2013/apr/23/ap-tweet-hack-wall-street-freefall.

39. Jake Zamansky, "The 'Twitter Crash' Is 'Flash Crash' Redux," *Forbes*, Forbes.com, May 1, 2013, http://www.forbes.com/sites/jakezamansky/2013/05/01/the-twitter-crash-is-flash-crash-redux/.

40. David Zeiler, "Why the Twitter Flash Crash Should Make You Angry," Money Morning, April 25, 2013, http://moneymorning.com/2013/04/25/why-the-twitter-flash-crash-should-make-you-angry/.

41. Richard Miniter, "Hacked! When Will We Start to Defend America's Computers?," *Gazette*, June 23, 2011, http://gazette.com/article/120320.

42. Rob Iati, "The Real Story of Trading Software Espionage," Wall Street & Technology, July 10, 2009, http://www.advancedtrading.com/algorithms/the-real-story-of-trading-software-espio/218401501.

43. "New Charges for Ex-Goldman Programmer in Code Theft Case," Reuters, August 9, 2012, http://www.reuters.com/article/2012/08/09/goldman-programmer-charges-idUSWEN697020120809.

44. "Rep. Kanjorski: $550 Billion Disappeared in 'Electronic Run on the Banks,'" Live Leak, February 7, 2011, http://www.liveleak.com/view?i=ca2_1234032281.

45. Richard W. Fisher, "Ending 'Too Big to Fail,'" remarks before the Conservative Political Action Conference, National Harbor, Maryland, March 16, 2013, transcript, Federal Reserve Bank of Dallas, http://www.dallasfed.org/news/speeches/fisher/2013/fs130316.cfm.

46. Steve Denning, "Banks Still Too-Big-To-Fail," *Forbes*, Forbes.com, March 24, 2013, http://www.forbes.com/sites/stevedenning/2013/03/24/banks-still-too-big-to-fail-six-things-the-fed-must-do/.

47. Editorial Board, "Rogue Banks Remain Too Big to Fail: Our View," *USA Today*, May 19, 2013, http://www.usatoday.com/story/opinion/2013/05/19/too-big-to-fail-15-capital-reserve-editorials-debates/2324843/.

48. "Historical Debt Outstanding—Annual 2000–2012," TreasuryDirect, last updated January 16, 2013, http://www.treasurydirect.gov/govt/reports/pd/histdebt/histdebt_histo5.htm.

49. Becket Adams, "Sound Like Cyprus? The SEC Proposed This Strict New Rule on Money Market Account Withdrawals," The Blaze, June 10, 2013, http://www.theblaze.com/stories/2013/06/10/sound-like-cyprus-the-sec-proposed-this-strict-new-rule-on-money-market-account-withdrawals/.

50. George Soros, "One Way to Stop Bear Raids," *Wall Street Journal*, March 24, 2009, http://online.wsj.com/article/SB123785310594719693.html.

51. Vedant Misra, Marco Lagi, and Yaneer Bar-Yam, "Evidence of Market Manipulation in the Financial Crisis," New England Complex Systems Institute, December 13, 2011, updated January 4, 2012, http://necsi.edu/research/economics/bearraid.html.

52. Matthew Vadum, "Stephen Lerner, SEIU Neo-Communist Union Boss, Uses #OWS to Spread Fear, Economic Mayhem," Breitbart.com, October 20, 2011, http://www.breitbart.com/Big-Government/2011/10/20/Stephen-Lerner--SEIU-Neo-Communist-Union-Boss--Uses--OWS-to-Spread-Fear--Economic-Mayhem.

53. Peter Schiff, "The FDIC Lacks the Resources to Cover Major Losses in a Systemic Failure," *Peter Schiff Blog*, March 24, 2013, http://peterschiffblog.blogspot.com/2013/03/the-fdic-lacks-resources-to-cover-major.html.

54. "Ten-Year Treasury Yield Tops 2%," *Wall Street Journal*, May 22, 2013, http://online.wsj.com/article/SB10001424127887323475304578498900160794578.html.

55. Mark Trumbull, "Tax Revenue to Hit Record This Year. So Is Spending 'the Problem'?," *Christian Science Monitor*, March 4, 2013, http://www.csmonitor.com/USA/DC-Decoder/2013/0304/Tax-revenue-to-hit-record-this-year.-So-is-spending-the-problem.

56. Jeff Cox, "Is the Dollar Dying? Why U.S. Currency Is in Danger," CNBC.com, February 14, 2013, http://www.cnbc.com/id/100461159.

CHAPTER FIVE

1. Jared Cummans, "Seven Warren Buffett Quotes on Gold Investing," CommodityHQ.com, October 2, 2012, http://commodityhq.com/2012/top-seven-warren-buffet-quotes-on-gold-investing/.

2. Mike Fuljenz, "'Buffett the Gold Slayer' Doesn't Understand Gold," Moneynews.com, July 1, 2013, http://www.moneynews.com/MikeFuljenz/Buffett-gold-stocks-understand/2013/07/01/id/512816?s=al.

3. Alan Greenspan, "Gold and Economic Freedom," in *Capitalism: The Unknown Ideal*, ed. Ayn Rand (New York: New American Library, 1966). Essay available through the Constitution Society, http://www.constitution.org/mon/greenspan_gold.htm.

4. "A History of Gold," *Daily Telegraph* (UK), December 4, 2010, http://www.telegraph.co.uk/finance/newsbysector/industry/mining/8180569/A-history-of-gold.html.

5. "Thomas Paine on Paper Money," Ludwig von Mises Institute, April 24, 2008, https://mises.org/daily/2942.

6. "Thomas Jefferson: 'Paper Is Poverty. It Is Only the Ghost of Money, and Not Money Itself,'" TheGoldStandardNow.org, http://www.thegoldstandardnow.org/jefferson.

7. "Geo. Washington on Unfunded Paper Money," BarefootsWorld.net, http://www.barefootsworld.net/gwpapermoney.html.

8. Nathan Lewis, "A Brief History of the Dollar," Huffington Post, November 6, 2009, http://www.huffingtonpost.com/nathan-lewis/a-brief-history-of-the-do_b_348253.html.

9. Harry C. Veryser, *It Didn't Have to Be This Way* (Wilmington, DE: Intercollegiate Studies Institute, 2012), 63.

10. Adrian Ash, "Governments Still Heavy-Handed 80 Years after FDR's Gold Confiscation," *Forbes*, Forbes.com, April 5, 2013, http://www.forbes.com/sites/greatspeculations/2013/04/05/governments-still-heavy-handed-80-years-after-fdrs-gold-confiscation/.

11. Richard G. Anderson, "U.S. Quantitative Easing: The 1930s," *Economic Synopses*, no. 17, 2010, http://research.stlouisfed.org/publications/es/10/ES1017.pdf.

12. Eric Rauchway, "How Franklin Roosevelt Secretly Ended the Gold Standard," Bloomberg.com, March 21, 2013, http://www.bloomberg.com/news/2013-03-21/how-franklin-roosevelt-secretly-ended-the-gold-standard.html.

13. Thomas E. Woods Jr., "The Great Gold Robbery of 1933," Ludwig von Mises Institute, August 13, 2008, http://mises.org/daily/3056.

14. Daniel Yergin and Joseph Stanislaw, *The Commanding Heights* (New York: Free Press, 1997), 60–64. Excerpt available at *Commanding Heights*, PBS, http://www.pbs.org/wgbh/commandingheights/shared/minitext/ess_nixongold.html.

15. Dhara Ranasinghe and Ansuya Harjani, "Bernanke Doesn't Understand Gold, Should We?," CNBC.com, July 19, 2013, http://www.cnbc.com/id/100898244.

16. Ralph Benko, "The Emerging New Monetarism: Gold Convertibility to Save the Euro," *Forbes*, Forbes.com, June 13, 2011, http://www.forbes.com/sites/ralphbenko/2011/06/13/the-emerging-new-monetarism-gold-convertibility-to-save-the-euro/.

17. Steve Forbes, "Advance Look: What the New Gold Standard Will Look Like," *Forbes*, Forbes.com, May 8, 2013, http://www.forbes.com/sites/steveforbes/2013/05/08/heres-what-a-new-gold-standard-could-look-like/.

18. Ralph Benko, "Fiat Money: The Root Cause of Our Financial Disaster," *Forbes*, Forbes.com, August 15, 2011, http://www.forbes.com/sites/ralphbenko/2011/08/15/fiat-money-the-root-cause-of-our-financial-disaster/.

19. "Inflation: The Value of the Pound, 1750–2002," Research Paper 03/82, House of Commons Library, November 11, 2003, http://www.parliament.uk/documents/commons/lib/research/rp2003/rp03-082.pdf.

20. Eric McWhinnie, "How Much Gold Exists in the World?," WallStCheatSheet.com, April 9, 2013, http://wallstcheatsheet.com/stocks/how-much-gold-exists-in-the-world.html/?a=viewall.

21. "The Many Uses of Gold," Geology.com, accessed September 2013, http://geology.com/minerals/gold/uses-of-gold.shtml.

22. Jeanette Rodrigues, "India Urges Resisting Gold as Curbs Fail to Stem Currency Slump," Bloomberg.com, July 2, 2013, http://www.bloomberg.com/news/2013-07-02/india-urges-resisting-gold-as-curbs-fail-to-stem-currency-slump.html.

23. "The New Era in Gold Repatriation Will Affect Everything," Daily Bell, March 5, 2013, http://www.thedailybell.com/28785/The-New-Era-in-Gold-Repatriation-Will-Affect-Everything.

24. John Browne, "German Gold Claw Back Causes Concern," January 22, 2013, Euro Pacific Capital Inc., http://www.europac.net/commentaries/german_gold_claw_back_causes_concern.

25. "The New Era in Gold Repatriation Will Affect Everything."

26. Browne, "German Gold Claw Back Causes Concern."

27. "The New Era in Gold Repatriation Will Affect Everything."

28. Amine Bouchentouf, "How Hedge Funds Influence Gold Markets," Seeking Alpha, June 27, 2013, http://seekingalpha.com/article/1525222-how-hedge-funds-influence-gold-markets.

29. Jason Tillberg, "The Hunt Brothers: How They Did It and What We Can Learn from It," Seeking Alpha, March 4, 2011, http://seekingalpha.com/instablog/170390-jason-tillberg/144117-the-hunt-brothers-how-they-did-it-and-what-we-can-learn-from-it.

30. Paul Craig Roberts, "Washington Signals Dollar Deep Concerns," PaulCraigRoberts.com, May 18, 2013, http://www.paulcraigroberts.org/2013/05/18/washington-signals-dollar-deep-concerns-paul-craig-roberts/.

31. Eric King, "Former U.S. Treasury Official—Fed Orchestrated Smash in Gold," KingWorldNews.com, April 12, 2013, http://kingworldnews.com/kingworldnews/KWN_DailyWeb/Entries/2013/4/12_Former_US_Treasury_Official_-_Fed_Orchestrated_Smash_In_Gold.html.

32.   Clara Denina, "Gold Rebounds after Biggest Quarterly Drop on Record," Reuters, July 1, 2013, http://in.reuters.com/article/2013/07/01/markets-precious-gold-idINDEE9600E120130701.

33.   Mark Skousen, "Are Precious Metals a Good Inflation Hedge?," Human Events, July 3, 2013, http://www.humanevents.com/2013/07/03/are-precious-metals-a-good-inflation-hedge/.

34.   "The Pros' Guide to Diversification," Fidelity, September 4, 2013, https://www.fidelity.com/viewpoints/guide-to-diversification.

35.   James Pethokoukis, "New Study: Gold Won't Save You from Hyperinflation or Zombie Apocalypse," AEI-Ideas (blog), January 22, 2013, http://www.aei-ideas.org/2013/01/new-study-gold-wont-save-you-from-hyperinflation-or-zombie-apocolypse/.

36.   David McAlvany and Kevin Orrick, "James Rickards: Currency Wars and $7,000 Gold," McAlvanyWeeklyCommentary.com, June 28, 2013, http://mcalvanyweeklycommentary.com/june-26-2013-james-rickards-currency-wars-and-7000-gold/.

37.   Katy Barnato, "Gold Prices Could Peak at $5,000: Bank of America," CNBC.com, September 21, 2012, http://www.cnbc.com/id/49119240.

38.   Matthew J. Belvedere, "'Gold Is Toast!' Why It Could Drop to $500: Pro," CNBC.com, May 15, 2013, http://www.cnbc.com/id/100739703.

39.   "What Is the Cost of Mining Gold?," VisualCapitalist.com, May 21, 2013, http://www.visualcapitalist.com/what-is-the-cost-of-mining-gold.

40.   Dan Vergano, "Gold on Earth Formed in Collision of Exotic Stars," USA Today, July 17, 2013, http://www.usatoday.com/story/news/2013/07/17/gold-neutron-star/2521311/.

CHAPTER SIX

1.   Floyd W. Parsons, "Buggy Whip Maker Still Doing Business," Milwaukee Journal, October 21, 1931.

2.   Jim Cramer, "There's Always a Bull Market," TheStreet.com, http://www.thestreet.com/static/rules25.html.

3.   "An Introduction to Sector ETFs," Investopedia, April 20, 2012, http://www.investopedia.com/articles/exchangetradedfunds/08/sector-etfs.asp.

4.   Russell Wild, "How to Diversify Your Sector ETF Investments," excerpt from Exchange-Traded Funds for Dummies, 2nd ed., Dummies.com, accessed September 2013, http://www.dummies.com/how-to/content/how-to-diversify-your-sector-etf-investments.html.

5.   Mark Riddix, "Is Active Investing Right for You?," Money Crashers, accessed September 2013, http://www.moneycrashers.com/is-active-investing-right-for-you/.

6.   Russell Campbell, "Don't Give Up on Active Investing—It's Worth Pursuing!," CFA Institute, July 12, 2013, http://blogs.cfainstitute.org/insideinvesting/2013/07/12/dont-give-up-on-active-investing-its-worth-pursuing/.

7.   Todd Renfro, "Passive Investors Shouldn't Rest on Laurels," Seeking Alpha, June 20, 2013, http://seekingalpha.com/article/1512962-passive-investors-shouldnt-rest-on-laurels-active-investing-may-be-the-future.

8.   Ren Cheng, "Active and Passive Investing: Both Are Essential to Long-Term Financial Market Health," Fidelity, June 2012, https://www.fidelity.com/bin-public/060_www_fidelity_com/documents/MillenniumBridge.614176.1.0.PDF.

9.   Ibid.

10.   Ted Schwartz, "Active versus Passive Investing: Should You Try to Beat the Market?,"
       ABCNews.com, March 25, 2013, http://abcnews.go.com/Business/active-versus-passive-
       investing-surprising-truths/story?id=18806687&singlePage=true.

11.   Prem C. Jain, "Is the Stock Market Efficient?," *American Association of Individual Investors
       Journal*, November 2010, http://www.aaii.com/journal/article/is-the-stock-market-
       efficient.touch.

12.   Eric Schurenberg, "How I Did It: John Bogle of the Vanguard Group," Inc.com, September
       25, 2012, http://www.inc.com/magazine/201210/eric-schurenberg/how-i-did-it-john-
       bogle-the-vanguard-group.html.

13.   Gillian Tett, "We Have Entered the World of Disaster Economics" (*Financial Times*),
       CNBC.com, July 23, 2012, http://www.cnbc.com/id/48294439.

14.   Michael Kling, "Merrill Lynch: U.S., Western World No Longer Call Shots for Rest of
       World," Moneynews.com, July 10, 2012, http://www.moneynews.com/StreetTalk/
       US-West-g-zero-economy/2012/07/10/id/444884?s=al&promo_code=F6D5-1.

15.   Shai Ahmed, "Western Economies: The New Great Risk?," CNBC.com, September 17,
       2012, http://www.cnbc.com/id/49057380.

16.   Jesse Colombo, "The Dot-Com Bubble," TheBubbleBubble.com, August 19, 2012, http://
       www.thebubblebubble.com/dot-com-bubble/.

17.   Shawna De La Rosa, "How Stocks Behave during Hyperinflation," Zacks.com, http://finance.
       zacks.com/stocks-behave-during-hyperinflation-8335.html.

18.   "Latin American Inflation," *Economist*, November 5, 1998, http://www.economist.com/
       node/175469.

19.   Alexandra Kirkman, "Bolsa Bargains," *Forbes*, Forbes.com, December 11, 2000, http://
       www.forbes.com/global/2000/1211/0325101a.html.

20.   Joe Weisenthal, "Here's What Happened to Stocks during the German Hyperinflation,"
       Business Insider, November 26, 2011, http://www.businessinsider.com/
       heres-what-happened-to-stocks-during-the-german-hyperinflation-2011-11.

21.   Tyler Durden, "Headlines from 2008: 'Zimbabwe Stock Exchange Soars as Others Crash,'"
       Zero Hedge, November 4, 2010, http://www.zerohedge.com/article/
       headlines-2008-zimbabwe-stock-exchange-soars-others-crash.

22.   John Paul Koning, "Zimbabwe: Best Performing Stock Market in 2007?," Mises.org, April
       10, 2007, http://mises.org/daily/2532.

23.   "Peter Schiff Warns of Martial Law," Infowars.com, October 5, 2013, http://www.infowars.
       com/peter-schiff-warns-of-martial-law/.

24.   John Morgan, "MarketWatch: Mom and Pop Investors May Be Buying at the Top Again,"
       Moneynews.com, August 16, 2013, http://www.moneynews.com/InvestingAnalysis/
       mom-pop-investors-retail/2013/08/16/id/520740?s=al.

CHAPTER SEVEN

1.   Reuters, "Dot-Coms Look beyond 'Stickiness' and 'Eyeballs,'" *USA Today*, August 17,
       2001, http://usatoday30.usatoday.com/tech/techinvestor/2001-08-17-dot-com-stickiness.
       htm.

2.   Kent German, "Top 10 Dot-Com Flops," CNET.com, accessed September 2013, http://
       www.cnet.com/1990-11136_1-6278387-1.html.

3.   Cristina Silva, "Federal Report: Home Flipping Drove Housing Bubble" (AP), Boston.
       com, December 12, 2011, http://www.boston.com/news/nation/articles/2011/12/12/
       federal_report_home_flipping_drove_housing_bubble/.

4.   "Historical Perspectives: Famous Bubbles," *Frontline*, PBS.org, accessed September 2013, http://www.pbs.org/wgbh/pages/frontline/shows/dotcon/historical/bubbles.html.

5.   "Risk-Free Interest Rate," Princeton.edu, accessed September 2013, http://www.princeton.edu/~achaney/tmve/wiki100k/docs/Risk-free_interest_rate.html.

6.   Jane McGrath, "How Do Bonds Work?," HowStuffWorks.com, accessed September 2013, http://money.howstuffworks.com/personal-finance/budgeting/bonds.htm/printable.

7.   Securities Industry and Financial Markets Association, "What You Should Know: Risks of Investing in Bonds," InvestingInBonds.com, accessed September 2013, http://www.investinginbonds.com/learnmore.asp?catid=3&id=383.

8.   David Waring, "The Yield Curve: What It Is and How It Works," LearnBonds.com, January 17, 2013, http://www.learnbonds.com/the-yield-curve/.

9.   Securities Industry and Financial Markets Association, "About Bills, Notes, and Bonds," Investinginbonds.com, accessed September 2013, http://www.investinginbonds.com/learnmore.asp?catid=9&subcatid=50&id=101.

10.   Mike Periu, "How the Federal Reserve Sets Interest Rates," OpenForum.com, July 14, 2011, https://www.openforum.com/articles/how-the-federal-reserve-sets-interest-rates/.

11.   "The Discount Rate," Board of Governors of the Federal Reserve System, October 15, 2013, http://www.federalreserve.gov/monetarypolicy/discountrate.htm.

12.   Tejvan Pettinger, "Quantitative Easing Definition," EconomicsHelp.org, December 8, 2012, http://www.economicshelp.org/blog/1047/economics/quantitative-easing/.

13.   G.I., "The Fed Acts, Just," Free Exchange, *Economist*, June 20, 2012, http://www.economist.com/blogs/freeexchange/2012/06/operation-twist.

14.   "Relationship between Bonds and Interest Rates," Wells Fargo Advantage Funds, accessed September 2013, http://www.wellsfargoadvantagefunds.com/wfweb/wf/education/choosing/bonds/rates.jsp.

15.   Rob Williams, "Should You Worry about Bond Funds If Interest Rates Rise?," Charles Schwab, April 23, 2013, http://www.schwab.com/public/schwab/resource_center/expert_insight/investing_strategies/bonds/should_you_worry_about_bond_funds_if_interest_rates_rise.html.

16.   John Waggoner, "Hidden Danger Lurks in Long-Term Bond Funds," *USA Today*, April 25, 2013, http://www.usatoday.com/story/money/columnist/waggoner/2013/04/25/investing-dangers-in-bond-funds/2113479/.

17.   "Understanding Duration," PIMCO, accessed September 2013, http://investments.pimco.com/MarketingPrograms/External%20Documents/understanding_duration_pu004.pdf.

18.   Jeff Cox, "Deflation Fears Send Investors Searching for Bonds, Dividends," CNBC.com, May 18, 2010, http://www.cnbc.com/id/37213693.

19.   Philip Moeller, "How to Prepare for a Deflationary World," *U.S. News & World Report*, February 1, 2012, http://money.usnews.com/money/blogs/the-best-life/2012/02/01/how-to-prepare-for-a-deflationary-world.

20.   Berkshire Hathaway letter to shareholders, 2011, available at http://s3.documentcloud.org/documents/320606/berkshirehathaway2011ltr.pdf.

21.   "Stocks Riskier Than Bonds? Not If You Think like Buffett," *Forbes*, Forbes.com, May 20, 2013, http://www.forbes.com/sites/iese/2013/05/20/stocks-riskier-than-bonds-not-if-you-think-like-buffett/.

22.   Charles Wallace, "Treasury TIPS: A Looming Disaster for Small Investors," DailyFinance.com, February 4, 2011, http://www.dailyfinance.com/2011/02/04/treasury-tips-a-looming-disaster-for-small-investors/.

23. "When Bonds Fall: How Risky Are Bonds If Interest Rates Rise," Welton Visual Insight Series, Welton Investment Corporation, accessed September 2013, https://www.welton.com/uploads/insight/Welton-When_Bonds_Fall_(Visual_Insight_Series).pdf.

24. Thomas Kenny, "Is There a Bond Bubble?," About.com, accessed September 2013, http://bonds.about.com/od/Issues-in-the-News/a/The-Bond-Bubble-Fact-Or-Fiction.htm.

25. Michael T. Snyder, "Have Central Bankers Lost Control? Could the Bond Bubble Implode Even If There Is No Tapering?," Seeking Alpha, July 5, 2013, http://seekingalpha.com/article/1534982-have-central-bankers-lost-control-could-the-bond-bubble-implode-even-if-there-is-no-tapering.

26. Snyder, "The Trigger Has Been Pulled and the Slaughter of the Bonds Has Begun," *The Economic Collapse Blog*, June 25, 2013, http://theeconomiccollapseblog.com/archives/the-trigger-has-been-pulled-and-the-slaughter-of-the-bonds-has-begun.

27. Wolf Richter, "Controlling the Implosion of the Biggest Bond Bubble in History," Zero Hedge, June 23, 2013, http://www.zerohedge.com/contributed/2013-06-23/controlling-implosion-biggest-bond-bubble-history.

28. Reuters, "Bond Losses of $1 Trillion If Yields Spike, BIS Says," CNBC.com, June 23, 2013, http://www.cnbc.com/id/100836919.

29. "Jim Rogers on Bond Bubbles, Buying Gold and the Japan Disaster," MarketWatch, *Wall Street Journal*, June 14, 2013, http://blogs.marketwatch.com/thetell/2013/06/14/jim-rogers-on-bond-bubbles-buying-gold-and-the-japan-disaster/.

30. Lauren Lyster, "Bond Bubble Will Be Bigger Catastrophe Than Real Estate Bust: Casey," Yahoo! Finance, January 17, 2013, http://finance.yahoo.com/blogs/daily-ticker/bond-bubble-bigger-catastrophe-real-estate-bust-casey-161402082.html.

31. "Sell US Treasuries Before They 'Crash,' Bank of America Says," Moneynews.com, June 3, 2013, http://www.moneynews.com/FinanceNews/Bank-of-America-Treasurys-Crash-Bonds/2013/06/03/id/507628?s=al&promo_code=13B1E-1.

32. Stephen Gandel, "Goldman Sachs Braces for Bond Market Blow Up" (Fortune), CNN.com, January 30, 2013, http://finance.fortune.cnn.com/2013/01/30/goldman-sachs-bond-market/.

33. Jill Treanor, "Bond Bubble Threatens Financial System, Bank of England Director Warns," *Guardian* (UK), June 12, 2013, http://www.guardian.co.uk/business/2013/jun/12/bond-bubble-threatens-financial-system.

34. Jeff Cox, "Long-Term Bond Bubble Getting Ready to Burst: Ross," CNBC.com, March 21, 2012, http://www.cnbc.com/id/46805820.

35. Agustino Fontevecchia, "Shutdown and Debt Ceiling Debate Prove U.S. Not Worthy Of AAA Credit Rating: S&P," *Forbes*, Forbes.com, September 30, 2013, http://www.forbes.com/sites/afontevecchia/2013/09/30/shutdown-and-debt-ceiling-debate-prove-u-s-doesnt-deserve-aaa-credit-rating-sp/.

36. "'Your History Is Wrong': Chris Wallace Presses Jack Lew for Straight Answers in Heated 'Default' Debate," FoxNews.com, October 8, 2013, http://nation.foxnews.com/2013/10/06/"your-history-wrong"-chris-wallace-presses-jack-lew-straight-answers-heated-'default'.

37. Kara Rowland, "White House Says Obama Regrets 2006 Debt Ceiling Vote," *Washington Times*, April 11, 2011, http://www.washingtontimes.com/blog/inside-politics/2011/apr/11/white-house-says-obama-regrets-2006-debt-ceiling-v/.

38. "United States of America Long-Term Rating Lowered To 'AA+' due to Political Risks, Rising Debt Burden; Outlook Negative," Standard and Poors, August 5, 2011, http://www.standardandpoors.com/ratings/articles/en/us/?assetID=124531652956.

39.   Karen Brettell, "Treasuries—U.S. Bonds Soar on Safe-Haven Bid despite Downgrade,"
       Reuters, August 8, 2011, http://www.reuters.com/article/2011/08/08/markets-bonds-
       idUSN1E7771RC20110808.

40.   Jeff Macke, "U.S. Is Broke, Can't Afford to Raise the Debt Ceiling Says Peter Schiff," Yahoo!
       Finance, September 26, 2013, http://finance.yahoo.com/blogs/breakout/u-broke-
       t-afford-raise-debt-ceiling-says-114000942.html.

41.   Alex J. Pollock, "Default and the Nature of Government," *Wall Street Journal*, March 14,
       2012, http://online.wsj.com/article/SB10001424052702304450004577277830065320286.
       html.

42.   John Griffing, "Monckton: Push 'Reset' on Dollar," WND, September 28, 2013, http://www.
       wnd.com/2013/09/monckton-push-reset-on-dollar/.

43.   Tom Mitchell, Gina Chon, Ben McLannahan, and Paul J. Davies, "China and Japan Warn
       U.S. on Default" (*Financial Times*), CNBC.com, October 7, 2013, http://www.cnbc.com/
       id/101091268.

44.   Tyler Durden, "Charles Gave Warns: 'Should the Fed Lose Control, the Downside Move
       in Markets May Be Terrifying,'" Zero Hedge, June 10, 2013, http://www.zerohedge.com/
       news/2013-06-10/charles-gave-warns-should-fed-lose-control-downside-move-markets-
       may-be-terrifying.

CHAPTER EIGHT

1.   Jon David Kahn, "Termites Feast on Woman's Life Savings," Breitbart.com, June 13, 2013,
       http://www.breitbart.com/InstaBlog/2013/06/13/Termites-Feast-On-Woman-s-Life-
       Savings.

2.   "Scrap Yard Workers in Queens Search for Couple Who Accidentally Trashed Life Savings,"
       CBSLocal.com, July 20, 2013, http://newyork.cbslocal.com/2013/07/20/scrap-yard-
       workers-in-queens-search-for-couple-who-accidently-trashed-life-savings/.

3.   Shira Medding, "Tel Aviv Search for Mattress Containing $1M Life Savings," CNN.com,
       June 10, 2009, http://www.cnn.com/2009/WORLD/meast/06/10/israel.mattress.money/.

4.   Bernard Condon, "AP Impact: Families Hoard Cash Five Yrs after Crisis" (AP), Yahoo!
       News, October 6, 2013, http://news.yahoo.com/ap-impact-families-hoard-cash-5-yrs-
       crisis-042042926.html.

5.   Ralph Benko, "U.S. Elites Begin to Confront the Paper Dollar," *Forbes*, Forbes.com, August
       29, 2011, http://www.forbes.com/sites/ralphbenko/2011/08/29/u-s-elites-begin-
       to-confront-the-paper-dollar/.

6.   Chris Mack, "Is This Time Different for the Dollar?," ResourceInvestor.com, January 24,
       2011, http://www.resourceinvestor.com/2011/01/24/is-this-time-different-for-the-dollar.

7.   Leslie P. Norton, "Coming: The End of Fiat Money," *Barron's*, Barrons.com, July 21, 2012,
       http://online.barrons.com/article/SB50001424053111904346504577531052271788084.
       html#articleTabs_article%3D1.

8.   John Griffing, "Monckton: Push Reset on the Dollar," WND, September 28, 2013, http://
       www.wnd.com/2013/09/monckton-push-reset-on-dollar/.

9.   Catherine Rampell, "As Low Rates Depress Savers, Governments Reap Benefits," *New York
       Times*, September 10, 2012, http://www.nytimes.com/2012/09/11/business/as-low-rates-
       depress-savers-governments-reap-the-benefits.html.

10.   John Matarese, "New Bank IRA Fees Eating into Savings," WCPO.com, July 7, 2011, http://
       www.wcpo.com/dpp/money/consumer/dont_waste_your_money/new-bank-ira-fees-
       eating-into-savings-.

11.   Pallavi Gogoi, "Bank Fees Quietly Coming Back Even after Backlash" (AP), Huffington Post, March 1, 2012, http://www.huffingtonpost.com/2012/03/02/bank-fees_n_1315828.html.

12.   Peter Rudegeair and Carrick Mollenkamp, "Analysis: U.S. Banks Get Ready for the Day When Deposits Shrink," Reuters, October 7, 2013, http://www.reuters.com/article/2013/10/07/us-banks-deposits-analysis-idUSBRE9960C220131007.

13.   Marcie Geffner, "FDIC Insures Bank Deposits to $250,000," Bankrate.com, accessed September 2013, http://www.bankrate.com/finance/savings/fdic-insures-bank-deposits-to-250-000-1.aspx.

14.   Jesse Hamilton, "FDIC Says Deposit Insurance Fund Should Recover by Late 2018," Bloomberg.com, April 23, 2012, http://www.bloomberg.com/news/2012-04-23/fdic-says-deposit-insurance-fund-recovery-expected-by-late-2018.html.

15.   U.S. Government Accountability Office, "Financial Audit: Federal Deposit Insurance Corporation Funds' 2012 and 2011 Financial Statements," February 2013, http://www.gao.gov/assets/660/652263.pdf.

16.   E. Scott Reckard, "In Major Policy Shift, Scores of FDIC Settlements Go Unannounced," Los Angeles Times, March 11, 2013, http://articles.latimes.com/2013/mar/11/business/la-fi-fdic-settlements-20130311.

17.   John Glover, "U.S. May Join 1933 Germany in Pantheon of Deadbeat Defaults," Bloomberg.com, October 14, 2013, http://www.bloomberg.com/news/2013-10-13/u-s-risks-joining-1933-germany-in-pantheon-of-deadbeat-defaults.html.

18.   Claes Bell, "Hackers Empty $900K Bank Account," BankRate.com, February 25, 2013, http://www.bankrate.com/financing/banking/hackers-empty-900k-bank-account/#ixzz2aC8RLd6g.

19.   "Could Bank Hackers Steal Your Money?," Bankrate.com, May 11, 2010, http://www.bankrate.com/system/util/print.aspx?p=/finance/savings/could-bank-hackers-steal-your-money-1.aspx&s=br3&c=checking&t=story&e=1&v=1.

20.   "DARPA Director Speaks of Offensive Capabilities in Cyber Security," Cybersecurity at the University of Texas at Dallas, March 21, 2012, http://cybersecurityutdallas.wordpress.com/category/uncategorized/page/2/.

21.   Dave Moore, "Who Pays When Your Bank Account Is Hacked?," NormanTranscript.com, July 15, 2012, http://normantranscript.com/x1301512034/Who-pays-when-your-bank-account-is-hacked.

22.   Nick Squires, "Cypriot Authorities Confirm Raid on Big Depositors," Telegraph (UK), March 29, 2013, http://www.telegraph.co.uk/finance/financialcrisis/9962244/Cypriot-authorities-confirm-raid-on-big-depositors.html.

23.   Neil Collins, "Cyprus Confiscation Could Happen in UK," Financial Times, March 22, 2013, http://www.ft.com/intl/cms/s/0/534b2eaa-92e9-11e2-b3be-00144feabdc0.html.

24.   Governor Jeremy C. Stein, "Regulating Large Financial Institutions," speech at the Rethinking Macro Policy II Conference, sponsored by the International Monetary Fund, April 17, 2013, transcript, Board of Governors of the Federal Reserve, http://www.federalreserve.gov/newsevents/speech/stein20130417a.htm.

25.   Federal Deposit Insurance Corporation and the Bank of England, "Resolving Globally Active, Systemically Important, Financial Institutions," Federal Deposit Insurance Corporation, December 10, 2012, http://www.fdic.gov/about/srac/2012/gsifi.pdf.

26.   Peter J. Wallison, "Dodd-Frank's Liquidation Plan Is Worse Than Bankruptcy," Bloomberg.com, June 11, 2012, http://www.bloomberg.com/news/2012-06-11/dodd-frank-s-liquidation-plan-is-worse-than-bankruptcy.html.

27.   Jerome Corsi, "Yes, Feds Can Take Your Deposits," WND, October 8, 2013, http://www.wnd.com/2013/10/yes-feds-can-take-your-deposits/.

28.   Andrey Ostroukh, "Russia to Grab Pension Money, Temporarily," *Wall Street Journal*, October 3, 2013, http://blogs.wsj.com/emergingeurope/2013/10/03/russia-to-grab-pension-money-temporarily.

29.   Alanna Petroff, "Europe Bank Rescue Plan Would Hit Investors," CNN Money, CNN.com, June 27, 2013, http://money.cnn.com/2013/06/27/news/world/eu-bank-rescue/index.html?iid=HP_River.

30.   Rex Nutting, "Money-Market Funds Are a Most Dangerous Investment," MarketWatch, *Wall Street Journal*, March 29, 2013 http://www.marketwatch.com/story/money-market-funds-are-a-most-dangerous-investment-2013-03-29.

31.   Justin Pritchard, "Money Market Funds—Risks and Benefits: How Money Markets Work," About.com, accessed September 2013, http://banking.about.com/od/investments/a/moneymarketfund.htm.

32.   Robert Lenzner, "There Could Still Be Runs on Money Market Funds," *Forbes*, Forbes.com, April 20, 2013, http://www.forbes.com/sites/robertlenzner/2013/04/20/there-could-still-be-runs-on-the-money-market-funds/.

33.   Arthur Brice, "Iran, Hezbollah Mine Latin America for Revenue, Recruits, Analysts Say," CNN.com, June 3, 2013, http://www.cnn.com/2013/06/03/world/americas/iran-latin-america/.

34.   "Hyperinflation," Prime Values, September 8, 2012, updated August 14, 2013, http://www.primevalues.org/investors-guide/hyperinflation.htm#.UlwPlhYfD9E.

CHAPTER NINE

1.   "Introduction to Annuities: The History of Annuities," *Investopedia*, accessed September 2013, http://www.investopedia.com/university/annuities/.

2.   "Annuities Made Simple," InsureYourHealthNow, 2013, http://www.insureyourhealthnow.com/annuities_madesimple.htm.

3.   "What Are the Different Types of Annuities?," Annuity FYI, updated July 22, 2013, http://www.annuityfyi.com/types-of-annuities.html.

4.   "Variable Annuities: What You Should Know," U.S. Securities and Exchange Commission, updated April 18, 2011, http://www.sec.gov/investor/pubs/varannty.htm.

5.   Ibid.

6.   "Explaining Types Of Fixed Annuities," *Investopedia*, February 23, 2011, http://www.investopedia.com/articles/retirement/05/071205.asp.

7.   "Equity-Indexed Annuities—A Complex Choice," FINRA, September 13, 2010, http://www.finra.org/investors/protectyourself/investoralerts/annuitiesandinsurance/p010614; and Stan Hathcock, "Behind the Indexed Annuity Curtain," MarketWatch, *Wall Street Journal*, January 5, 2013, http://www.marketwatch.com/story/behind-the-indexed-annuity-curtain-2013-01-14?pagenumber=1.

8.   Keith Dennis, "What Are Bonus Annuities?" About.com, accessed September 2013, http://annuities.about.com/od/annuityquestions/a/What-Are-Bonus-Annuities.htm; "Index Annuities Are a Safety Trap," *Money Magazine* Investor's Guide 2011, CNN Money, CNN.com, January 17, 2011, http://money.cnn.com/2011/01/17/pf/index_annuities_safety_trap.moneymag/index.htm.

9.   "Variable Annuities: Beyond the Hard Sell," FINRA Investors, August 31, 2009, http://www.finra.org/investors/protectyourself/investoralerts/annuitiesandinsurance/p005976.

10. InvestorGuideStaff, "Annuities as an Investment For Retirement," InvestorGuide, January 25, 2013, http://www.investorguide.com/article/11702/annuities-as-an-investment-for-retirement-igu/.

11. "Annuities Made Simple."

12. Shelby J. Smith, "Are Annuities Offered by Insurance Companies Safe?," *Retirement Planning Blog*, November 11, 2008, http://www.theretirementpros.com/blog/2008/11/are-annuities-offered-by-insurance-companies-safe/.

13. "Guaranteed Investment Contracts," Financial Web, accessed September 2013, http://web.finweb.com/investing/guaranteed-investment-contracts.html#axzz2bhxO9JBQ.

14. *Encyclopedia of Business*, 2nd ed., s.v., "Guaranteed Investment Contract," by Anandi P. Sahu, http://www.referenceforbusiness.com/encyclopedia/Gov-Inc/Guaranteed-Investment-Contract-GIC.html#b.

15. Ibid.

16. Ibid.

17. Steve Vernon, "What Happens If Your Insurance Company Fails," CBS News, February 9, 2012, http://www.cbsnews.com/8301-505146_162-57373586/what-happens-if-your-insurance-company-fails/. The figure for insurance company failures represents institutions with which the National Organization of Life and Health Insurance Guaranty Associations was involved.

18. "How Can I Assess the Financial Strength of an Insurance Company?," Insurance Information Institute, accessed September 2013, http://www.iii.org/individuals/life/buying/strength/.

19. "The Pros and Cons of Annuities," YourInvestmentAdvise.com, accessed September 2013, http://www.yourinvestmentadvise.com/annuity2.html.

20. Jack Marrion, Geoffrey Vanderpal, and David Babbel, "Real World Index Annuity Returns," Wharton Financial Institutions Center, December 27, 2010, http://annuity123.com/Portals/1/whitepapers/F_Wharton%20Financial%20Real%20World%20Index%20Annuity%20Returns.pdf.

CHAPTER TEN

1. "Alternative Investments—Redefining Diversification," BlackRock, Inc., accessed September 2013, http://www2.blackrock.com/us/individual-investors/products-performance/alternative-investments.

2. Barry Ritholtz, "A Hedge Fund for You and Me? The Best Move Is to Take a Pass," *Washington Post*, May 24, 2013, http://articles.washingtonpost.com/2013-05-24/business/39489985_1_hedge-funds-private-investment-partnerships-investors.

3. *Investopedia*, s.v. "Alpha," accessed September 2013, http://www.investopedia.com/terms/a/alpha.asp.

4. Sheelah Kolhatkar, "Hedge Funds Are for Suckers," Businessweek.com, July 11, 2013, http://www.businessweek.com/articles/2013-07-11/why-hedge-funds-glory-days-may-be-gone-for-good.

5. Geri Terzo, "What Are Net Worth Requirements for a Hedge Fund?," The Motley Fool, http://wiki.fool.com/What_Are_Net_Worth_Requirements_for_a_Hedge_Fund%3F.

6. Ritholtz, "A Hedge Hund for You and Me?"

7. "Rich Managers, Poor Clients," *Economist*, December 22, 2012, http://www.economist.com/news/leaders/21568740-investors-have-paid-too-much-hedge-fund-expertise-better-focus-low-costs-star.

8. Ritholtz, "A Hedge Hund for You and Me?"

9. Ibid.

10. Nathan Vardi, "The World's Richest Billionaire Hedge Fund Managers and Traders," *Forbes*, Forbes.com, March 4, 2013, http://www.forbes.com/sites/nathanvardi/2013/03/04/the-worlds-richest-billionaire-hedge-fund-managers-and-traders/.

11. "Going Nowhere Fast," *Economist*, December 22, 2012, http://www.economist.com/news/finance-and-economics/21568741-hedge-funds-have-had-another-lousy-year-cap-disappointing-decade-going.

12. Ritholtz, "A Hedge Hund for You and Me?"

13. Kolhatkar, "Hedge Funds Are for Suckers."

14. Robert Lenzner, "Bernie Madoff's $50 Billion Ponzi Scheme," *Forbes*, Forbes.com, December 12, 2008, http://www.forbes.com/2008/12/12/madoff-ponzi-hedge-pf-ii-in_rl_1212croesus_inl.html.

15. "Did Bernie Madoff Run a Hedge Fund?," StreetID, October 9, 2012, http://streetid.com/newsblog/?p=2371.

16. "Hedge Fund Founder Raj Rajaratnam Sentenced in Manhattan Federal Court to 11 Years in Prison for Insider Trading Crimes," press release, Federal Bureau of Investigation, October 13, 2011, http://www.fbi.gov/newyork/press-releases/2011/hedge-fund-founder-raj-rajaratnam-sentenced-in-manhattan-federal-court-to-11-years-in-prison-for-insider-trading-crimes.

17. Matthew Goldstein, "Steven Cohen Throws a Party despite His Fund's Indictment," Reuters, July 28, 2013, http://www.reuters.com/article/2013/07/28/us-sac-fund-party-idUSBRE96R0BQ20130728.

18. Lynn Stout, "How Hedge Funds Create Criminals," *Harvard Business Review Blog Network*, December 13, 2010, http://blogs.hbr.org/cs/2010/12/how_hedge_funds_create_crimina.html.

19. "Brutal Gingrich Ad Ties Romney to Soros," FoxNews.com, February 6, 2012, http://nation.foxnews.com/newt-gingrich/2012/02/06/brutal-gingrich-ad-ties-romney-soros.

20. "Insider Trading Conviction of Soros Is Upheld," *New York Times*, June 14, 2006, http://www.nytimes.com/2006/06/14/business/worldbusiness/14iht-soros.1974397.html?_r=0.

21. Joanna Slater, "When Hedge Funds Meet Islamic Finance," *Wall Street Journal*, August 9, 2007, http://online.wsj.com/article/SB118661926443492441.html.

22. Larry Summers, "Sovereign Wealth Funds Should Agree to Standards to Allay fears," *New Perspectives Quarterly*, January 25, 2008, http://www.digitalnpq.org/articles/economic/238/01-25-2008/larry_summers.

23. Eric Uhlfelder, "Best 100 Hedge Funds," *Barron's*, Barrons.com, May 18, 2013, http://online.barrons.com/article/SB50001424052748704253204578469283806191260.html#articleTabs_article%3D0.

24. Tim McLaughlin, "Blackstone and Fidelity Offer Hedge Fund Taste to Retail Crowd," Reuters, August 13, 2013, http://www.reuters.com/article/2013/08/13/uk-blackstone-fidelity-hedgefunds-idUSLNE97C00820130813.

25. Daniel Solin, "Why Hedge Funds for Retail Investors Are a Bad Idea," *U.S. News & World Report*, August 22, 2013, http://money.usnews.com/money/blogs/On-Retirement/2013/08/22/why-hedge-funds-for-retail-investors-are-a-bad-idea.

26. *Investopedia*, s.v. "Financial Asset," accessed September 2013, http://www.investopedia.com/terms/f/financialasset.asp.

27. Tony Romm "Facebook Goes Public," Politico.com, May 18, 2012, http://www.politico.com/news/stories/0512/76485.html.

28. Dan Primack, "Facebook's Pre-IPO Pricing History," CNN Money, CNN.com, May 18, 2012, http://finance.fortune.cnn.com/2012/05/18/facebooks-pre-ipo-pricing-history/.

29. Paul Sullivan, "Lights. Camera. Invest! Putting Filmmaking in the Portfolio," *New York Times*, April 27, 2012, http://www.nytimes.com/2012/04/28/your-money/filmmaking-as-an-alternative-investment.html?pagewanted=all.

30. Sullivan, "Investing in a Racehorse without Breaking the Bank," *New York Times*, May 4, 2012, http://www.nytimes.com/2012/05/05/your-money/investing-in-a-racehorse-without-losing-your-shirt.html?pagewanted=all.

31. "Own a Race Team—How to Buy a Nascar Team," Athlete Promotions, accessed September 2013, http://www.athletepromotions.com/own-a-nascar-team.php.

32. Glenn E. Morrical, Jennifer W. Berlin, and Robert M. Loesch, "Finder's Fees: Folklore and Fact on Regulation," VCExperts, https://vcexperts.com/buzz_articles/1275.

33. "Finder's Fee Agreements," Private Equity 101, February 20, 2010, http://www.privateequity101.com/2010/02/finders-fee-agreements.html; and "What Are Going Rates for Finder's Fees?," Answers on Startups, accessed September 2013, http://answers.onstartups.com/questions/3844/what-are-going-rates-for-finders-fee.

34. Constance Gustke, "Six Alternative Investments for Fat Returns," FoxBusiness.com, December 1, 2011, http://www.foxbusiness.com/personal-finance/2011/12/01/six-alternative-investments-for-fat-returns/.

35. Casey W. Riggs, "Stock Options versus Stock Warrants—What's the Difference?," *Strictly Business Law Blog*, November 2, 2012, http://www.strictlybusinesslawblog.com/2012/11/02/stock-options-versus-stock-warrants-whats-the-difference/.

36. "What Is Convertible Debt?," WiseGeek, accessed September 2013, http://www.wisegeek.com/what-is-convertible-debt.htm.

37. Asheesh Advani, "Raising Money Using Convertible Debt," *Entrepreneur*, May 14, 2006, http://www.entrepreneur.com/article/159520.

38. Constance Gustke, "6 Alternative Investments for Fat Returns," Bankrate.com, http://www.bankrate.com/finance/investing/alternative-investments-fat-returns-1.aspx#ixzz2dTpmSQI2.

39. Clark, Josh, "How Microlending Works," How Stuff Works, August 18, 2009, http://www.howstuffworks.com/microlending.htm.

40. Gustke, "Alternative Investments for Fat Returns."

41. Tamara E. Holmes, "Now Is a Great Time to Invest in a Rental," Bankrate.com, MSN Real Estate, accessed September 2013, http://realestate.msn.com/article.aspx?cp-documentid=23972039.

42. "The Investor's Guide to REITs," National Association of Real Estate Investment Trusts, 2011, http://www.reit.com/~/media/PDFs/UpdatedInvestorsGuideToREITs.ashx.

43. "Direct Real Estate Investment vs REITs," My Financial Independence Journey, June 5, 2013, http://myfijourney.com/2013/06/05/direct-real-estate-investment-vs-reits/.

44. Brandon Turner, "Investing in Rental Property," *The Bigger Pockets Blog*, April 23, 2013, http://www.biggerpockets.com/renewsblog/2013/04/23/investing-in-rental-property/.

45. Tara Siegel Bernard, "Rental Investment May Seem Safer Than It Really Is," *New York Times*, March 29, 2013, http://www.nytimes.com/2013/03/30/your-money/investing-in-a-rental-home-isnt-as-safe-as-it-may-seem.html?pagewanted=all.

46. Pat Curry, "Investing in Gems for Fun and Profit," Bankrate.com, accessed September 2013, http://www.bankrate.com/brm/news/investing/20031103a1.asp.

47. Aimee Picchi, "Diamonds: Investors' Best Friends?," MSN Money, accessed September 2013, http://money.msn.com/exchange-traded-fund/diamonds-investors-best-friends.

48. Andreas Travillian, "Know These 8 Rules before Investing in Diamonds and Gems," Yahoo! Finance, April 30, 2013, http://finance.yahoo.com/news/know-8-rules-investing-diamonds-150648931.html.

49. "How to Buy Futures," MarketWatch, *Wall Street Journal*, accessed September 2013, http://www.marketwatch.com/getting-started/futures.

50. "Investing in Futures and Commodities," Wells Fargo Advisors, https://www.wellsfargoadvisors.com/financial-services/investment-products/futures-commodities.htm; and Amer Keefer, "How to Invest in Futures," The Nest, http://budgeting.thenest.com/invest-futures-3690.html.

51. Ibid.

52. See the Global Food Exchange website at http://globalfoodexchange.org.

53. International Food Security Source, "Global Food Exchange and IFS Fund Announces Its Founders Will Be Presenting at the Accredited Members Spring Micro Cap Investor Conference in Las Vegas," press release, Market Wired, February 19, 2013, http://www.marketwire.com/press-release/global-food-exchange-ifs-fund-announces-its-founders-will-be-presenting-accredited-members-1758749.htm.

54. "Overview," Commodity HQ, accessed September 2013, http://commodityhq.com/commodity/industrial-metals/.

55. Carl Delfeld, "Investing in Rare Earth Metals," Investment U, May 31, 2012, http://www.investmentu.com/2012/May/rare-earth-metals-investing.html.

56. Tim Worstall, "Investing in Rare Earth Metals: Don't Do It!" *Forbes*, Forbes.com, May 3, 2012, http://www.forbes.com/sites/timworstall/2012/05/03/investing-in-rare-earth-metals-dont-do-it/.

57. Jeff Stouffer, "Timber Investing for the Average Investor," The Motley Fool, April 24, 2013, http://beta.fool.com/jlstouffer/2013/04/24/timber-investing-now-a-program-for-the-average-i-3/31719/.

58. Investment U Research Team, "Investing in Timber," Investment U, accessed September 2013, http://www.investmentu.com/research/timber-investing.html.

59. *Investopedia*, s.v. "Master Limited Partnership," accessed September 2013, http://www.investopedia.com/terms/m/mlp.asp.

60. Ethan Sacks, "Spider-Man Comic, Amazing Fantasy #15, Sells for Record $1.1 Million," *New York Daily News*, March 9, 2011, http://www.nydailynews.com/entertainment/spider-man-comic-amazing-fantasy-15-sells-record-1-1-million-article-1.112875.

61. "Princess, Ty Beanie Baby Bear," TV Collector, updated November 4, 2013, http://www.tycollector.com/the-scoop/princess-bear.htm.

62. Charles Passy, "So You Think You Want to Invest in ...," *Wall Street Journal*, October 29, 2012, http://online.wsj.com/article/SB10000872396390443684104578064800307480808.html.

63. Teresa Levonian Cole, "Returns on Property v. High-End Collectables," House and Home, *Financial Times*, February 22, 2013, http://www.ft.com/intl/cms/s/2/7883dbf4-76c9-11e2-8569-00144feabdc0.html#axzz2dOgLW8mg.

64. Rob Griffith, "Collectibles: A Way to Invest and Have Fun at the Same Time," *Independent*, May 1, 2010, http://www.independent.co.uk/money/spend-save/collectibles-a-way-to-invest-and-have-fun-at-the-same-time-1959574.html.

65.   "Avoiding 'Prohibited Transactions' in Your IRA," *Investopedia*, September 18, 2010, http://www.investopedia.com/articles/retirement/03/073003.asp.

66.   Sara Callan, "New U.K. Law Allows Collectibles in Retirement Portfolios" (*Wall Street Journal*), *Sun Sentinel*, November 27, 2005, http://articles.sun-sentinel.com/2005-11-27/business/0511250489_1_mutual-funds-bordeaux-and-burgundy-wine.

CHAPTER ELEVEN

1.   David Chilton, *The Wealthy Barber: Everyone's Commonsense Guide to Becoming Financially Independent*, 3rd ed. (New York: Three Rivers Press, 1997).

2.   Benjamin Graham, Jason Zweig, and Warren E. Buffett, *The Intelligent Investor: The Definitive Book on Value Investing; A Book of Practical Counsel* (New York: Collins Business, 2006).

3.   William Proctor, *The Templeton Touch* (West Conshohocken, PA: Templeton Press, 2012).

4.   Charles D. Ellis, *Investment Policy: How to Win the Loser's Game* (Burr Ridge, IL: Irwin Professional Publishing, 1992).

5.   Manisha Thakor and Sharon Kedar, *On My Own Two Feet: A Modern Girl's Guide to Personal Finance* (Avon, MA: Adams Business, 2007).

6.   Norman Berryessa, *Global Investing: The Templeton Way* (New York: McGraw-Hill, 1988).

7.   Erik Davidson, *Investing in Separate Accounts* (New York: McGraw-Hill, 2002).

8.   "Robert Duggan," *Forbes*, Forbes.com, accessed September 2013, http://www.forbes.com/profile/robert-duggan-1/.

9.   Davidson, *Investing in Separate Accounts*.

10.   Ellis, *Investment Policy*.

11.   Ibid.

12.   *Wikipedia*, s.v. "1937," accessed September 2013.

13.   "Group of 7, Meet the Group of 33," *New York Times*, December 26, 1987, http://www.nytimes.com/1987/12/26/opinion/group-of-7-meet-the-group-of-33.html.

14.   "Templeton Maxims: 10 Principles for Investment Success," Franklin Templeton Investments, http://www.dryassociates.com/images/maxims.pdf.

15.   Mark J. Perry, "The U.S. Economy Is Bad, but the 1980s Were Worse," *Encyclopedia Britannica Blog*, January 21, 2009, http://www.britannica.com/blogs/2009/01/the-economy-is-bad-but-the-80s-were-worse/.

16.   James Joyner, "History of American Income Tax Rates," Outside the Beltway, http://www.outsidethebeltway.com/history-of-american-income-tax-rates/.

17.   Daisy Luther, "Power Outage Picnic," The Organic Prepper, http://www.theorganicprepper.ca/power-outage-picnic-02062013.

18.   Luther, "Getting Started: Prepping for a Two-Week Power Outage," LewRockwell.com, July 2, 2013, http://archive.lewrockwell.com/luther/luther40.1.html.

19.   NSIC Institute, Oklahoma Wesleyan Institute, http://nsic.org.

CHAPTER TWELVE

1.   Bob Veres, "The Price Clients Pay for Worst-Case Forecasts," Advisor Perspectives, August 27, 2013, http://advisorperspectives.com/newsletters13/pdfs/The_Price_Clients_Pay_for_Worst-Case_Forecasts.pdf.

2.   Juan Zarate, *Treasury's War: The Unleashing of a New Era of Financial Warfare* (New York: PublicAffairs, 2013).

3.	Kate Brannen, "Mike Mullen Focuses on Debt as Security Threat," Politico.com, December 6, 2012, http://www.politico.com/story/2012/12/mike-mullen-focuses-on-debt-as-security-threat-84648.html.

4.	Zarate, *Treasury's War*.

5.	Annalyn Censky, "What Is Naked Short Selling?," CNN Money, CNN.com, May 19, 2010, http://money.cnn.com/2010/05/19/news/economy/naked_short_selling_wtf/.

6.	"Germany's Naked Short-Selling Ban: What the Analysts Say; Germany's Surprise Clampdown on the 'Naked Short-Selling' of Bank Shares, Government Bonds and Credit Default Swaps Has Alarmed City Analysts, Who Believe It Could Make Europe's Financial Crisis Even Worse," *Guardian*, May 19, 2010, http://www.theguardian.com/business/2010/may/19/germany-naked-short-selling-ban-analysts.

7.	Matthew Dalton, "Euro Strengthens as Fears Fade," *Wall Street Journal*, January 11, 2013, http://online.wsj.com/news/articles/SB10001424127887324442304578235843274207164.

8.	Jim Brunsden, "EU Gets Deal on Naked Sovereign CDS Curbs, Short-Selling Rules," Bloomberg News, October 18, 2011, http://www.businessweek.com/news/2011-10-18/eu-gets-deal-on-naked-sovereign-cds-curbs-short-selling-rules.html.

9.	John Chapman, "CDS: Modern Day Weapons of Mass Destruction," *Financial Times*, September 11, 2011, http://www.ft.com/intl/cms/s/0/1c81fdf8-d4b9-11e0-a7ac-00144feab49a.html#axzz2kImq3w9e.

10.	Adam Taggart, "Rep. Ken Ivory and Dan Griffiths: Creating a Financial Emergency Plan for States: Utah Is Pioneering a Bold New Model," Peak Prosperity, May 19, 2013, http://www.peakprosperity.com/featuredvoices/81915/rep-ken-ivory-dan-griffiths-creating-financial-emergency-plan-states.

11.	Dan Griffiths, "Financial Ready Utah: Peace in Preparedness," State Budget Solutions, May 6, 2013, http://www.statebudgetsolutions.org/blog/detail/financial-ready-utah-peace-in-preparedness.

12.	"Rep. Matt Krause Files Bill to Create Fiscal Risk Management Commission," press release, Texas House of Representatives, February 27, 2013, http://www.house.state.tx.us/news/press-releases/?id=4344&session=83&district=93&bill_code=2465.

13.	Emily Ramshaw and Aman Batheja, "Tarrant Lawmaker Seeks to Create Texas Bullion Depository," *Texas Tribune*, March 22, 2013, http://www.star-telegram.com/2013/03/21/4721036/tarrant-lawmaker-seeks-to-create.html.

14.	Michelle Smith, "James Richards: Texas Law Would Protect Its Gold from Government Seizure," Moneynews.com, March 25, 2013, http://www.moneynews.com/Markets/gold-Rickards-Texas-depository/2013/03/25/id/496123.

15.	U.S. Cyber Command, U.S. Strategic Command, http://www.stratcom.mil/factsheets/Cyber_Command/.

16.	René Obermann, "Uniting for Cyberdefense," *New York Times*, February 19, 2013, http://www.nytimes.com/2013/02/20/opinion/global/uniting-for-cyberdefense.html?_r=0.

17.	Scott Borg and Elad Yoran, "A New Approach to Cyber Defense," FoxBusiness.com, April 3, 2013, http://www.foxbusiness.com/technology/2013/04/03/new-approach-to-cyber-defense/.

18.	Richard A. Fleetwood, "U.S. Civil Defense History," Survival Ring, May 2009, http://www.survivalring.org/community/library/civil-defense-history/#ixzz2kOiK0M44.

19.	*American Blackout*, National Geographic Channel, November 13, 2013, http://channel.nationalgeographic.com/channel/american-blackout/.

20. "Maine Setting Standard for EMP Defense; Legislature Working to Protect against Event That Could Change Civilization," WND, February 24, 2013, http://www.wnd.com/2013/02/maine-setting-standard-for-emp-defense/.

21. "Franks Launches Caucus to Address EMP Threat, Introduces 'SHIELD Act,'" press release, U.S. Congressman Trent Franks, February 16, 2011, http://franks.house.gov/press-release/franks-launches-caucus-address-emp-threat-introduces-shield-act.

22. "Space Weather: The Impact on Earth and Its Implications for Business," Lloyd's of London, 2013, http://www.lloyds.com/~/media/Lloyds/Reports/360/360%20Space%20Weather/7311_Lloyds_360_Space%20Weather_03.pdf.

23. Frank Gaffney Jr., "Doing Something about Space Weather," Center for Security Policy, June 17, 2013, http://www.centerforsecuritypolicy.org/2013/06/17/doing-something-about-space-weather/.

24. "Credit and Liquidity Programs and the Balance Sheet," Board of Governors of the Federal Reserve System, September 20, 2013, http://www.federalreserve.gov/monetarypolicy/bst_recenttrends.htm.

25. David Callahan, "The Most Bogus Employment Number: Discouraged Workers," Demos, September 6, 2013, http://www.demos.org/blog/9/6/13/most-bogus-unemployment-number-discouraged-workers.

26. Richard Rubin, "Offshore Cash Hoard Expands by $183 Billion at Companies," Bloomberg.com, March 8, 2013, http://www.bloomberg.com/news/2013-03-08/offshore-cash-hoard-expands-by-183-billion-at-companies.html.

27. Daniel J. Mitchell, "More Compelling Evidence That America's Corporate Tax System Is Pointlessly Destructive," Cato at Liberty, Cato Institute, August 14, 2013, http://www.cato.org/blog/more-compelling-evidence-americas-corporate-tax-system-pointlessly-destructive.

28. Mitchell, "America's Corporate Tax System Ranks a Miserable 94 out of 100 Nations in 'Tax Attractiveness,'" International Liberty blog, July 11, 2013, http://danieljmitchell.wordpress.com/2013/07/11/americas-corporate-tax-system-ranks-a-miserable-94-out-of-100-nations-in-tax-attractiveness/.

29. "U.S. Acquirers Cut Taxes by Relocating to Europe after Mergers," CNBC.com, August 13, 2013, http://www.cnbc.com/id/100957874.

30. Jeff Sommer, "How to Unlock That Stashed Foreign Cash," New York Times, March 23, 2013, http://www.nytimes.com/2013/03/24/your-money/how-companies-could-unlock-stashed-foreign-earnings.html?pagewanted=all&_r=0.

31. Julie Bort, "Cisco's John Chambers Repeats Threat to Ship Jobs Overseas If Tax Laws Don't Change," Business Insider, May 16, 2013, http://www.businessinsider.com/ciscos-john-chambers-threatens-to-ship-jobs-overseas-2013-5#ixzz2eQ57Q8aB.

32. James Pethokoukis, "CBO: Obama Stimulus May Have Cost as Much as $4.1 Million a Job," AEI-Ideas (blog), May 30, 2012, http://www.aei-ideas.org/2012/05/cbo-obama-stimulus-may-have-cost-as-much-as-4-1-million-a-job/.

33. Ashe Schow, "President Obama's Taxpayer-Backed Green Energy Failures," Foundry, Heritage Foundation, October 18, 2012, http://blog.heritage.org/2012/10/18/president-obamas-taxpayer-backed-green-energy-failures/.

34. Marc A. Thiessen, "Forget Bain—Obama's Public-Equity Record Is the Real Scandal," Washington Post, May 24, 2012, http://www.washingtonpost.com/opinions/forget-bain-obamas-public-equity-record-is-the-real-scandal/2012/05/24/gJQAXnXCnU_story.html.

35. Darius Dixon, "DOE IG: 100+ Stimulus-Related Criminal Probes," Politico.com, November 2, 2011, http://www.politico.com/news/stories/1111/67444.html.

36. Greg Pollowitz, "Why the Government Should Not Play Venture Capitalist," *National Review Online*, September 1, 2011, http://www.nationalreview.com/planet-gore/276069/why-government-should-not-play-venture-capitalist-greg-pollowitz.

37. R. Maxwell, "Apple Seeks to Build a Solar Farm to Power Data Center in Reno, Nevada," Phone Arena, July 2, 2013, http://www.phonearena.com/news/Apple-seeks-to-build-a-solar-farm-to-power-data-center-in-Reno-Nevada_id44805.

38. Mark Garrison, "How Much Would Apple's Overseas Cash Help the U.S. Economy?," Marketplace, May 21, 2013, http://www.marketplace.org/topics/business/how-much-would-apples-overseas-cash-help-us-economy.

39. Damien Carrington, "Germany's Renewable Energy Revolution Leaves UK in the Shade," *Guardian*, May 30, 2012, http://www.theguardian.com/environment/2012/may/30/germany-renewable-energy-revolution.

40. "Oil Economics," Fuel Freedom, 2013, http://www.fuelfreedom.org/the-real-foreign-oil-problem/oil-economics/.

41. Patti Domm, "U.S. Is on Fast-Track to Energy Independence: Study," CNBC.com.com, February 11, 2013, http://www.cnbc.com/id/100450133.

42. Morgan Korn, "U.S. to Pass Saudi Arabia in Energy Production, IEA Says: Huge Foreign Policy, Economic Implications," Yahoo! Finance, November 12, 2012, http://finance.yahoo.com/blogs/daily-ticker/u-pass-saudi-arabia-energy-production-iea-says-170907660.html.

43. Michael Bastasch, "White House Praises Oil Drilling While Blocking It on Federal Land," Daily Caller, September 3, 2013, http://dailycaller.com/2013/09/03/white-house-praises-oil-drilling-while-blocking-it-on-federal-land/#ixzz2eQQhqtgd.

44. Ibid.

45. Stacy Curtin, "The Fracking Revolution: More Jobs and Cheaper Energy Are Worth the 'Manageable' Risks, Yergin Says," Yahoo! Finance, February 3, 2012, http://finance.yahoo.com/blogs/daily-ticker/fracking-revolution-more-jobs-cheaper-energy-worth-manageable-171414515.html.

46. Ibid.

47. "Obama Administration Imposes Five-Year Drilling Ban on Majority of Offshore Areas," Committee on Natural Resources, November 8, 2011, http://naturalresources.house.gov/news/documentsingle.aspx?DocumentID=2679.

48. Kevin D. Freeman, "Why Our Shale Boom Is So Important to Us and Such a Threat to Russia and OPEC," GlobalEconomicWarfare.com, August 9, 2013, http://globaleconomicwarfare.com/2013/08/why-our-shale-boom-is-so-important-to-us-and-such-a-threat-to-russia-and-opec/.

49. Freeman, "Fracking and Hacking; Why Energy Is the New Front in Economic Warfare," GlobalEconomicWarfare.com, October 7, 2012, http://globaleconomicwarfare.com/2012/10/fracking-and-hacking-why-energy-is-the-new-front-in-economic-warfare/.

50. Summer Said and Benoit Faucon, "Shale Threatens Saudi Economy, Warns Prince Alwaleed," *Wall Street Journal*, July 29, 2013, http://online.wsj.com/news/articles/SB10001424127887323854904578635500251760848; and Timur Moon, "Oil Price Slips as Saudi Prince Alwaleed bin Talal Warns of West's Fracking Boom," *International Business Times*, July 29, 2013, http://www.ibtimes.co.uk/articles/495259/20130729/prince-alwaleed-talal-oil-price-shale-gas.htm.

51. Freeman, "Can Environmental Rules Be Secret Weapons?," GlobalEconomicWarfare.com, August 16, 2012, http://globaleconomicwarfare.com/2012/08/can-environmental-rules-be-secret-weapons/.

52.   Robert Toews, "Former CIA Head Ties Oil, Terror," *Stanford Daily*, February 25, 2010, http://www.stanforddaily.com/2010/02/25/former-cia-head-ties-oil-terror/.

53.   Dana Hull, "How 'Teslanaires' Made Fortunes on Tesla Motors Stock," *San Jose Mercury News*, August 21, 2013, http://www.mercurynews.com/business/ci_23912622/how-teslanaires-made-fortunes-tesla-motors-stock.

54.   Ashlee Vance, "Revealed: Elon Musk Explains the Hyperloop, the Solar-Powered High-Speed Future of Inter-City Transportation," Businessweek.com, August 12, 2013, http://www.businessweek.com/articles/2013-08-12/revealed-elon-musk-explains-the-hyperloop.

55.   Mary Ann Milbourn, "Boone Pickens Invests in O.C. Natural Gas Fueling Firm," *Orange County Register*, August 21, 2013, http://www.ocregister.com/articles/energy-333968-pickens-company.html.

56.   "Overregulation: The Problem We Can't Outproduce," *The Optimistic Conservative Blog*, August 13, 2012, http://theoptimisticconservative.wordpress.com/2012/08/13/overregulation-the-problem-we-cant-outproduce-with-some-words-from-reagan/.

57.   "Skyrocketing Number of Regulations Burden Economy," Smarter Government Washington, August 21, 2013, http://smartergovernmentwa.org/skyrocketing-number-of-regulations-burden-economy/.

58.   Patrick McClaughlin, "The Economics of Regulation Part 1: A New Study Shows That Regulatory Accumulation Hurts the Economy," Mercatus Center at George Mason University, July 16, 2013, http://neighborhoodeffects.mercatus.org/2013/07/16/the-economics-of-regulation-part-1-a-new-study-shows-that-regulatory-accumulation-hurts-the-economy/; and Ronald Bailey, "Federal Regulations Have Made You 75 Percent Poorer," Reason.com, July 21, 2103, http://reason.com/archives/2013/06/21/federal-regulations-have-made-you-75-per.

59.   Bailey, "Federal Regulations Have Made You 75 Percent Poorer."

60.   Ibid.

61.   Alyene Senger, "Obamacare Hassle: A 127-Million-Hour Paperwork Burden," *Foundry*, Heritage Foundation, February 7, 2013, http://blog.heritage.org/2013/02/07/obamacare-a-127-million-hour-burden/.

62.   James L. Gattuso, "Reforming Regulation: Some Sensible Steps," Heritage Foundation, July 25, 2012, http://www.heritage.org/research/reports/2012/07/how-to-reduce-red-tape-and-reform-government-regulation.

63.   William McBride, "What Is the Evidence on Taxes and Growth?," Tax Foundation, December 18, 2012, http://taxfoundation.org/article/what-evidence-taxes-and-growth.

64.   "Simplify Tax Code With Blank Slate: Our View," *USA Today*, July 22, 2013, http://www.usatoday.com/story/opinion/2013/07/22/simplify-tax-code-blank-slate-editorials-debates/2576665/.

65.   "How FairTax Works," FairTax.org. 2013, http://www.fairtax.org/site/PageServer.

66.   Nathan Lewis, "Flat Tax vs. Fair Tax vs. Herman Cain's 9-9-9 Plan," *Forbes*, Forbes.com, October 13, 2011, http://www.forbes.com/sites/nathanlewis/2011/10/13/flat-tax-vs-fair-tax-vs-herman-cains-9-9-9-plan/.

67.   Al Cardenas and John McLaughlin, "Do We Need More Immigrants?," Human Events, August 5, 2013, http://www.humanevents.com/2013/08/05/1078-words/.

68.   Nathan Cotto, "Gov. Richard Lamm on the Immigration Plan to Destroy America," *Washington Times*, September 2, 2012, http://communities.washingtontimes.com/neighborhood/conscience-realist/2012/sep/2/richard-lamm-plan-destroy-america/.

69.   "Does Illegal Immigration Pose a Terrorist Threat to the United States?," ProCon.org, 2013, http://immigration.procon.org/view.answers.php?questionID=000786.

70. Mark Landsbaum, "Al-Qaeda's Illegal Immigration Threat," FrontPage Magazine, March 3, 2005, http://archive.frontpagemag.com/readArticle.aspx?ARTID=9387.

71. Igor Volsky, "Congressman Says Bombings Reveal Danger of Immigration Bill: 'Radical Islamists … Are Trained to Act Hispanic,'" ThinkProgress, April 17, 2013, http://thinkprogress.org/immigration/2013/04/17/1879411/congressman-says-bombings-reveal-danger-of-immigration-bill-radical-islamistsare-trained-to-act-hispanic/.

72. "Colleges Teach Students How to Hate America," Cincinnati.com, May 18, 2013, http://news.cincinnati.com/article/20130519/EDIT/305190025/Colleges-teach-students-how-hate-America?nclick_check=1.

73. Victor Skinner, "Columnist: Too Many Educators Want Our Kids to Hate America," EagNews.org, http://eagnews.org/columnist-cites-examples-of-educators-teaching-students-to-hate-america/.

74. "Air Force Training Calls Founding Fathers and Southerners Terrorists While Ignoring Islamists Who Brought Down the Trade Centers," NC Renegade, August 24, 2013, http://ncrenegade.com/editorial/air-force-training-calls-founding-fathers-and-southerners-terrorists-while-ignoring-islamists-who-brought-down-the-trade-centers/.

75. Peggy Noonan, "Patriots, Then and Now," *Wall Street Journal*, March 30, 2006, http://online.wsj.com/article/SB122512408935772391.html.

76. "U.S. History Quotes about God and the Bible," USA Christian Ministries, http://www.usachristianministries.com/us-history-quotes-about-god-and-the-bible/.

77. WhoWasRonaldReagan.com, posted June 16, 2013, http://whowasronaldreagan.com/80/2013/06/16/if-we-ever-forget-that-we-are-one-nation-under-god-then-we-will-be-a-nation-gone-under-ronald-reagan-3/.

78. Conrad Black, "Collapse of American Influence Recalls Disintegration of Soviet Union, Fall of France," *New York Sun*, September 7, 2013, http://www.nysun.com/foreign/collapse-of-american-power-recalls-dis/88400/.

APPENDIX

1. John Templeton, *Discovering the Laws of Life* (New York: Continuum, 1994), 13.

2. C. Robert Allred, "Life's Greatest Investment," Sermon Archive, November 24, 2002, http://www.bobssermons.com/sermons/archive/021124.html.

3. John Templeton, "A New Way to Think about Money," Looking Glass Coaching, Inc., posted November 9, 2010, http://mysuccessfilledlife.com/2010/11/09/a-new-way-to-think-about-money-by-sir-john-templeton/.

4. Winston Churchill, "Never Give In," speech given at Harrow School, Britain, October 29, 1941, transcript, Churchill Centre, http://www.winstonchurchill.org/learn/speeches/speeches-of-winston-churchill/103-never-give-in.

Index